IT HAPPENS
EVERY DAY

MORE PRAISE FOR ROBIN SAX'S *IT HAPPENS EVERY DAY*

"Robin Sax's gift to the criminal justice system is helping victims—especially children—articulate the unspeakable. Sex crimes happen every day, but advocates like Sax are far from common."

—Vanessa Leggett, true crime author

"Sax is at the top of her game. A strikingly upfront view into the world of one the most high-profiled district attorney offices in the country, Sax gives a disturbing account of the sexual predator and the means used to stop him. It's what the public doesn't see behind closed doors—very compelling."

—Stacey Dittrich, former sex crime detective and
author of *The Devil's Closet*

"This book again shows Sax's dedication, devotion, and 100 percent commitment to helping victims and families. The education aspect is top notch, and if we can't help the children, I don't know whom we can help."

—Dana Pretzer, *Scared Monkeys Radio*

IT HAPPENS EVERY DAY

INSIDE THE WORLD OF A SEX CRIMES DA

ROBIN SAX

FOREWORD BY NOTED
LOS ANGELES DEFENSE ATTORNEY
MARK GERAGOS

Prometheus Books

59 John Glenn Drive
Amherst, New York 14228-2119

Published 2010 by Prometheus Books

It Happens Every Day: Inside the World of a Sex Crimes DA. Copyright © 2010 by Robin Sax. All rights reserved. No part of this publication may be reproduced, stored in a retrieval system, or transmitted in any form or by any means, digital, electronic, mechanical, photocopying, recording, or otherwise, or conveyed via the Internet or a Web site without prior written permission of the publisher, except in the case of brief quotations embodied in critical articles and reviews.

Inquiries should be addressed to
Prometheus Books
59 John Glenn Drive
Amherst, New York 14228–2119
VOICE: 716–691–0133, ext. 210
FAX: 716–691–0137
WWW.PROMETHEUSBOOKS.COM

14 13 12 11 10   5 4 3 2 1

Library of Congress Cataloging-in-Publication Data

Sax, Robin.
    It happens every day : inside the world of a sex crimes DA / by Robin Sax.
        p. cm.
    ISBN 978–1–59102–758–4 (hardcover : alk. paper)
    1. Child sexual abuse—United States. 2. Child sexual abuse—Investigation—United States. 3. Sexually abused children—United States. 4. Sex crimes—United States. 5. Sex offenders—United States. I. Title.
HV6570.2.S385 2009
363.25'9536—dc22

2009021868

Printed in the United States on acid-free paper

The materials contained in this book have been prepared for informational purposes only and are not intended to constitute medical advice, legal advice, or professional counseling services. Transmission of the information is not intended to create, and receipt does not constitute, a physician-patient, attorney-client, or counselor-patient relationship. The materials in this book do not represent the opinions, policy, or philosophy of the Los Angeles County District Attorney or the Los Angeles County District Attorney's Office.

To my children,
Hannah, Jason, and Jeremy,
forever and always

CONTENTS

PART I: BEHIND THE ONE-WAY MIRROR: ASKING THE MOST DIFFICULT QUESTIONS

CONTENTS

PART II: BEHIND COUNSEL TABLE: TIME FOR COURT

CONTENTS

AUTHOR'S NOTE

I wrote this book from the personal and highly opinionated perspective of Robin Sax, the individual, the advocate, and the lawyer. This book does not represent the opinions or views of the Los Angeles County District Attorney, the District Attorney's Office, or any other part of Los Angeles County government. At the time that I wrote this book, I was very much a deputy DA. However, in the time since I began this project until now, I have turned into a former prosecutor. My decision to leave the DA's office in no way changes my beliefs and opinions expressed here. The only difference is that instead of advocating for change one victim, one case, at a time, I now do so on a macro level, openly, loudly, through print, TV, and other media.

While the job of a prosecutor intersects with many other disciplines—like advocate, therapist, social worker, and police officer—my job is very much about what is legal and not legal, what will and will not hold up in court, and what the criminal process will do for and to the victim and the perpetrator.

So while I discuss in this book the different roles and perspectives of the many professionals involved in child sexual assault cases, please keep in mind that as the prosecuting attorney I will always have one eye focused on the law and what will get me a conviction in court.

AUTHOR'S NOTE

This book is not intended to supply legal advice, and nothing in it should be taken as legal advice. Every case differs, laws vary state to state, statutes are amended year to year. So if you have any questions about your legal rights and responsibilities, be sure to consult your lawyer.

Now, a word about gender. As politically correct as I try to be, the reality is that most perpetrators are men and most victims are female. That is not to say, as you will read, that there are not male victims or female perpetrators. In order to streamline this book, I take the statistical approach and refer to perps as "he" and victims as "she."

Also, while all the cases in this book are true, the names of the victims in cases where I have had direct involvement have been changed to protect the privacy of the victims.

FOREWORD

Mark Geragos

For more than twenty-five years I have spent my professional career defending those accused of committing crimes. I have had battles with hundreds if not thousands of prosecutors all over the United States. Some I remember, some I would rather forget. But one prosecutor whom I will never forget, and would not want to, is the author of this book, Robin Sax. I first met her years ago while defending a man she was prosecuting. Since then we have sat on opposite sides of the court-room, taking opposite sides of the same arguments. And while we may not agree on what the law should be, we both agree that trial advocacy skills, tenacity, and, most important, passion is what makes the difference in a courtroom.

It may seem strange that someone who has made a career out of defending people would write the foreword of this book. I am writing it because not only do I agree with Robin that child sexual assault is widely misunderstood, but I think it is important that prosecutors, defense attorneys, legislators, judges, and lobbyists should always look to see how we can make our system better.

At the outset, in the interests of full disclosure, I should again state that, many times, Robin and I do not agree on the law. Further, I confess that I do not agree with all of the suggestions she makes in this book.

However, I do think this book does something that no other book out there does: it challenges us to start a dialogue, not just as individuals but as a society, on how to protect some of the most valuable yet vulnerable citizens—our children.

Any crime committed against a child is horrible. Trust me, I have kids. I know the worries and concerns you, the reader, and everybody has for children. Child abuse concerns me, too. And you may be surprised that I am going to say this, but sex crimes against children are some of the most heinous crimes committed.

Maybe it is because of the outrageous nature of these crimes that the whole category has become so sensationalized. This book does what needs to be done. It brings the issue of child sex crimes off the sensationalized shelf and uncovers its hidden secret—that child sex crimes affect virtually every family in the United States. If it is not you or your family, then it is someone you know. Society does not need another heart-wrenching tale of child sex crimes that falls somewhere in between a fictional thriller and a nonfiction autobiography. What our society needs is a sober discussion about these issues based on reality, not on what sells newspapers.

As a defense attorney, I fervently believe that words matter and that the right word can make all the difference, but so can the wrong word. So when I say that a discussion is needed, I do mean a discussion. Our criminal justice system depends on all the people involved and requires them to work together to keep the system functioning. As much as everyone would like cases to be black and white, they almost never are. If they were, I wouldn't have a job. It takes good prosecutors and good defense attorneys to make the system work.

A prosecutor has to know his or her boundaries. How far is she willing to go to obtain a conviction? How much of the victim's privacy is she willing to sacrifice? How can she use the evidence to prove what no one else saw? And the defense attorney is fighting the same battle. Just being accused of something like sexually assaulting a child is enough to ruin the defendant's life, even if the accused is factually innocent. And as one defendant said after being acquitted, "Where do I go to get my reputation back?"

On the other hand, there is the equally nettlesome task of dealing with prosecution witnesses who are hardly candidates for sainthood. How far does the attorney tread into those areas, even if the judge allows you any meaningful cross-examination in an effort to save your client?

Regardless of which side the attorney is on, or what she has to prove or rebut, it comes down to the people, the prosecution witness, and the accused. Prosecutors and defense attorneys learn to understand human nature in way that few other people do. So the decisions that these attorneys make, on their own or in discussions with each other, shape the way society views crime. But there are not enough discussions that go on between prosecutors and defense attorneys outside of the courtroom. That is why this book is so important. It starts a discussion that is long overdue.

Child sex crimes are unique because the victims are considered more vulnerable. More important, child victims are often less able to cope with the crimes committed against them. Because these crimes are different, and because these victims are different, this discussion is even more vital. It is up to us as prosecutors, as defense attorneys, as parents, and as people to protect our children. It is up to us to learn what the crimes and the perpetrators look like. It is up to us to find out what is really going on. Having the ability to come to this discussion and learn the realities from someone on the front lines makes all the difference.

In this book, Robin shares what she knows and what she thinks should be done. As I said at the onset, I disagree with much of the way she would change the world. But I, like many defense attorneys, have a response. And just like that, the discussion has begun—without the media flash and without the sensationalism. Addressing the issues presented in this book, whether in agreement or counterargument, raises awareness of what it really means for children to be victims of sex crimes. And with awareness, real awareness, comes prevention.

FOREWORD

It's almost axiomatic that Robin was meant to write this book. Not just because she has the experience or because it fits her job description. Not just because she's seen the worst and wants to talk about it. Robin was meant to write this book because she has wielded an enormous amount of power through her exercise of professional discretion. She had made the decision to prosecute and the decision to let the case go. She has made the call on when a case is one that the community should decide, and when to protect the victim from public scrutiny. She has seen past the obvious and won impossible cases. She weeds out cases to ensure justice. She advocates tirelessly for victims. Prosecutors like her make sure that defense attorneys like me are always at our best.

INTRODUCTION
MAKING A DIFFERENCE, ONE CASE AT A TIME

There is no greater concern in a society than the well-being of its children. Whether it is providing a healthier earth or protecting kids from wars, terrorism, criminals, abuse, and so on, we pride ourselves on shielding our young. And with good reason—children are ill equipped to take on the perils of our world on their own.

The premise of this book is that we are failing to protect our children from sexual assault—*failing miserably*—and we need to do something about it. Why focus on this when there are thousands of other compelling causes out there? The answer is that child sexual assault has become a social epidemic, and its breeding ground is not a dark alley but our own homes, schools, and churches.

According to the Department of Justice's crime statistics, 67 percent of sexual assault victims are juveniles, and one in seven is under six years old. Twenty percent of girls and 17 percent of boys will be molested before their eighteenth birthdays. Combined statistics show there is a sexual assault every two minutes in the United States, and two-thirds of those victims are children. If that's not enough to horrify you, try this: *93 percent of juvenile sexual assault victims are attacked by someone they know.* This epidemic isn't driven by strangers. The explosive growth comes from attacks by family members, friends, teachers, coaches, neighbors—the very people the child trusts.

While the numbers can vary depending on who is reporting and what methodology is used, the fact is that child sexual assault happens every day. It happens in homes, schools, cars, beaches, parks, and alleys across the country. As a sex crimes prosecuting attorney, I personally review at least five new *reported* cases of sexual assault every day, and the Justice Department estimates that for every four reported cases, there are an additional six sexual assaults that go unreported. It's a measure of the breadth of this problem that I am only one of a thousand or more prosecutors in Los Angeles County, eighty or so of whom work on sex crime cases.

In addition to the new reports that come in, I receive hundreds of e-mails, anonymous calls from families, and information calls from law enforcement about how to approach a potential report of child sex assault. I get these calls because people recognize that child sexual assault is different from other crimes, including adult rape.

For most people, these differences tend to make people very apprehensive about reporting a possible child sex abuse crime. But the fact that a child may be at risk also makes people desperate for information, which leads them to the Internet (inconclusive and unable to deal with specific situations), defense attorneys (expensive and not always skilled with children), or to the media (in the business of revealing, not keeping, secrets).

Of course, the best-case scenario is that the quest for information leads people to the answers they're seeking. But people under stress are prone to jump to conclusions, misunderstand, or simply end up with wrong or incomplete information.

The reason I decided to write this book is to highlight what really happens when a district attorney prosecutes a child sexual assault case. Readers will learn how these cases are investigated, which ones go to trial, what special methods are used in the courtroom to deal with juvenile witnesses, what happens if someone is convicted, and what happens if someone is not.

I will also introduce readers to all the players in the system, from victim to defendant, from cop to prosecutor, from judge to jury, and explain how they all work together to bring about justice.

While not all jurisdictions handle child sexual assault cases in exactly the same way, in the last twenty years the "team approach" as been one of the most positive advances made in handling these cases. It's what we use in LA. The team approach ensures that information from a variety of individuals and agencies—law enforcement, child protective services (CPS), medical personnel and mental health professionals—is shared in order to properly support the victim as well as to build strong cases against the perpetrators of these crimes.

And though there are a lot of treatises and journal articles, and other professional literature, out there about the multidisciplinary team approach, there is little if anything that tells a normal person on the street about how child sexual assault cases are really handled by prosecutors, detectives, courts, jurors, and child services.

This book separates the truth from the spin, debunks the myths, and gets blunt about what works and what needs to be changed. This book doesn't come out of academia, it comes from the trenches—where I prosecute child sex crimes, day in and day out.

You've heard the saying "What happens behind closed doors should stay behind closed doors"? Whoever coined that phrase wasn't a sex crimes prosecutor. That, in a nutshell, is what makes this epidemic of child sex crimes possible. If what goes on behind closed doors is a sex crime against a child, it should not remain private. It's a crime. If it happens anywhere in LA County, then it's definitely my business to bring it out from behind closed doors and into a courtroom.

As a deputy district attorney in my special unit, I handle some of the most heinous crimes against the most defenseless members of our society. I don't do stop-and-robs (e.g., liquor store hold-ups), drug sales, burglaries, and so on. Instead, I'm assigned to a special unit where I handle all phases of cases that involve sex crimes against children, from the initial interview through the investigation, the trial, and the sentencing.

This means I have to keep a lot of different hats on my hat rack. Sometimes I'm in the investigator's role, digging out evidence. Or I'm the interviewer asking a child victim difficult, embarrassing, and very invasive questions. Other times, I'm an advocate for children who often cannot speak for themselves. And at yet other times, I'm an educator lecturing on law enforcement to college students, or speaking at community meetings about how we can all better protect our kids both inside and outside the criminal justice system. And, of course, there are the times when I am a litigator, exchanging verbal blows with defense attorneys, judges, or witnesses.

Some days I wear only one hat, as when I am in trial, advocating all day in front of one court on one case. But most days, I am juggling all my hats, trying to keep the right one on my head and my head on my body.

For example, take my schedule for today. It's pretty representative of my average day. I don't need an alarm to get up at the crack o' early. My body knows what six hours of sleep feels like, and when it's over, I'm up.

Today, it was 5:15 a.m. when I hit that magical six-hour mark. I planned that to give me an hour of quiet calm before the day begins at full speed. Ah, one whole glorious hour to myself. Do I work on my book? Write my sentencing motion that's due to the court in a couple of days? Review my speech that I am giving at 8:30 a.m.? (Nah, waste of time. Internet safety is my bread and butter and I can do that one with my eyes closed.)

Should I read the files I have for court today to make sure I have plea bargain offers for the defense attorneys? As I check my e-mail, contemplating what I am going to tackle first, my phone rings. Damn! It's a 213 number. I know what that means. It's an LA cop and someone is in custody.

"Hi, Robin? It's Sharlene from Robbery/Homicide."

I groan, fearing the worst—is some abused kid dead? "What've you got, Sharlene?"

"Well, remember that Monahan* rape case?"

"Uh huh," I sigh, dreading that cluster of a case.

"Well, he's in custody, the press is calling, and you need to decide what you're going to do by 10 a.m. today."

"You've got to be kidding me," I say, trying to sound incredulous. But I know it's no use. So much for that glorious hour to myself. The next hour belongs to the People of the State of California as I review a multi-count rape case with every issue imaginable rolled into one. Now I've got to figure out what to do before the press calls, the judge asks questions, or my boss e-mails me.

And I love it. The adrenaline is pumping through my veins, the aroma of strong, black coffee is revving me up, and once again I'm in the thick of doing the job I feel I was born to do.

I love that the cops know to call me, that they know I'll be awake, available, and immediately ready to handle the case. I love that my passion for protecting child victims is still as hot as ever, and I love knowing that I will do whatever it takes to reach a fair and reasoned decision on this case—even by 10 a.m. this morning.

What amazes me is how many of these calls I get, every single day, from police officers, social workers, hospitals, and others who are just as dedicated as I am. It amazes me how many victims are in the emergency room at the wee hours of the night having a "rape kit" done. And what's even more amazing is how much there is to child sexual assault about which no one ever hears.

This book is about the stuff that never makes the news, the parade of "no-name" defendants and Jane (and some John) Doe victims that fills our courtrooms but is somehow not "newsworthy." Sometimes my life feels like a TV show, but the stuff I see is the real deal. I see the good and the bad of the system, the most inspiring and most pathetic victims, the progress and stagnation of the criminal justice system, the characteristics of the predators, and the sick or abused wives who support them.

---

* Pseudonym for a high-profile defendant.

I see the great advances in scientific evidence coupled with the budget-challenged labs of even major metropolitan cities. (Can you imagine a city with a population topping a million running a Sexually Exploited Children's Unit off a DOS operating system? I can.) I see stuff you wouldn't believe. I see stuff that defies all reason or logic. I see stuff I can't believe. And every time I think I've seen it all, a case with something I never imagined lands on my desk.

In this book, I will show you the criminal justice system that you don't hear about on the news. I will make sense of the amorphous parts of child sexual assault and explore what's right and wrong about the system.

My perspective comes from the belief that knowledge is power. The more people know about the inner workings of the system from a real-life DA, the better equipped we'll all be to protect kids—yours and mine.

This book is divided into two parts. Part One, "Behind the One-Way Mirror," deals with the investigation portion of child sexual assaults, what makes a case "fileable," and why some cases never get filed. Part Two, "Behind the Counsel Table," opens up the entire court process. It will pick apart the trial strategies of both sides. It will show you how six-year-old witnesses are completely different from teenaged witnesses, and how both are completely different from adult witnesses. And you'll learn what really happens when the lawyers huddle with the judge at a "sidebar" conference during a trial.

Throughout the book (and as always), I will be brutally honest. My credibility is everything. So I will tell it like it is, even if I think that you or my colleagues won't like what I have to say. If something makes me angry, you'll see the anger. If something breaks my heart, I will do my best to put the tears on the page. And I'll warn you now—my language isn't always ladylike. When you live in the dark world of sex predators who prey on children, you get crass and dark. But you'll come to expect the passion that drives the words and maybe, just maybe, that passion will grow in you, too.

PART I
BEHIND THE ONE-WAY MIRROR

Asking the
Most Difficult Questions

CHAPTER ONE
IT TAKES A TEAM

It was a month before her quinceniera (celebration for fifteen-year-old girls in Mexican culture) when Liliana jumped in her dad's truck to go hand deliver invitations for the biggest celebration of her life. Before making it to the first home to deliver the invites, Liliana's dad pulled off into a parking lot. She knew what it meant. It had happened hundreds of times before. He would take her to the back, pull down her pants, put his penis inside of her, and moan slowly until "he was done." He would caution her not to tell, and remind her that he loved her. It would be the same today. After all, nothing had changed, even when Liliana reached out to her mother, several years before, and told her what she was suffering at the hands of her own father. Her mom's only response was to buy her a lock for her bedroom door. So for three years, instead of raping her in the middle of the night, he would simply take her to the back of his truck, just as he did on that Thursday morning.

Even though Liliana had expectations of what would happen in that parking lot, she would never have guessed how that day would change the course of her life. A concerned citizen saw "a man" (her dad) take a young girl in the back of the truck and immediately called 911. What happened in the hours to come was a top-notch example of a modern, coordinated team effort to carefully and gently interview Liliana; medically examine her; arrest her dad (and mom); care for her siblings; provide a safe, comfortable home for Liliana; and arrange for immediate crisis intervention and a long-term psychological support plan for her.

In the "old days" (pre-team approach), Liliana would have had to tell and retell her story to a series of people, each performing his or her individual task with little coordination with each other, as her case made its way to a courtroom: the initial police officer on the scene, the investigating detective, the prosecutor, the doctor or nurse who conducted her medical examination, and the social worker(s) from the Department of Children and Family Services.

The system of handling child abuse cases is changing, but that change does not happen overnight or without setbacks. For example, as the investigation into Liliana's case continued, it was revealed that there were at least six prior reports of suspected abuse involving her, and that several different government agencies from different cities were involved, with no coordinated effort to remove the abuser or her from her home. Each investigation was proceeding separately and at a different level of completeness, and there had not been one unified interview of Liliana.

" **T**here is no 'I' in TEAM." You've seen the poster—you know the one I'm talking about—the one in the in-flight airline catalogs. The saying is so overused it drives everybody up a wall, me included. But as tired and corny as the motto is, it captures the core of the multidisciplinary team approach to handling child abuse cases, from first report through prosecution and beyond.

The proper handling of a child sexual assault case can be difficult and complex. The interview of the traumatized and terrified young victim must be done carefully, with compassion, and without implicit "suggestions" from the interviewer. The interviewer must be careful to allow the victim to tell his or her story, not become the storyteller using the victim's voice. Suggestive questioning is somewhat like leading questions in court. These are questions within which the answers are included or implied. Even seemingly benign multiple-choice questions can be suggestive. For example, were you in the bedroom or in the living room? is equally suggestive because it does not allow the child to come up with her own answer or, even worse, implies that the act only could occur in a room. (In some situations it could be somewhere else, like a car.)

Resources must be brought together for the victim and the family. Special arrangements must be made for the victim's safety. The evidence must be collected in compliance with constitutional and other requirements and and it must be properly preserved. And the list goes on.

Multidisciplinary teams with representatives from health services, social services, law enforcement, and legal service agencies are the best way to handle the many facets and complexities of child sexual assault cases. Together, the team members can coordinate the assistance and resources needed by the victim and the family, streamline the investigation, prepare for prosecution, and better serve both victims and society. A multidisciplinary team can do more combined than each agency can do alone, and do it more quickly and without unnecessary repetition of work already done.

While working as part of a group, each member still plays his or her individual role—the prosecutor files the case, the law enforcement member leads the investigation, and so on. Not all cases require the same team members. For instance, a representative from child protective services may not be necessary if the perpetrator is a stranger and the parents are providing appropriate support for the victim.

But while each member has specific tasks, the team approach affords a coordination that ensures that the most effective use will be made of each member's strengths. For example, by working as a team, the Department of Children and Family Services (or whatever the local child protective services agency is formally titled) and law enforcement can jointly decide when the best time is to interview, for example, the offending parent, allowing both to capitalize on the element of surprise. Coordinating the agencies' efforts also decreases the chances of mistakes that might weaken or compromise the investigation or the prosecution, such as too many interviews (which may give rise to a claim of suggestion), key questions not asked at the opportune time, prematurely tipping off the offender to the investigation, and so on. The adage "Too many cooks in the kitchen spoils the broth" can apply to the prosecution of child sexual assault cases, too!

The team environment combines the knowledge and skills of different professionals with a diversity of backgrounds, training, and experience. This collaborative effort can help team members—all of whom are passionate about protecting children—provide unmatched professional resources for the child and devise a customized plan that will result in the best decisions in each case.

Of course, such collaborative efforts are not always pure sweetness and light; there can be a measure of strife among the troops. Each professional has his or her own perspective and, to a degree, his or her own objectives. Team members can become frustrated by working together, and may even occasionally long for the "bad old days," when each team member worked on his or her own. But such differences usually disappear through communication and attention to the ultimate goals of protecting the victim and prosecuting the wrongdoer.

So, without further ado, let's meet the members of the team (in alphabetical order).

THE ADVOCATE

The advocate is the spokesperson for the victim and is literally in charge of the victim's care. The advocate is the bridge between the victim and the "system," not only for communicating the victim's needs to the system but also for explaining the system to the victim. On my multidisciplinary team, our advocate acts as the liaison between all the agencies, keeps us all coordinated and focused on the best interest of the child, and assures that all support and resources are available for everyone on the team.

This may sound like a lot of work, and it is. The advocate is the oil that makes the whole machine run smoothly, constantly checking with all of the team members to ensure we are all providing and getting the necessary support, communication, and information to and from each other. Furthermore, especially at a time (as with this writing) when the economy is sunk and crime is on the rise, the expeditious handling of cases becomes even more important. It is usually the advocate who makes sure that a case is not collecting dust on someone's desk.

Advocates must understand the many ways the lives of intrafamilial sexual abuse victims and their offenders are inextricably linked. The dynamics of these familial relationships often dictate the victim's interactions, behaviors, actions, and decisions with and toward each other. It is the understanding and the kindness of advocates that give many victims the comfort, support, and ability to handle the criminal justice system.

Sensitivity to how the definition of family may vary across cultural, religious, ethnic, and class lines in today's society is also necessary. Advocates take the "family" as it is, whether two same-sex partners and children, two opposite-sex partners and children, extended families, single-parent families, or whatever set of relationships the victim considers family. While statutory definitions of family may affect some legal options, it is the meaning and the emotion attached to the relationships between family members that create and sustain the dynamics an advocate uses to help the victim.

These family dynamics are critical—over 85 percent of child sexual assault cases involve relationships where the victim and the perpetrator know each other, usually due to a familial relationship. The advocate helps others in the team understand how these family dynamics affect the victim and the case, such as the following:

- It is not unusual for children to feel love toward the offender. This can be further complicated by physical, emotional, and economic dependence on the offender. Victims do not necessarily want the relationship to end; they just want the abuse to stop. They are forced to cope with the contradictory feelings that this love, dependence, and abuse evoke. These may manifest themselves in ostensibly mixed messages from the child about the perpetrator and the abuse experienced.
- The perpetrator often uses threats and coercion against the victim to maintain secrecy. Because the offender is often a parent or parentlike figure who is trusted by the victim, the victim is likely to believe it if the offender says something bad will happen if the child discloses the abuse.
- Children react to the sexual abuse in a variety of ways, ranging from acting out to becoming a model child. Some children—especially if they are older siblings—may also focus efforts on protecting other children in the home.
- Children need the help and attention of their primary caregivers in many ways as they learn life's skills, and they may prefer the attention of sexual contact—despite its painful aspects—to not getting any attention at all.
- Some children may be too young or isolated to be aware that sexual abuse is not "normal," and too afraid of the offender's threats and demands for secrecy to learn otherwise.
- Some children may experience sexual gratification, intensifying their shame and self-blame.
- Anger, rage, and helplessness may overwhelm victims, leading to self-abusive and/or destructive behaviors.

THE DETECTIVE

Patrol or "street" cops are the first to respond to a report of child sexual abuse. They conduct a preliminary investigation, trying to get basic facts like the five W's: who, what, where, when, and why. Sometimes the preliminary investigation includes bringing in a forensic specialist, for example, to lift fingerprints, look for DNA, examine blood, and so on. Following the preliminary investigation, the case is assigned to a specific detective for further investigation.

Detectives, unlike patrol officers, are specially assigned to a specific "desk" or "table." Every police department has its own organization of these, but let's take the Los Angeles Police Department as an example. In the LAPD, all sex crimes—adult and juvenile—are categorized together under Major Assault Crimes, except if the abuse is by a biological family member, in which case it goes to the Assault against Children Unit (ACU).

In Los Angeles, as soon as the police take a police report, it is classified by the type of crime and assigned to a detective specializing in that type of case. Once the detective gets the initial police report, he or she will immediately send it to the district attorney's office for review. (The district attorney, or "DA," is also called the prosecutor.) This is quite different from what happens in any other criminal case. In other cases, a prosecutor won't become involved until after the detective has completed his investigation—when it has come time to make the decision of whether to file formal charges in court. But in sex crimes, DAs are brought into the loop almost from minute one to review the case, participate in the investigation, and otherwise assist the team of professionals working the case. Prosecutors are brought into these cases early on because they are complicated and are extremely dependent on rapport building with the victim and the victim's family. Since prosecutors know what is legal and what is illegal, what it takes to prove a case, the elements of a crime, and so forth, the prosecutor has a greater chance of success by being involved up front.

THE DOCTOR/NURSE PRACTITIONER

It is natural for people to assume that the medical examination of a sexual assault victim must be a traumatic, invasive procedure that causes the victim extreme discomfort, pain, and embarrassment.

Well, not so. Given the advances in technology, the medical exam usually is neither invasive nor painful, and in fact can be a great source of comfort for the victim. One example of that technology is the colposcope—a binocular optical instrument used to magnify the genital area to assess the extent of the damage caused by the child's abuser. The colposcope does not touch the child and a camera records the conditions in order to avoid further examinations.

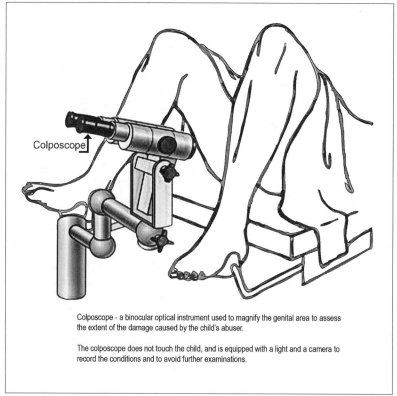

Colposcope - a binocular optical instrument used to magnify the genital area to assess the extent of the damage caused by the child's abuser.

The colposcope does not touch the child, and is equipped with a light and a camera to record the conditions and to avoid further examinations.

Photo Illustration by Rikki Sax

Also, prosecutors and investigators are aware of the sensitivity of any pictures of the child's genitals or body parts taken during an examination, and to avoid embarrassment and unwanted exposure that these pictures may bring—either for investigative purposes or for use during trial—prosecutors and investigators usually adopt procedures that work to protect the child. Some examples include taking pictures of the victim without her face on the photograph, waiting to have the medical professionals identify and explain the examination and the related pictures. Medical exams can provide key evidence in child sexual assault examinations. The exam itself may show how an assault occurred and can often reveal physical or scientific evidence on the victim.

Since juries are conditioned to expect scientific and physical evidence, an investigative team would be remiss in not pursuing an exam. Clearly, the best type of evidence from a medical exam would be some sort of physical injury that corroborated a victim's words. However, there are other benefits to a medical exam, including finding hairs, fibers, DNA, or other scientific evidence. A medical exam can also show that the medical findings or medical conclusion is consistent with the account of abuse that the victim alleged. And, lastly, it shows how serious both the investigative team was investigating and the victim was in disclosing the abuse from the beginning.

While in most medical situations, consent is required by a parent or a guardian before an exam takes place, it is not required when it involves child abuse. Representatives from child protective service agencies or local law enforcement can authorize an exam even if a parent refuses to do so.

Medical and physical exams are important because they can provide powerful evidence for prosecutors in criminal cases. This is particularly true in child sexual assault cases because children often do not or cannot provide authorities with the full story of the acts committed against them. Medical exams can help prosecutors and investigators to better understand and reveal what happened from the damage the abuse caused.

The exam also allows the care provider to detect, diagnose, and treat any sexually transmitted diseases, as well as hidden internal trauma of which the child or parent may not be aware. Knowing the full extent of the injuries also helps the doctors educate and counsel the child regarding the damages—emotional, physical, and psychological—that he or she may have suffered at the hands of the abuser.

Dr. Elliott Schulman at UCLA Rape Treatment Center adds a component to his medical exam that I have seen be very beneficial for child victims. Regardless of the victim's age or whether the abuse involved vaginal penetration, he prepares and provides the victim with a certificate of virginity. His view, and one I share, is that a person can lose her virginity only by consensual intercourse. Many children are desperately concerned they will no longer be considered virgins in the eyes of God, family members, or a future spouse. Dr. Schulman's certificate of virginity has made many children come out of the medical exam feeling comforted after enduring trauma.

In the practical world of a prosecutor preparing cases for trial, I see the strategic benefit of medical exams as well. Because jurors are inclined to expect that police investigations should have a "no stone goes unturned" approach, jurors do not like cases where there has been no medical exam. Even if, as often happens, the medical examination produces no relevant evidence, still the fact that an exam was conducted shows the state's multidisciplinary team was fair and thorough. (And later an expert can be brought in to explain why no evidence was expected, for example, in a fondling case.)

THE FORENSIC INTERVIEWER

The forensic interviewer is a key person in any investigation of child sexual assault. He or she must be able to gain the victim's trust, elicit information the child oftentimes has strong emotional reasons to withhold and may not even understand, and do it all without suggesting a desired answer from the impressionable child. Who conducts the interview varies from state to state and city to city, but it is generally a qualified forensic interviewer whose sole responsibility is to conduct the interview. In my office it is the prosecutor, while others rely on a detective or a child services worker. As a matter of practice, I believe it jeopardizes the case and subjects the prosecutor to the witness stand if he or she conducts the interview.

Despite the importance and difficulty of the initial victim interview, and the official sound to the term *forensic interviewer*, there is unfortunately very little formal forensic interviewer training or education. Most forensic interviewers, myself included, become such through practical, on-the-job experience. Through practice, observation, and a smattering of classes, I have learned to question children in a way that is effective without being suggestive or leading. I have found the teachings of University of Southern California Professor Tom Lyon, who advises on questioning children witnesses at trial, particularly helpful in conducting initial forensic interviews:

Children are presumptively competent as witnesses, and should not be disqualified by age-inappropriate competence questions.

Despite what people may think, the law considers children competent to testify unless proven otherwise, just like any other witness. But ask an eight-year-old to define "truth" and his confusion may make it look like he's not competent. Philosophers have debated that question for centuries. But ask the child what happens if he tells a lie and his answer immediately reveals he understands the crucial distinction between lying and telling the truth.

Child witnesses should be given an age-appropriate oath.

"Do you solemnly swear or affirm . . ." doesn't mean much to a six-year-old, and God can be a difficult concept for adults, let alone children. ("How could there be a God if He let this happen to me?" is a question I actually got from a thirteen-year-old incest victim.) A simple promise to the judge and everyone in the courtroom to say only what is so and not make things up should suffice.

Child witnesses in dependency cases who are reluctant to testify and/or at risk of emotional harm should be allowed to testify in chambers.

Children in court know the stakes are huge, even if they don't know the exact specifics—the fate of a parent, of their family, or whom they'll live with may be hanging in the balance. And if that weren't enough to terrify a victim, putting her alone up in the witness box with the judge peering down at her and the alleged abuser sitting at the defense table in front of her is sure to do it. Even judge's chambers can be intimidating enough. I try for the comfort of the judge's office, where a child can see pictures of the judge's family on his desk, paintings or posters on the wall, book shelves, and other décor to create a more normal and relaxed atmosphere that humanizes the judge and the proceedings. This can be key support for the child to be forthright and open when the questioning gets to the core—and very traumatic—issues.

All questioning on direct-examination and cross-examination of child witnesses must be age appropriate.

Specific types of age-inappropriate questions:

A. Closed-ended questions
B. "How many" questions
C. "What time" questions[1]

Anyone who has kids (as I do) knows that if you ask a young kid a "when" question, the answer is either "right now," "yesterday," or "tomorrow." That's not always accurate, but it's the best they can do. In addition, if you ask a child how many times something happened, such as how many times did your daddy touch your pee-pee, kids seem to always answer "five." I don't know the exact theory as to why kids choose five so often, but it seems to be the number of choice for something that has happened a lot of times without their keeping track. This doesn't mean the kid is lying or has a memory problem, it's just the way a kid's brain works. As a prosecutor I have to avoid these "how many times" and "on what dates" kinds of questions and prove my case some other way. For example, say Mommy testifies she worked every Wednesday and left her children with Uncle Ron, who had Wednesdays off, and had done so for a couple of years. I can then ask the children what happened on days when her mom was working and Uncle Ron was babysitting.

Child witnesses should be given instructions on the role of a witness.

A. "Don't know" instruction:

The "don't know" instruction reminds children that just because a lawyer or judge asks them a question, that doesn't mean they have to know the answer. An example I use is to ask the child, "What did I have for breakfast?" If the child guesses eggs, cereal, or anything, I say, "You're guessing—the accurate answer is 'I don't know.'" If I asked my own kids what I had for breakfast, they'd have to say, "I don't know," because I always pick up breakfast on my way to court in the morning, so there's no way they could know. "I don't know" is a perfectly acceptable answer and is the only truthful answer if you simply don't know.

B. "Don't understand" instruction:

Asking clear, simple questions is a skill that, frankly, some lawyers just don't have. So it's important to explain to a kid that just because a grown-up asks a question doesn't mean the question makes sense. If you don't understand a question, just say so and whoever asked it will say it a different way or clear it up some other way.

C. "You're wrong" instruction:

I tell the child witness that just because I'm an adult doesn't mean I can't make a goof now and then. If I say something incorrect or wrong, then please make sure to correct me. You won't get in trouble and I'm certainly not going to be angry about it.

D. Ignorant interviewer instruction:

Children tend to assume that adults know all the facts. As a result, they sometimes leave things out thinking the adults already know. I tell children I know nothing and this is the time to tell me everything. I personally take this instruction a little further by explaining I don't know her family, her friends, or what life for the victim is like.

Children should be asked open-ended, rapport-building questions at the beginning of their testimony.

Casual, ice-breaking questions are critical for everyone, but especially for a child sexual assault victim. You wouldn't start a meeting, let alone a courtroom examination, talking about the witness's private parts, assaults, or "good touch versus bad touch." The best rapport-building questions are those about everyday stuff—what grade are you in, what's your favorite subject, do you like sports, do you like coloring books, do you ever watch *Sesame Street* and is Elmo your favorite character? Apart from putting children at ease, these questions also give the questioner and the jury a sense of their cognitive and developmental abilities, how well they concentrate, and how well they articulate their answers.

Children should be asked to provide a narrative of the alleged abuse whenever possible.

Just like in the initial interview, the way to get the most genuine and accurate description of the abuse is to ask the child to say in her own words from beginning to end what occurred. There's another benefit besides getting the unvarnished truth: letting kids tell their story from beginning to end with as little interruption as possible often results in little nuggets of key information, previously not remembered or omitted, coming out. And telling their story this way lets children move quickly through the anxiety of describing the icky stuff. Sometimes the defense objects that my questioning "calls for a narrative," but that's easily handled by every now and then interjecting a "What happened next?" question. Juries want to hear stories, so the witnesses tell the story.

THE PROSECUTOR

The prosecutor—that's me. Let me take you inside my office. Most people think lawyers work in big fancy offices with dark wood paneling, fantastic views, and classical music softly piped in. They sit in fancy black leather chairs behind an acre of marble-topped desk.

Well, not me. My office is a cubbyhole stacked a mile high with files, books, and papers. The only thing I have clear access to is my computer, where I spend most my day. I do have a desk, I think, but I haven't seen it for a month, and right now where I last remember seeing it looks like a storage bin. Every day brings new cases to be reviewed and balanced—"juggled" might be a better word—with the cases I've already filed and their motions, witness interviews, and other trial prep work still undone.

I have police reports with paper clips and yellow stickies with notes to follow up with the detectives to dig into this point, follow up that point, and generally make sure the case doesn't fall through the cracks.

Plus reminders to me to keep the victims and their families updated on the case's progress and upcoming court dates they might want to attend.

Every new case means a victim who needs to be interviewed, by someone (i.e., me) who has studied every detail in her file. Like a hospital emergency room, we have to prioritize cases whether or not we like it—victims in the most immediate danger must come first. But how to tell "the most immediate danger"? We look for a several things, for example:

- Is the victim "in love" with the perpetrator, and so will the victim actively try to keep the sexual activity continuing?
- Does the alleged perpetrator have continued access to the victim?
- What is the age of the perp?
- What's the seriousness of the alleged abuse, for instance, intercourse versus touching?

In addition, I work with five or six detectives and four or five patrol officers whom I've encouraged to call me for advice any time they have a doubt about what the law requires them to do—do I need a search warrant? Can I look for pornography on the suspect's computer?

I am one of five prosecutors on my "team." Because we handle a very large geographical area, we are split among the West District and the Central District of Los Angeles, and further split among specializations. For example, my multidisciplinary team handles only child sexual assault where the perpetrator is an adult (over eighteen years old) and the victim is a minor.

Cases are sent to us at the DA's office via fax from detectives throughout the day. We first determine if the case qualifies for a "team interview," which means the facts alleged support filing charges. While many prosecutors (including me) are accused of being gung-ho and overzealous, we do not move forward with a prosecution unless, after careful evaluation of the victim's (and other's) description of the abuse, we are convinced we can actually prove the truth of those statements in court beyond a reasonable doubt. While the perception may be that we file and prosecute everything, the reality is that less than 50 percent of the cases that come across our desks result in formal charges being filed. And why is that?

The decision of whether or not to file a criminal case, and the choice of what crime to charge, are among the most important functions of a prosecutor. The first hurdle is that there must be probable cause to believe the defendant committed the crime to warrant even filing the charges. But lurking beyond this first hurdle is the ultimate test: there must be enough credible evidence to convince a jury the defendant is guilty "beyond a reasonable doubt" before the defendant will be convicted.

No matter how tempting it may be simply to file a case, a prosecutor has a duty to make sure that a case can be proven in court before he or she files it. This duty relates to perhaps the most important qualities of a lawyer—honesty, integrity, and ethics. Prosecutors who cannot properly assess the provability of a case and over-file lose their credibility and thereby jeopardize the chances of success with their entire caseload.

To that end, when looking at whether a case should be filed, the factors a prosecutor will consider are:

1. Has a crime been committed?
2. What crime was committed? (Which penal code section is involved?)
3. Who committed the crime? (What is the identity of the perpetrator?)
4. What connects the defendant to the crime? (What kind of corroboration is there?)
5. What defenses are available? (What will the defendant say?)
6. How strong is the victim's testimony? (Is it believable and can it be corroborated?)

It does no one any good to file charges simply for the sake of filing them. It is more traumatizing to any victim, particularly a child, to bring charges and then see the defendant later found "not guilty."

I use the words of my fellow prosecutor Cathie Stephenson in my detective classes at the Los Angeles Police Academy and elsewhere across the country: "What you file should be a function of what you want the outcome to be." In plain terms, this means prosecutors need to avoid the urge to charge every case, and to look to the actual likelihood they will achieve the outcome they seek—usually, a conviction. I'll talk more about this in chapter 11, where we'll discuss plea bargaining and sentencing. More time and resources should be allocated based on what you want the outcome to be.

In some child sex abuse cases, there is no useful evidence from the medical examination and no corroborating testimony to back up the victim's description of the abuse. Such cases often come down to little more than a "he said/she said" dispute between the victim and the alleged abuser. Such cases are generally not filed, often to the dismay of the victim and the outrage of the family. Under our laws, the defendant is always presumed innocent until proven guilty. This means that, by law, if the balance between the prosecution's evidence and the defendant's evidence is equal, the result must go in the defendant's favor.

To tip the scales far enough to find the defendant guilty beyond a reasonable doubt, prosecutors look for evidence to corroborate or support the victim's description of the abuse. It is rare that the victim's testimony alone is enough for a case to be filed.

I've devoted a whole chapter of this book to the kinds of corroborating evidence we look for in child sexual assault cases, but let me summarize the main kinds here:

1. DNA evidence
2. Medical evidence such as physical injuries consistent with the victim's report
3. Defendant's confession, admission, or statements confirming the victim's report
4. Defendant's criminal record or prior conduct, whether or not convicted

5. Pretext calls—the victim calls the perpetrator and talks about the abuse, often leading the perpetrator to make an admission of some kind. This is not entrapment but perfectly legal.
6. Testimony of similar abuse from other victims of the same perpetrator
7. Information only the victim would know (e.g., unusual scars on the genitals of the suspect, what a hotel room where the abuse allegedly took place looks like)
8. Other witnesses, including people to whom the victim immediately disclosed the abuse and who can corroborate the victim's disclosure to the authorities

THE SOCIAL WORKER

The social worker member of a multidisciplinary team is usually a person employed by the Department of Children of Family Services or Child Protective Services. It is the social worker's responsibility to direct the state's response to an allegedly abusive situation. This means the social worker assesses whether a child may be in danger, is being abused, or is being neglected—and what the state can and should do about it.

While many people view the social worker's sole job as the removal of kids from abusive situations, most social workers will tell you that their role is to provide the counseling, education, oversight, and other resources needed to keep the family together. Their goal is family stability, not to make every threatened child a ward of the state, while making sure that children who need to be protected from an abusive situation get that protection. As you can imagine, this is no easy or obvious task. In order to help them make these decisions, the social worker participates in all phases of the investigation of the alleged child abuse in order to better determine whether a child is need of protective services, foster care, or other solutions.

Social workers are involved in more cases than one might think.

Besides the obvious cases where the offender is a family member living with the victim, social workers also become involved when an offender who has abused children outside his family has kids of his own who may be at risk. Social workers must also evaluate the ability of the non-offending parent or family members to provide the support needed by the victim. Finally, social workers assist the prosecution team in making sure the victim is accessible and not subjected to improper influences at home during the pendency of a case.

You can't talk about the team without at least mentioning certain very involved and concerned people who are not on the team and who should not participate in the investigation. This will sound harsh, but the parent of the child victim (or her guardian) is not on the team, nor is any lawyer hired to pursue the victim's civil claim for damages against the perpetrator.

Caring parents often don't like to be told that they are not allowed to observe or participate in the interview process. However, no matter how good the parent's intentions may be, there is no good that can come from a parent participating in the process. Sometimes the parent tries to answer for the child when she is having trouble with a question, the child has trouble being completely forthright and open in front of the parent, the parent's emotional reaction to what comes out dominates the interview, or a whole host of other very understandable matters of human nature can impede the interviewer's efforts to get to the bottom of what has happened. Leaving the parent outside the interview room is terribly hard, but the outcome is not only better for the child but better for the case as well.

A parent's role is usually limited to escorting the child to the interview room and being present through the introduction to the key people involved, including the interviewer. Parents are encouraged to be supportive in this escort and "breaking the ice" process, as children are very sensitive to both the verbal and the nonverbal cues coming from the parent. A child who senses a parent's discomfort with the process may carry that discomfort into the interview room and be even more reluctant and torn about answering questions.

The primary reason for keeping parents out of the interview process is to minimize any pressure or prompting—intentional or completely subconscious—that may affect the interview. The goal of the interview is a clean disclosure without any suggestions, coaching, pressure, or the like, and so the best approach is for the victim to speak only to a trained interviewer. Plus, the parents are likely to be excluded from the courtroom while the child testifies at trial, so it is better for the team to assess the child's ability to articulate facts and statements without the parents present.

A view of the interview room from the observation area

Photo Illustration by Rikki Sax

Concerned parents, however, should take heart. Multidisciplinary teams—including prosecutors, social workers, and psychologists—consist of highly trained professionals who are sensitive to any discomfort a child might feel relating to the interviewer's gender, tone, or questions, and team members will immediately identify and address these concerns to make sure the child feels safe and comfortable during the interview.

One final word: civil attorneys have no place on the prosecution team or as part of the investigative process. Their good intentions in wanting to make sure that their victim/clients' interests are preserved for a later civil damages lawsuit are understood and supported. However, I have found that the involvement of civil lawyers in the criminal process only undermines the criminal case. I'll go even further: it is my preference as a prosecutor that any civil case be filed only *after* completion of the criminal case. I know the victim and the victim's family are entitled to bring a civil suit for damages, but filing it too soon can make it appear that the victim has a financial motivation for making a sexual assault report. I try to remind victims and their civil law counsel that since the standard of proof in a criminal case is much higher than in a civil case, if they help me get a conviction, the civil case will pretty much be a slam dunk.

CHAPTER TWO

THE FAX NEVER STOPS BUZZING

New Cases Every Day

It's Friday. It's supposed to be a quiet day. Most of my detectives are off on Friday because they work ten-hour shifts Monday through Thursday. But not this Friday. This particular Friday has shaped up to look like a Monday after a three-day weekend—people drinking too much, partying too hard, getting into trouble. I pull the first case off the fax machine. A twelve-year-old girl named Brianna was at a parade watching the floats with her dad when she was groped by a guy. The grope might seem minor to some (a squeeze to the buttocks), but a little digging reveals much more. The butt squeezer is a registered sex offender and his description is a near-perfect match to a suspect in at least two unsolved cases. So I have to get Brianna in for an interview and locate those other victims from the past, maybe get a line-up put together instead of just pictures, to see if this is the same guy.

As I am scheduling the interview of Brianna, I get a call from Detective Leslie Trapnell from Santa Monica Police Department. "You're not going to believe this," she said. "Try me," I say. "Well, Thomas Beltran has been accused yet again of sexually touching one of his students. That makes at least fourteen victims out there we know about, and who knows how many we don't?" Beltran was a thirty-year veteran ESL teacher.

Leslie continues, "Robin, we've got to move fast on this before the school district, the parents, and the media get wind of it. You know, schedule interviews, write a search warrant, set up surveillance on his house, and just get all of our ducks in a row immediately." She continues as I am thinking, "So much for dealing with the case of the thirteen-year-old girl who is madly in love with her thirty-nine-year-old biological uncle. That'll have to slide until Monday. Same for the statutory rape case between the fifteen-year-old and nineteen-year-old."

On any given day, I can get anywhere from one to ten new cases to review, consult on, and decide whether or not to file criminal charges. They are all different—often bizarrely so—but they all have one common denominator. If the case finds its way to my desk, it will involve a sexual assault of a child by an adult. It is my job to examine the circumstances and conclude whether a case can be made. That's what I do. And for all the years I've been doing it, each case still grabs my gut with an Ironman-strong fist.

Here are some of the differences. The abused child's age can range from two to seventeen years old. The victim's age means I can expect a totally different level of cooperation and disclosure. Older children may have immediately told an adult about the abuse they have endured, while a younger victim may have kept "the secret" locked up for many years. Some parents act appropriately concerned and supportive, while others are shaking nervous. Some show no emotion at all. There are kids who speak English and others for whom we've got to track down an interpreter before we can even ask them their names. Some cases involve legal residents, others illegal immigrants, and some a mix. There are people who've grown up respecting law enforcement and others who've heard bad stories or had a negative experience themselves and don't trust the cops, the lawyers, or any part of the system. There are cases with an isolated one-time situation and others that involve years and years of protracted abuse. Every case has its own steaming-hot emotional soup of anger, fear, love, hate—or all the above.

While some might think my days are filled with the same kinds of cases, in fact the variety of these cases never ceases to amaze me. While many in our society tend to lump all sexual assaults together, there is much variation. Victims are not all the same, nor are all the perpetrators. There is nothing typical or expected about the crimes themselves, except that each will affect the victim's outlook on life, decisions, and relationships for the rest of his or her life.

Whenever I ask a group of people what is "sexual assault," the usual response is that it is some form of unwanted intercourse—basically rape. But there are many kinds of illegal sexual assault beyond just rape or unwanted sexual intercourse. And all can leave scars that can be just as devastating as rape, oral copulation, or finger penetration.

ADULT VERSUS CHILD SEXUAL ASSAULT

The prosecutor's offices of some cities group all sex crimes together, child or adult, but I am fortunate to be in a highly specialized unit where all I do is prosecute sex crimes perpetrated by adults against children. Juveniles accused of sex crimes are handled by my office's juvenile divisions, and adult sex crimes are handled by the general sex crimes unit downtown. Separating sex crime prosecution depending on whether the victim is a child or an adult is the most sensible approach. The law treats these crimes differently. And so should we! Let's take a moment to see how.

Actions that are perfectly legal for adults may be illegal when one of the parties is a child. The acts that we are talking about in the realm of sex crimes are intercourse, sodomy, oral copulation, penetration of the vagina by something other than a penis (like a finger or an object), or touching an intimate private part of another person. Adult sex crimes are less about *what* was done and more about *how* the act was accomplished, primarily, whether there was consent.

There are basically only seven ways to commit an adult sex crime: accomplishing a sex act by force, fear, violence, duress, undue influence, intoxication, or incapacity. Each of these has its own specific legal definition, yet all basically involve the appearance of consent while the circumstances show that actual consent was not in fact present. If a sex crime is perpetrated by force or violence, it may appear that someone is willing (or consenting), that is, she is not fighting the perpetrator off, but the act is being complied to under a threat or actual force or violence. Force is legally defined as an amount of force that is greater than the amount it would take to complete the act without it.

Consent is generally defined as the "positive cooperation" in a particular act. Therefore, in the realm of sex acts, consent requires that all participants understand the nature and the extent of the act and are exercising free will in choosing to participate. If the circumstances show that a participant does not understand what is happening, then his or her failure to say no or to exercise some other outward resistive action does not amount to consent.

There are two primary defenses to adult sex crimes: either "it wasn't me" or "sure it was me, but it was consensual." The problem for prosecutors is to find evidence that will counter whichever defense is raised. For example, if the defense is "not me," then DNA evidence linking the defendant to the crime would provide strong corroboration. But if the defense is "it was consensual," then DNA evidence isn't much help—it doesn't prove whether there was consent.

WHAT'S DIFFERENT ABOUT CHILD SEXUAL ASSAULT?

While the main dispute in many adult sex crime cases centers on the question of whether there was or wasn't consent (including the ability to consent), consent is not an issue in most child sexual assault crimes. When the victim is a child, there is no consent. Period. Children do not have the capacity to consent to a sex act as a matter of law. Over and over again, I hear children describe actions imposed on them that I know are sexual in nature, yet the children have no understanding that it is sexual or even why the offender wants to do them. They simply do not understand sex.

Another difference between adult sex crimes and child sexual assault is that the age of the offender matters, as well as that of the victim. Legislatures have tried to realistically recognize the normal sexual and cognitive development in children and to fashion their state laws accordingly. One big age-related distinction is the age of majority, which varies somewhat state to state. Many states go further in categorizing child sex crimes by the age of the victim. For example, some states draw a line at the age of ten, making sex crimes committed against children under ten subject to a life sentence even for the first offense. Some states have a division in crimes according to whether the child is fourteen or younger versus fifteen or older.

Besides the victim's age, some laws take into account the difference in ages between victim and perpetrator. For example, a fourteen- or fifteen-year-old having sex with a nineteen-year-old is treated differently in some states than a fourteen- or fifteen-year-old having sex with thirty-year-old.

WHAT ARE THE DIFFERENT KINDS OF CHILD SEX CRIMES?

I find that many people still envision a typical child molester as a creepy old man skulking around in a tattered overcoat, leering at unwitting young girls. The truth is that most molesters look perfectly normal and in fact use normal adult positions of trust or responsibility relative to a child as the means to accomplish the abuse.

Child sexual assault may involve a variety of different actions or behaviors. It includes the conduct most people think of first when they hear a term like "child sex crimes": rape, sodomy, oral copulation, finger penetration, digital penetration, and other physical contact aimed at sexual gratification. *Digital penetration* can be defined as penetration with any object. Most people get confused with the word *finger* being used as *digit*.

While rape is a serious crime that calls for thorough investigation, the fact is that evaluating child sex crimes is more complicated. There many other forms of child sex abuse that can have equally damaging short- and long-term effects that have nothing to do with intercourse or penetration.

For example, there is a category of child sex crimes generally known as *sexual molestation*. Unlike sexual assault, where there is some kind of physical contact, molestation may not involve any physical element, although the perpetrator's behavior is still intended to use the child for sexual gratification. A classic example is when the creepy old man I mentioned above yanks open his overcoat to expose himself to a group of children. But this general category also includes many other forms of inappropriate behavior, such as photographing children at the beach in bathing suits, hiding a video camera in a dressing room, or sending sexually explicit letters or e-mails both about children and to children.

Another general category of child sex crimes is often referred to as *sexual exploitation*, which usually means some form of victimizing children for sexual gratification or financial profit. Child pornography falls into this category, whether the offender creates the child pornography, possesses it, sells it, or shows pornography to a child. Even more upsetting are cases where the exploitation involves child prostitution. Obviously a child prostitution case will often involve sexual assault and molestation. But the difference with exploitation, and an evil difference it is, is the financial gain to the perpetrator—that is, the child's pimp.

All child sex abuse cases pull on my heartstrings, but cases where kids are being abused for financial profit are particularly upsetting. One of the worst I've ever handled involved a girl I'll call Kimmie. Kimmie was fourteen years old and one of five children. Her mama had each with a different man who likely didn't know he'd fathered a child. Kimmie was Mama's only girl and had to help with the household chores and help care for the other children. There is nothing wrong with children having to do such chores, but what was very wrong and disgusting was the other work Mama had Kimmie do. She told Kimmie that to get clothing, books, or school supplies, Kimmie had to earn money. (What Kimmie didn't know was the money she was earning went largely to support her mother's drug addiction.) Earning money meant giving her body to the men her mother brought by. The men could do what they wished—touch her, kiss her, and lick her.

Kimmie told me it wasn't so bad—all she had to do was lie there and pretend to enjoy it. In fact, Kimmie got angry at us for even investigating her case at all. She knew what she doing, she said, and it was her own free choice to do it. She didn't have a problem with letting men grope her body and couldn't believe that she was being taken into foster care because of it.

Kimmie's story illustrates one of the harshest truths about child sexual assault. Besides the multiple levels of abuse by Mama acting as a madam and then by the men who actually physically did the abuse, Kimmie herself was drawn into the abuse emotionally and psychologically to the point of trying to defend it. The effects will likely be with her for the rest of her life.

Kimmie's case is a rather extreme example of the differences between adult and child sexual assault and why we take child sexual assault so seriously. By pimping out her own daughter, Mama subjected her daughter to abuse by multiple people, degraded her, exposed her to disease, and taught her to accept it all as normal. It is my responsibility to protect Kimmie and punish Mama, whether or not fourteen-year-old Kimmie thinks it is a good idea.

My tools for protecting Kimmie and prosecuting her mother are the child sex crime laws on the books. But not all levels of sexual abuse are prosecutable. Certain behaviors may be sexually inappropriate, but they are not necessarily crimes. Only if the legislature passes a law making the behavior a crime can I start prosecuting it.

So when do people go to jail? Child sex crime laws generally look to four things: the specific sexual act, the intent of the person doing the act, the age of the victim, and the age of the perpetrator. Prosecutors use these factors to determine whether a crime has been committed and, if so, which one. Cases like hard-core rape and sodomy are easy to categorize as crimes, so let's take something with a little more gray area to illustrate how these four factors are actually used: let's look at lewd and lascivious acts.

"Lewd and lascivious acts" is a phrase that you hear a lot on the news and in some of the police and prosecutor TV dramas. It sounds bad. It is bad. And it happens all the time. So many L&L cases came across my desk during my first couple of years as a prosecutor that I lost count.

Why is that particular charge so common? Because it's easy to prove and get a conviction. Most states define a lewd and lascivious crime as touching with sexual intent a child younger than a certain age. Thus, as a prosecutor, all I had to show was the victim's age, some kind of touching occurred, and the defendant did it to get some kind of sexual stimulation. If an adult male fondles a thirteen-year-old's breasts through her blouse, for example, I pretty much have a case.

L&L actions are also common because opportunities for physical contact present themselves on a regular basis, and may or may not be with sexual intent. Take the example above of the man fondling the young girl's breasts through her blouse. What if the man is a dentist who, while working on the girl's teeth, repeatedly brushes his forearm across her chest? Or take the example of a forty-year-old man touching the penis of a six-year-old boy—of course, we're outraged. But if the man is a doctor examining the penis as part of a routine physical examination of the boy, it's not a sexual crime. Not every touch is with sexual intent and a person's intent, being invisible, can be difficult to discern. My point is twofold. First, to illustrate how something as apparently black and white as a lewd and lascivious charge can quickly blend into gray; second, to sound a word of caution, all too often when we hear of someone in a position of responsibility (doctor, teacher, coach, etc.) touching a child's private parts, we talk ourselves into thinking the best instead of suspecting—and guarding against—the worst.

To further complicate things, the touching doesn't have to be of the child's private parts to be lewd and lascivious. Some states allow for lewd and lascivious acts to be filed even if the touching is on a nonsexual organ, so long as the touching is done with sexual intent. For example, an adult who runs his fingers through a young girl's hair and says, "I want to have sex with you," can be charged with a lewd and lascivious act.

I actually had a case where a thirty-two-year-old stranger approached a six-year-old girl at the park and put his hand on her shoulder and said, "I want to make babies with you." The act of touching (on the shoulder) combined with the intent (the statement) was enough for me to file what California calls a lewd act on a child charge. Was I being overzealous? Some might think so, pointing out, "Geez, he didn't even do *anything*." I could not disagree more. I think this kind of offender is precisely the kind the state needs to identify, monitor, and register as a sex offender. He is, by his own admission, sexually stimulated by children *and* he has acted on that unnatural urge—he asked a six-year-old girl to have sex with him. In my book, he's a classic pedophile.

Which brings me to one of my pet peeves. Excuse me while I sound off. Our criminal justice system makes way too much of a distinction between a crime that is completed and one the offender has tried his best to complete but has failed. This happens not just in sex crimes but other crimes as well. Take, for example, a woman who points a gun at her cheating boyfriend, fully intending to blow his brains out. But just as she's squeezing the trigger a car on the street outside backfires, the sound throws off her aim, and her shot goes high. She did everything necessary to commit the crime of murder, and only a twist of fate kept her from succeeding. Yet the prosecutor can only charge attempted murder, which carries a significantly lesser penalty (in California, half of the time of a completed murder). So, the defendant gets half the punishment because her aim was a little bit off. Unbelievable! Outrageous!

The same applies to sexual assault. If a man entices a young girl into his car, strips her, and is about to have intercourse when she manages to twist out of his grasp and run away, is the man half as culpable just because the victim got away before he was done? Why must the victim suffer a completed crime before the offender can get the serious time associated with that crime? This is a question that I ask myself almost every day.

So how do I answer it? I answer it by doing my job to file the maximum charges legally possible from the onset. This doesn't mean I try to get a life sentence in every case, but it does mean that if the warning signs of a child sex offender are there, it is my job as prosecutor to use every bit of legal ammunition the law gives me to see that the offender is held accountable, registered, and monitored. We need to know who in our communities presents a danger to our children.

Let's take a quick look at other common child sex crimes. Rape probably doesn't need much description: it is penetration of a female vagina with a penis. That much is true for both adult and child rape, but as we've seen, the question of whether the penetration was consensual or against the victim's will is not at issue in child rape cases. Children under a certain age are automatically considered to be unable to consent to sexual intercourse purely by their being under age. The law does not waste time trying to figure out if a minor gave consent.

Rape isn't the only sexual penetration crime. Sodomy is penetration of the anus by a penis. Digital penetration by foreign object involves the vagina or anus being penetrated by something other than a penis. Oral copulation, while not a penetration crime, qualifies for criminal charges when an adult puts his or her mouth on the child's sexual organ, or causes the child to put his/her mouth on the adult's sexual organ.

Statutory rape under most state laws is consensual sex between a victim who is between fifteen to eighteen years of age and an offender who is over eighteen. Statutory rape presents problems for law enforcement, prosecutors, and judges alike. For many people, a nineteen-year-old having sex with his seventeen-year-old girlfriend doesn't seem like criminal behavior. However, having sex with a minor is a chargeable crime, and the minor's age means her consent is irrelevant. The law doesn't consider minors to have the capacity to decide whether or not they consent to sexual behavior with an adult.

As a practical matter, however, few prosecutors consider it a proper use of the justice system's resources to bring statutory rape charges where there is less than a three-year age difference and the victim is at least sixteen years old. Nonetheless, a number of these cases continue to be filed. Why is that?

The reality is that in my world, 90 percent of statutory rape charges are filed by either the parent of the victim, or by the victim herself after being dumped by the older boyfriend.

If any of the above crimes are between blood relatives, then the crime of incest has also been committed—at least in those states that consider incest illegal, and most do.

I already mentioned sexual exploitation crimes against children, such as child prostitution and child pornography. I want to go into child pornography a bit more because while all of us would agree that child prostitution is a heinous crime, many consider child pornography to be sick and disgusting but relatively harmless. I disagree.

First, research shows that there is nearly a one-to-one correlation between possessing child pornography and contact sex crimes against children. In fact, government studies show each child pornography possessor has fourteen to thirty-one molestation victims on average before being caught.

Second, the United States is the number one producer and consumer of child pornography in the world.

Third, to generate child porn, the child must be tricked or forced (or worse) into engaging in obscene acts.

Finally, in many of my cases the perpetrator uses sexual pictures of children as a way to "groom" his victim. The pictures tend to normalize, at least in the impressionable mind of a child, the sex activity the perpetrator wants to do with the victim. Every parent has heard her son or daughter try to use the argument "but *everyone* is doing it." That's what the perpetrator is doing by showing child pornography pictures to a victim.

Take, for example, a recent case where child porn was used on a popular social networking site to promote this "it's okay, everybody's doing it" mentality in the victims. In that case, a man pretended to be a female classmate and asked boys to send naked pictures or videos of themselves to "her." When they complied, he used the pictures for two purposes. One was to help persuade other boys to get naked for him by showing them that many other boys had, as proven by the pictures. The other use was for blackmail. The man insisted that the boys who sent pictures meet him in person, or else he'd show the pictures to the other kids in their class and tell them the boys were gay. According to what was reported, thirty boys sent pictures, and seven were actually sexually abused before anyone told the police.

In the end, child pornography and other forms of sexual exploitation need our attention just as much as actual sexual assault. Particularly because child porn is crime scene evidence.

TYPES OF PERPS

Speaking of bad guys—who are these people? Many ask, what kind of a sicko would do these things to kids? Unfortunately, I know a lot of them. And it's quite possible that you've come across one or two, whether or not you know it. There is no cookie-cutter type of person who victimizes children sexually. That's why it is so important for parents to keep an eye on all the people in their children's lives, not just the ones who seem visibly dangerous or untrustworthy. As a matter of fact, in my experience it is more often someone the family trusts who wreaks the most havoc on kids and their families.

Like child sex crimes, there are categories of child sex offenders. The primary ones are: pedophiles, molesters, opportunists, and predators. I'm going to define these specifically, but please don't leave this chapter thinking these are the only kinds of sex offenders. The person you are suspicious of may not fit into one of these categories as I describe them. That doesn't necessarily mean he is innocent, and it doesn't mean he can't be caught and prosecuted if he is sexually abusing children. Listen to your gut—if you or your child gets the willies from the way some adult is interacting with him or her, then do something about it. I don't mean going around and making reckless accusations, but why not talk to the person about your concern? Talk to his or her supervisor, the police, a counselor, a minister, or a friend. Your gut may be right. And even if not, it's better that you are wrong and took responsible action than that you live with the risk of your child becoming a victim.

Psychologists, sociologists, and criminologists use the term *pedophile* to describe someone with an unnatural sexual interest in children. By this definition, you could be a pedophile purely by thinking dirty thoughts about children, even if you never had any actual contact with a child. But, as the law tends to do, it waits for action before it labels someone a pedophile. Legally, a pedophile is someone who has been convicted of, or is awaiting charges on, child sexual assault. You have to be accused of sexually assaulting a child to be a pedophile, at least in the eyes of the law. But for most of us, if someone is turned on by the thought of sexually molesting a child, we think that person is a pedophile, even without committing the crime.

Another kind of child sex abuser is called an *opportunist*. Unlike pedophiles, opportunists are not sexually fixated solely on children; they "take the opportunity" to have sex with partners their own age as well. For example, a thirty-year-old who has sex with a twelve-year-old could be called an opportunist or a pedophile, depending on whether the act was a one-time isolated act (opportunist) or whether there is a consistent, ongoing preference for or fixation on children (pedophile).

One problem with the term *opportunist* is that perpetrators often use it to transfer blame to the child victim. I have seen perpetrators who, instead of accepting responsibility for their actions, try to blame the circumstances or the victim for presenting the opportunity for the sexual assault.

Next is the *molester*. Molesters get excited from touching sexually but without any performing any penetration. The touch is still unlawful but it falls short of rape, sodomy, or other penetration crimes. The touch doesn't need to be skin to skin. It can be through clothing, a towel, or some other covering. Additionally, acts like flashing genitals, showing pornography to a child, and deviant sexual behavior, like bondage or defecation/urinating in public or on another's personal property, are all considered molesting acts. The law doesn't try to list all possible molesting behavior. The whole point is the sexual gratification intent of the molester, not the precise actions or behavior he exhibits.

Last and definitely worst of all are the *predators*. Predators are worse not because of what they do, but because of the frequency. If someone has sex with a child, he or she is a pedophile. If someone has sex with children repeatedly, that person is a predator. Seems straightforward enough, doesn't it? But keep in mind, there's a widely held belief that most child sex offenders will keep molesting or assaulting over and over again until physically stopped. Counseling and other forms of rehabilitation are thought to be inconsequential in stemming the behavior. So a "one-time only" pedophile or opportunist may be a predator who hasn't been pursuing children for long or who got caught early. The odds are that he has sexually offended a child before and will do so again.

Fortunately, the law hasn't incorporated these terms, at least when it comes to charging, convicting, and sentencing child sex offenders. Each instance of an illegal sex act with each victim is a separate crime and will be tried and sentenced as such, regardless of whether a sociologist might label the offender an opportunist or a predator.

THE VICTIMS/THE SURVIVORS

The best thing you can do to better understand the prevalence of child sex crimes is to stop thinking of all victims as angelic eight-year-old girls. Heart-wrenchingly enough, I've seen hundreds of such angelic victims. But I've also seen hundreds of scantily clad teenage girls or hormonal teenage boys who "got what they were asking for," as their assaulter or even some law-abiding citizens might put it.

The child's behavior may have been deliberately provocative and may have in fact inflamed the passions of the attacker, but that doesn't excuse the attack and will not prevent its prosecution. If a ten-year-old walked up to you and said he or she wanted to have sex with you, would you? Of course not. Why? Aside from the absence of attraction, you know that children are still figuring stuff out, still in the process of learning how to be a responsible adult, still developing their judgment skills. That's why consent is never a valid defense to a charge of child sexual assault—no matter how old the child looks or acts, he or she doesn't have the ability to understand the nature and consequences of his or her decisions. For the same reasons the law doesn't allow children to vote, drink, smoke, form binding contracts, and so on, it doesn't recognize children as having the ability to consent to sex.

I still remember a case that is a great illustration of this "children cannot consent to sex" principle. Cassie was fifteen and a half and loved watching her brother's basketball games at his school. She attended them so regularly that she became the honorary score keeper and started accompanying the team to most of their away games. Cassie's mom was supportive and did not think there was reason to be alarmed. Not only did her son play on the team, but she also knew the coach was married and had a son on the team as well.

Through her score keeping, the coach had plenty of opportunities to interact with and get to know Cassie. He built a friendship with her by acknowledging her diligence in score keeping and complimenting how pretty she looked and how mature she acted. He volunteered to drive Cassie and her brother home from practice and games, and soon was phoning her under the guise of official team business.

Cassie enjoyed the attention and the responsibility, and she found the coach much more mature and kind than any of the boys she knew. Cassie knew he was forty-seven, but his athletic energy and personality made him seem younger, and besides, she always liked older men. Barely three months after they met, the coach asked Cassie to meet him at the gym, where he "confessed" he loved her. Curious and flattered, she went to the beach with him and, in her words, they "made love." The relationship and sex continued for two years. They had sex everywhere they could yet managed to keep their secret. Cassie told her mom and friends she had a "boyfriend" but lied and said that it was a boy from another school. It was all a fairy tale to Cassie, even though her prince was married and more than thirty years older.

One day Cassie stopped by the gym as a "surprise" for the coach and caught him making out with another student. Cassie was crushed, and like any teenager suffering a broken heart, she spilled her guts to her friends. "How could he?" After that, it took just a day before the gossip made its way around town and the coach was in custody. Cassie, still in love with the coach, was furious with his arrest. After all, it was a totally consensual relationship, and she didn't want it to end.

While a teenage minor's acquiescence may affect how people perceive the acts, everyone needs to be aware that often the only reason a child is targeted is because the adult wants to use his or her authority, position, or other control to get the child to consent to satisfying their adult sexual desires. When the child is dependent on the adult for care, nurturing, education, shelter, and so on, the coercion is particularly egregious. The minor may feel his or her life is at risk if he or she resists the adult's wishes.

Just because juveniles look like adults doesn't mean they are, even when they deliberately dress up to look like adults. Children, no matter whether they are six or sixteen, no matter how short their skirts are or how much makeup they have on, deserve to be protected against adult perpetrators. And until more people realize that children are children— that they do not have the capacity to truly consent to sexual content— and recognize the need to protect all children against child sexual abuse, my fax will continue buzzing all day long.

CHAPTER THREE

THE CASES THAT PUSH THE ENVELOPE

Vince was a sixteen-year-old high school junior who missed his bus and was running, trying to get to school on time. So when a woman pulled over and offered him a lift, he gratefully hopped in her Toyota. She asked if he wanted a haircut, saying she owned a beauty salon. Vince declined the offer and the woman gave him a business card for her salon. Later when I asked Vince why he got into the car, he just shrugged and said, "She didn't look dangerous or anything."

Once she had Vince in the car, the woman pulled over and began rubbing his leg and groin area over his clothing. She told Vince to "pull it out." Vince was unable to exit the car, and the woman unzipped his pants, exposed his penis, and began to stroke it, using both hands. This went on for approximately ten minutes. Vince stated his penis became erect, but he did not ejaculate. Finally, some pedestrians came close and the woman stopped. When they had passed, the woman unlocked the car door and let Vince get out.

Vince immediately ran to school. Once there, he ran into a male cousin and told him what had happened. "You lucky dog!" the cousin laughed. His advice was to "just blow it off." This did not sit well with Vince. After all, Vince was a cadet, a teenager who volunteered at the police station. From his experience, he knew that the police were the people to call. As Vince was walking to the main office, he ran into the school resource officer who was the LAPD person on this particular campus. Vince reported what happened and the resource officer immediately called a detective to come to the campus. From there, Vince was brought to the Center to meet me.

While the detective was driving Vince to meet with the rest of the team, other patrol officers went to the beauty shop on the card and, sure enough, a woman named Ota matching Vince's description was there. Ota was arrested and when the police ran her criminal history, they found that not only was Ota registered sex offender, but "Ota" was in fact "Oto"—a man.

There are cases that are "different" from what people expect when they think of child sex crimes. These are the cases where something doesn't fit the stereotypes, whether it's the nature of the victim, what a perpetrator looks like, or what the circumstances of an assault are. Many of these "different" cases are encrusted with myths and misconceptions. Because they are less expected, they are more likely to go unnoticed or unreported. This chapter will turn the spotlight on four of these "different" kinds of cases and bust the myths and misconceptions that can make it hard to discover and prosecute them.

MALE VICTIMS

Sexual abuse of boys is vastly understudied, underreported, and misunderstood. According to RAINN (Rape Abuse Incest National Network), 2.78 million men in the United States have been victims of sexual assault. The Justice Department's statistics say one in six boys will be sexually abused before his eighteenth birthday. RAINN also reports that one in thirty-three American males will be raped at some point in his lifetime or suffer an attempted rape.

There are a lot of myths in our society about the sexual victimization of males. Let's debunk some of the main ones.

"MOST SEXUAL ASSAULTS OF MALE CHILDREN ARE PERPETRATED BY HOMOSEXUAL MALES."

Sexual assault is not about sexual preference. Sure, some child molesters have gender and/or age preferences, but the vast majority of those who seek out boys are not homosexuals. Frankly, it is of no importance to me whether the perpetrator is heterosexual or homosexual. Anyone who assaults a child, regardless of the victim's sex or the perpetrator's sexual preference, has one label: pedophile.

While professionals know that this is a myth and usually dismiss it, the thought can consume a victim. A boy who is molested by a male perpetrator often fears that if he reports it, he will be perceived as a homosexual. Or worse, he fears he will "turn gay" due to the male-on-male abuse. I know, that's an old-fashioned notion in our enlightened society, but believe me, to a teenager, being gay or being perceived as gay when you're not is a big, big deal. So the effect of this myth is that boys who suffer male-on-male abuse are reluctant to report it. Those statistics I started this section with may be too low if the majority of these crimes are going unreported.

"SEXUALLY ASSAULTED BY A FEMALE? YOU DESERVE A HIGH FIVE."

There is a widespread attitude that boys who "get laid" by an older woman should consider themselves lucky. Society has generally supported the notion that a boy initiated into a heterosexual relationship by an older woman is simply undergoing a rite of passage.

The reality is that sexual assault of a minor has the same damaging effects for boys and girls. It is coercing a child to engage in an activity that he or she is not physically, mentally, or developmentally able to understand, appreciate, or consent to. The sexual decision is being made by the adult, and that's assault.

To illustrate this stereotype, recall the case of thirty-four-year-old teacher Mary Kay Letourneau who molested her thirteen-year-old student. This case caused much debate on the equal treatment between men and woman with respect to criminal molestation and sexual assault in American culture. Fortunately, Judge Linda Lau, the judge who sentenced Letourneau, applied the law and sentenced her to eighty-nine months in prison and to register as a sex offender, a status that will be with her for the rest of her life. But to this day, people wonder and question whether Mary Kay Letourneau was a criminal, a woman in a loving relationship, or herself a victim.

"BOYS ARE TOUGH AND DON'T GET ALL SOPPY AND 'WIMP OUT' AFTER A SEXUAL ASSAULT."

The effects of sexual assault are devastating for males and females alike. But the perception that males are supposed to be "strong" and tough it out makes the chances of disclosure, and therefore help and recovery, even lower for boys than for girls.

In truth, what matters is not the sex of the victim, but that he or she is a child. Male children are just as clueless about sex; intimidated by adults; subject to the same pressures of dependency, trust, and need for affection; and are similarly vulnerable to their perpetrators. As in all sexual assaults, the perpetrator uses his or her age, status, and power to take advantage of a young boy for sexual purposes. Boys deserve just as much support in prosecuting their abusers as girls.

The acts that qualify as sexual assault are the same for males as females, with the exception (in some states) of rape. Male sexual assaults include unwanted touching, fondling, or groping of a male's body including the penis, scrotum, or buttocks, even through his clothes. Male rape is any kind of sexual assault that involves forced anal sex, including any amount of penetration of the anus.

When it comes to children under fourteen, I tend to file the same sexual assault charges for the same sexual acts, whether the victim is a boy or a girl. Recall that when a state's statute says any sexual touching of a child under a certain age (fourteen here in California) is a crime, all I have to prove is touching with a lewd intent, that is, for sexual pleasure. By filing a lewd and lascivious act charge for a victim under fourteen, I can get a conviction with fewer details than, say, a sodomy charge. And if the victim of a sodomy is having trouble testifying to the specifics about the penetration (what child wouldn't?), an L&L is a great way to go.

Some states define rape as including any forced sex act that includes some form of penetration without distinguishing the type. For example, Rhode Island treats oral, anal, and vaginal penetrations all as rape. Such statutes help us recognize that all forms of rapes, regardless of the sex of the victim, cause great harm and are all criminal. So long as states (like California) do not define *rape* to include anal penetration as well as vaginal penetration, then male and female sexual assault will continue to be viewed differently by victims, juries, and the public. And that sexual disparity means I will continue to have a hell of a time getting boys who have been raped to tell me exactly what happened.

Most people simply cannot wrap their minds around the concept that a male can be a victim of sexual assault. This perception comes from the stereotypes our society has about males. All guys want sex, right? And if they don't, surely they can fight off a woman's advances? Well, no and no, as we'll see in the next section.

FEMALE PERPS

Fourteen-year-old Danny and his cousin Ron were sound asleep on Danny's grandmother's floor when Danny was awoken by someone licking his penis. "What the hell!?" He shot up from a deep sleep and his yelling woke up Ron. "What the fuck?" screamed Ron. All the ruckus caused Grandma to run in and turn on the lights, illuminating her daughter orally copulating her own son. Grandma called 911 and Danny's mom was arrested.

When Danny came to meet with me at the Center he was mortified. At fourteen years old he was just beginning to become interested in girls and really did not know what to make of his own mother licking his penis. He had no idea what to think. He tried to explain that she was probably just doing drugs (like she was known to do), or maybe she'd mistaken him for someone else. But then why did she keep at it even after Danny screamed and the lights came on?

What Danny didn't know is that his mom's blood was tested for alcohol and drugs and came back clean. Mom, at least according to her blood test, was both straight and sober.

Statistics show that most child sexual assaults are perpetrated by men, most often against girls. Of course, statistics in this area are problematic. They're pretty good with *reported* sex crimes, but how many more crimes go unreported? There are all sorts of reasons why the statistics about the number of female perpetrators are skewed. One is that male victims are less likely to report female abusers—remember the reaction Vince got from his cousin at school when he told him about a "woman" masturbating his penis? Another is simply the lack of education and information in the public arena, which has left a misperception that women don't commit these kinds of crimes, and certainly not against their own children.

Women do perpetrate sexual assault against children—even their own children. I know what you're thinking—*that's sick!* I couldn't agree more, but wait a minute. Be honest now, compare how sick you feel it is for a mother to have sex with her son to your reaction to the "father assaults daughter" scenario we've been talking about thus far. Do you feel a difference? I feel a difference, as a human being and a mother; but as a prosecutor, I see none.

I probably hold the same views about this that many of you do. I think moms are, by nature or nurture, inherently more protecting, more nurturing, and more strongly bonded with their children than are their male counterparts. (I am all about women's rights and equality, but I'm also a firm believer in acknowledging and respecting *real* differences between men and women. A mom's role as a parent and a caregiver is one.)

Things outside of the norm, such a female perpetrators, require special care. Not only does the team have to put aside their attitudes and preconceptions to properly investigate and support the victim, but an "outside the norm" case has to be as understandable, credible, and criminal as any other to the jury. Women as perpetrators, though less common, should be regarded with the same scrutiny by a jury that can ultimately understand and convict.

DIVORCE/CUSTODY CASES

What do you think when you read that in the middle of a particularly nasty divorce case, allegations of sexual abuse were suddenly brought up? If you're like most people, you tend to discount the charges of sex abuse, thinking it's just another way for one of the parents to attack the other in hopes of getting full custody of the children. Well, maybe that's true in some cases. But my experience is just the opposite: divorce proceedings are far more likely to open the door to disclosure of *true* cases of abuse than to generate false reports.

Let me give you an example. Bella was a twelve-year-old girl whose parents were divorcing. Bella was working on an extra-credit project for school one day that required Internet research. While online, she inadvertently clicked on a pornographic Web site. Upon seeing the pornographic images, Bella became hysterical, crying out of control, and spewed out to her mother that a teacher at school had been touching and penetrating her vagina for over a year. Bella's mom immediately called the police and right after that she called her soon-to-be ex-husband, Samuel.

In the course of the investigation, I learned that Samuel had moved out of the family home just ten days prior to the disclosure. While the two parents apparently couldn't make it as a married couple, they did do one heck of a job as parents. Samuel supported Bella and her mom's decision to call the police, and he participated in the interviews, counseling, and court appearances. And while all the time there was a divorce case going on with the custody of the kids at issue, that dispute had absolutely no effect on Bella's sexual assault case.

I bring up this example because it is important to note that just because a divorce case is going on at the same time as sexual abuse claims are disclosed does not necessarily mean there is some reason to treat the abuse disclosure as inherently unreliable.

There is no doubt that a charge of abuse can change the landscape of a divorce or custody case. It's also true that a divorce or custody case in the background can make a child sexual assault case more difficult to investigate and prosecute. However, every disclosure of an alleged child sex crime warrants a complete and thorough investigation. I have seen, all too many times, prosecutors and law enforcement blow off the investigation and simply decide to back-drawer a disclosure because there is a pending divorce case. This is a mistake.

But it's a mistake for more reasons than just the fact that every disclosure deserves a complete and thorough investigation. We know that children may decide to disclose a previously hidden sexual assault when they experience an atmosphere of safety and unconditional acceptance. One thing divorce can do is change the atmosphere in the home. If the perpetrator is no longer in the picture on a regular basis, it stands to reason a child may then feel able to bring the abuse to light.

In contrast, fear of spending time alone with the abusive parent may cause a child to come forward and disclose the abuse. On the other hand, seeing the mother standing up to the father may give the child the strength she needs to disclose, if the abuser is the father or someone on his side of the family. My point with all these examples is the same: the change in circumstances associated with a divorce can *help* children come forward with *true* disclosures of abuse.

Like other sociological aspects of criminal sexual assaults, there are many studies that evaluate sexual assault claims arising during the pendency of a divorce and/or custody disputes. University of Michigan doctoral student Ellen DeVoe conducted a study in the mid-1990s that concluded about 67 percent of abuse accusations coming out at the same time as a divorce or custody proceeding are probably true, 21 percent appear to be false or possibly false, and 12 percent were indeterminable.[1]

A more recent study says that out of 169 cases of child sexual abuse allegations arising in marital relations courts, only 14 percent were deliberately falsified allegations.[2] This means that the overwhelming majority were legitimate reports. So what's the support for the opposite, conventional wisdom view? So far as I'm aware, only one-off anecdotal reports like "I heard about a case once where this wife got her daughter to say . . ."

Kathleen Colburn Faller took a more disciplined approach in her article "Possible Explanations for Child Sexual Abuse in Divorce."[3] She identified four situations that might lead to allegations of sexual abuse arising in the context of a divorce case:

1. Abuse leads to divorce.
2. Abuse is revealed during a divorce.
3. Abuse is precipitated by divorce.
4. Improbable allegations are made during a divorce situation.

Taking each of her four scenarios, one can see that the very dynamics of divorce may in fact lead to accurate, not false, disclosures of sexual assault.

ABUSE MAY LEAD TO DIVORCE

In my mind, discovering that a spouse has been abusing a child would be the no-brainer reason for divorce. Yet researchers Elizabeth A. Sirles and Colleen E. Lofberg found that only about half of nonoffending parents decided to divorce the offending parent after the sexual abuse was disclosed to the authorities.[4]

As I discuss in chapter 9, it still amazes me how many wives take the side of their offending husbands/boyfriends over their kids. And most times, "taking the side of" the offender means a lot more than not kicking him out of the house. In my experience, mothers often choose to believe the offender, and reject, deny, or refuse to believe their child's disclosure of the abuse. What's the kid to do then?

ABUSE MAY BE REVEALED FOR THE FIRST TIME DURING A DIVORCE

There are many reasons why legitimate allegations of sexual abuse will surface for the first time in the course of a divorce. As I mentioned before, a child may feel safer after the parents separate and thus able to disclose. The corollary may be true as well. A child going back and forth from one parent's house to the other's may feel anxious about having to spend more time alone with the offending parent and disclose as a result.

Parents, even under the best of circumstances, may have difficulty admitting to themselves (let alone others) that a spouse may be behaving in a way that is immoral and wrong, or even criminal. It is not uncommon for the nonoffending parent to be reluctant to accept a child's disclosure of sexual abuse as long as the parent is still invested in keeping the marriage together. This phenomenon, by the way, isn't exclusive to child sexual assault. We see this same denial in hopes of preserving the marriage all the time when a battered wife refuses to blame her abuser and insists on believing his apologies and promises to change. Once a nonoffending parent accepts that the marriage relationship must end, she may become more open to hearing and believing her child's disclosure. Children sense this kind of shift, and feeling that they are more likely to be believed encourages them to disclose.

Even when abuse precedes a divorce and indeed causes it, that abuse may not be disclosed until well after the divorce papers have been filed and the case is proceeding. A protective parent may not initially mention sexual abuse because of a desire to protect the children from the trauma of openly accusing the other parent and testifying against him in court, to protect the child from the stigma of being labeled as sexually abused, out of shame for having married a molester, or fear of the prospect of CPS investigations and court hearings.

Such a parent may naively hope to get custody and restricted visitation without mentioning the sexual abuse. But when this does not happen, the protective parent is then forced to disclose the sexual abuse to protect the children from spending time in the offending parent's custody.

In addition, some protective parents have themselves been abused by the offender and may initially fail to disclose the abuse when they file for divorce out of fear of retaliatory abuse. And again, they may only disclose the child abuse when they must do so to protect their children.

ABUSE MAY BE PRECIPITATED BY THE DIVORCE

This is probably the most rare scenario, at least as far as I have encountered in my experience. But perhaps that's just because the only way I'd know that a divorce precipitated the abuse is if the offender or his lawyer told me, and they don't usually go around making that kind of admission to prosecutors.

Certainly many individuals become intensely distressed during a divorce, and some perhaps may sexually offend as a result. The offender may be expressing anger at the nonoffending spouse for leaving the marriage, seeing the sexual abuse of a child very dear to the nonoffending spouse as a way of punishing the spouse. Such individuals may not have offended prior to the divorce but because of the divorce find more opportunities to offend and fewer resources to resist the urge to do so. The individual may have had a sexual attraction to children all along but been able to resist it through the sexual release of the marriage. A rejected spouse may become dependent and needy, and then turn to the child for support, affection . . . and more.

FALSE ALLEGATIONS MAY BE MADE DURING DIVORCE PROCEEDINGS

There are parents who have a vendetta and misuse the criminal justice system to support their custody claims. I wouldn't be thorough or fair if I didn't acknowledge this. In addition, a divorcing spouse may not intentionally file a false claim but may have developed a distorted perception of what is happening between her children and her spouse. She may truly believe that sexual abuse is occurring when it is not.

So the only answer to the questions about claims of abuse that surface during divorces is, as I said earlier, to make no assumptions or guesses—either the disclosure of abuse is false or it is true. Instead, the proper response is what we aim to do with every case: conduct a diligent, thorough investigation in order to establish whether an allegation of sexual assault is in fact valid. This includes:

1. Having a forensic interviewer conduct conduct a nonsuggestive, nonleading interview.
2. Looking for corroboration via medical, scientific, and physical evidence.
3. Conduct pretext calls, interview the suspect, and administer a polygraph or voice stress test.
4. Interview all available witnesses.
5. Investigate both the suspect and the victim before, after, and during the assault as there is more to a sex case than just the act (this includes prior sex assaults, other crimes, and juvenile crime history).

When a disclosure of abuse comes out during the course of a divorce or custody proceeding, it is particularly important to understand why the child disclosed this assault on this particular day. Let me illustrate with a case where the "why now?" question had an unusual answer. My fellow prosecutor Jill Starishevsky in New York had a case where a nine-year-old girl named Alice suddenly came forward with a report that she had been repeatedly raped by her stepfather since she was six. She had told no one before, so why did she disclose it now?

The answer was Oprah. One day, Alice was watching an episode of *The Oprah Winfrey Show* about children who were physically abused. The episode was called "Tortured Children" and watching the show empowered the girl with this simple message: *If you are being abused, tell your parents. If you can't tell your parents, go to school and tell your teacher.*

The girl got the message and the very next day went to school and told her teacher. How powerful is that? I mean really. Everyone knows you do what Oprah tells you to do.

If the jury doesn't hear why a victim has waited until now to disclose the abuse, jurors may think the delay is a reason not to believe the victim. Putting the reasons for disclosure right in front of the jury makes the victim's account of the abuse more understandable, and thus more credible.

There is one other relation between abuse and divorce that I need to talk about. As I've discussed elsewhere, abusers tend to target vulnerable or needy children, those who may feel an unfilled need for attention and affection, those who may feel alone and without the support of family and friends. Unfortunately, that can describe a lot of kids whose parents are going through divorce. Often, divorcing parents have so much of their mental and emotional attention focused on their own battle that there is little left over for their children. This can leave the children especially vulnerable to sexual predators. In fact, in some cases I've used divorce and its effect on the children as corroboration for why this particular child was victimized, as opposed to other children.

DEVELOPMENTALLY DELAYED

Susie took the bus to her school, a school specifically designed for children who are developmentally delayed (the now politically correct term for kids we once called "retarded," then later called "mentally challenged"). Each day her bus driver, Mr. Bill, picked her and the other kids up and drove them back. Susie liked Mr. Bill. As a matter of fact, Susie would tell her mom almost daily, "Me love Mr. Bill."

Every morning and every afternoon, Susie's mom was at the bus stop to send Susie off and to welcome her home. At the school, the counselor, Ms. Smith, accompanied the kids off the bus. On the bus, there were ten other kids who rode with Susie to school. Never in a million years would the school or Susie's mom think there was danger of Susie or any other kid on the bus being molested. The school itself was a premiere institution that prided itself on forty-five years of education with the best staff available.

After twelve-year-old Susie's checkup, the doctor phoned Susie's mom and said that Susie's blood work showed she was four and a half months pregnant. Mom was stunned, dismayed, mortified. The doctor, as a statutorily mandated reporter of any signs of abuse, reported the per se suspected child abuse to the "hotline." Both the Department of Family Services as well the Los Angeles Sheriff's Department were notified. Susie was immediately brought to the Center for a medical exam and interview with me.

All Susie would say in the interview was "Me love Mr. Bill. Me marry Mr. Bill. Me and Mr. Bill having a baby." After the birth, a DNA test confirmed that Mr. Bill, the forty-seven-year-old bus driver for the school, was indeed the father.

But suppose Mr. Bill had used a condom and there was no pregnancy and no DNA evidence to corroborate the disclosure by Susie. It would have been very difficult to proceed with this case without anything more.

If I've said it once, I've said it a million times—but it's so darn important I'll say it again! Offenders seek out the weak, the lonely, the needy, and those unable to defend themselves. Why? *Because victims make good victims.* Victims of developmental delay or any other physiological, sociological, psychological disadvantage make easy targets for abuse. Their impediments call into question their ability to accurately describe what happened, whether they experienced or only imagined the abuse they disclose, and whether they even know the acts against them were abusive, let alone wrong. And their actual age may make it difficult to convince a jury what their actual developmental age is.

I've already pointed out the massive underreporting of child sexual assault generally. But that's even more of a problem with developmentally delayed kids. According to research conducted in 1989 for Vancouver Centre for Human Development, an estimated 90 percent or more of people with developmental disabilities will experience sexual assault at some point in their lives. That's a stunning statistic—nine out of ten! And even more troubling is that sexual abuse of this highly vulnerable part of our population goes undetected and unreported even more often than sexual assaults on other types of victims.

What reports we do get of assaults on developmentally delayed children usually come from someone who is statutorily mandated to report signs of abuse, like a physician who finds a child is pregnant or has a sexually transmitted disease, or an alert teacher who may have seen or heard something that made her suspect child sexual abuse. Such mandated reporters, as they are called, do not need conclusive proof before they can report, and they don't need to conduct an investigation. All one needs before making a report is some reason to suspect there has been some sort of abuse.

Of course, before we can prosecute, we need some sort of corroboration, just like with any other case of sexual assault. And the reality is that with a victim whose ability to articulate the abuse is weak due to a disability, the level of corroboration may need to be greater.

So what to do? First, all team members need special training in dealing with and interviewing children who have special needs. And "special needs" doesn't mean just developmentally delayed kids. Autism is different from Asperger's, which is different from ADHD. While every team member can't be an MD with a psychiatry certification, it is important that the members of the team are aware of and trained to deal with the needs and abilities of developmentally delayed victims. Even if the jurisdiction has a forensic interviewer who is equipped to interview a developmentally disabled child, the prosecutor must also be able to elicit an adequate description of the abuse from the child on the stand. If the prosecutor cannot get the child to answer the questions in court, there may be serious issues about whether the child is qualified as a witness and can present any evidence at all.

While there are specific nuances and greater myths when it comes to the sexual abuse of developmentally disabled victims, there are some basic facts:

1. Sexual abuse of developmentally disabled victims is often committed by a person the victim knows.
2. Developmentally disabled victims often delay in disclosing the abuse and their difficulties in articulation may cause disclosures to be misinterpreted or go unnoticed entirely.
3. Just as perpetrators look for known weaknesses in a victim, there are offenders who specifically look for people with disabilities because they know that they will have difficulties disclosing, and their dependence on the abuser will often be a gateway to initiate the abuse.

As if all this were not enough, there is an even more sinister side to sexual abuse of the developmentally delayed. I realized this only after reading an article by Dr. Charles Schulbert, Kathi Makaroff, William Holmes, and Sharon Cooper in which they say:

> Myths that propagate the development of psychological justification of a hate crime include the following:
>
> The dehumanization myth: perpetrators may feel their abusive behavior is not really injuring another person because the person with a disability is less than a full member of society.
>
> The "damaged merchandise" myth: the individual with a disability is worthless and has nothing to lose.
>
> The "feeling no pain" myth: people with disabilities have no feelings and are immune to pain and suffering.
>
> The "disabled menace" myth: individuals with disabilities are different, unpredictable, and dangerous, promoting fear in others.
>
> The "helpless" myth: individuals with disabilities are helpless and therefore unable to take care of themselves, making them vulnerable to abuse and manipulation.[5]

This passage started me thinking that anyone who commits a sex crime against a developmentally disabled victim is really committing a hate crime and should suffer the enhanced sentences like those found in the hate crime sections of various state penal codes. In California, we have increased penalties for crimes against dependent adults, but they don't seem to apply the same reasoning and enhanced penalties for crimes against children who are developmentally disabled. And really, a developmentally disabled child is doubly vulnerable, and therefore, the persons preying on them should be doubly punished. We need to change the law.

CHAPTER FOUR
FIRST MEETINGS AND IMPRESSIONS

The court finally adjourns for the lunch recess and I rush to the Center to meet my 1 p.m. interview. I get there and the victim advocate has already discussed the process with the victim. She knows what to expect. The rest of my team is assembled. I turn to Lucy, the victim.

Lucy could not be more different from the stereotypical high school girl from Malibu. She doesn't have sun-bleached blond hair, doesn't have a perfect tan, doesn't like school, and doesn't have many friends. But she does have every fifteen-year-old girl's desperate yearning to fit in.

I pull my chair a little closer to begin my interview about what brought her to the Center when I instantly recognize the potent smell of last night's drinks combined with today's vomit. I ask her simply, "What happened?"

And what comes out is an all-too-familiar story. Lucy was at a Halloween party at another kid's house. She came with another friend (but had no clue what happened to her), drank too much, passed out, and woke up with some naked guy lying on top of her. She remembered no details other than her Halloween costume, which she no longer had on, was a French maid's outfit.

The second she staggered home the next day her mom saw her condition and called the police.

The victim interview is the single most important part of the investigation and prosecution process. It is here where two key questions are answered. One, was a crime committed? And, two, can the victim describe what occurred with enough credibility to withstand cross-examination should I file the case in court? The importance of this first interview is something of which most children are keenly aware, despite our constant assurances that it is only one piece of the investigation process.

Setting the interview up is often almost as difficult as conducting it. The victim advocate schedules the meeting so all members of the team can attend, which is always a challenge with court schedules, other meetings, filing deadlines, and the ever-present bureaucratic logistics of each agency.

Equally if not even more challenging can be the task of getting the victim to commit to come to the interview in the first place. Advocates have heard every excuse imaginable and know those excuses are most often masks for the victim's fear, embarrassment, apathy, denial, and so on. The advocate gently heads off excuses with offers of transportation, promises of therapeutic referrals, and guarantees of an expert investigative team. Even so, no one really knows if the interview is actually going to happen until every team member and the victim are physically together in one room at the same time.

HOW THE INTERVIEW IS CONDUCTED

There is no single correct way to conduct a child victim interview, but there are literally hundreds of ways to screw them up. The techniques used in traditional crime investigation or even adult sex abuse cases will not work with children. As any parent knows, preschoolers, grade schoolers, and adolescent children all communicate very differently, especially with adults, and each must be approached on his or her level of communication.

In addition, as the interviewer, I must be mindful of the dynamics of the abuse, the individual child's developmental status and capabilities, and the subtle cues of fear, withdrawal, and denial the victim sends me. Now add the fact that the semantics and word choices need to be carefully crafted (yet appear spontaneous) in order to meet the legal standards and evidentiary hurdles that will undoubtedly come up in court later on. It's enough to send even an efficient multitasker into a tizzy.

As prosecutor, I must be poised, comfortable, and patient as I gradually press up against and through the victim's the comfort zone, trying to get to the details of how the child has been abused. A key concept that I and everyone else on the team needs to know and accept is that this is an interview, and not an interrogation.

If the victim isn't in the hospital, the interview usually begins with the child being brought into a special kids' waiting room set up by my office. Picture a child-friendly, pastel-colored room filled with all kinds of distractions—toys, coloring books, children's magazines. But time and time again, I find there is no way to really distract the child from the reason for this meeting, even though in some centers there are enough toys around to occupy a class of fifty kids.

The child is met by a volunteer who knows something has happened to the child, but doesn't know what, where, when, or by whom—and doesn't ask. The volunteer makes small talk until the baton is passed to the advocate, the person who organized the meeting in the first place. The volunteer is the first in a series of steps designed to ease a probably nervous and scared child. At the same time, it is critical for the volunteer to avoid any discussion or contact that might influence what the child has to say about the abuse.

After saying hello, the advocate immediately walks the child to an interview room for preparation for what is about to come. Again, the effort is to make a strange place and process less intimidating. Key parts of the room are pointed out—the places where everyone will sit, the speaker, and of course, the one-way mirror.

The mirror is often the source of many questions by victims and their parents. Who wouldn't be worried about a room with a big one-way mirror on one wall, where unknown others are watching from the other side? My team's practice is to tell children and their parents straightaway that yes, the entire process will be observed through the mirror. We do this because the child has probably been lied to and deceived by the abuser, and we need to show we're different. Also, by telling children the truth, my team is modeling honesty for them. Finally, we can gain rapport with the victim by starting on the side of open communication, encouraging him or her to trust us with the truth. And since truth is the cornerstone of the justice process, we must begin our pursuit of it from the get-go.

So we show them the observation room and let them see what it is like. We tell them the different roles of the different people and tell them why everyone is observing. We also tell them if the phone rings in our room, it'll be someone in the observation room reminding me to ask something I forgot. But in general the kids quickly come to ignore the mirror. For example, sometimes a kid will say "I'm hungry" and moments later the advocate, who has been in the observation room, comes running in with a snack. I have heard kids say, "Wow! That's magic!" because they really do forget they are being observed.

The orientation process has other purposes in addition to calming the victim's immediate fears or concerns. It also provides the advocate with a quick assessment of the child's developmental capabilities. A greeting and some initial small talk is usually all that is necessary for an experienced advocate to assess a child's mental status and development for the real interview yet to come. The third purpose of the orientation is educational: to inform the victim who the team members are, what the role of each is, and which of them will be sitting behind the mirror.

With the team members assembled in their respective places and the child oriented as to who is observing, the interview is now ready to begin. Enter me, the DA who has been described to the child and parents by the advocate as "the lady who is going to ask you some questions."

So, what questions do I ask and how do I ask them? The best questions are those that simply get the child to start talking and explaining in his or her own words what occurred. These kind of open-ended questions are the most reliable since they avoid even the appearance of suggesting what the interviewer might expect or want to hear. In a perfect world, all of my interview questions would be nothing more than questions like "Tell me more about that . . . ," "Go on . . . ," and "What happened next?"

Unfortunately, we don't live in a perfect world. More often, the interview will go something like this one with a young girl named Tina.

> "He grabbed me from behind, blindfolded me, and pushed me into a van," Tina tells me.
>
> I felt like I'm in a bad movie as I listen to Tina's abrupt words. "Tell me more," I say.
>
> "Well, then he pulled down my pants and stuck it in."
>
> Of course, I have more questions and I am anxious to ask them: "Did you get a glimpse of him?" "Did he say anything?" "Do you know if he had a weapon?" "When did you find out you were pregnant?" "Why didn't you tell anybody?" But I squelch them and instead just ask, "Tell me what happened again."
>
> She sighs. "He grabbed me from behind, blindfolded me, and pushed me into a van, pulled down my pants, and stuck it in."
>
> "Tina, you are safe here," I tell her. "Are you sure there isn't something else you want to tell me? Has anyone else ever touched you?"
>
> "No, I swear," she says, flushing slightly, then turns away.

Tina clearly has more to tell, but getting it out of her when she doesn't want to tell me while avoiding any appearance of suggesting the answer I suspect is true is tough. I'll get back to Tina and what she wasn't telling me a little later in this chapter. For now, let's stick with what happens during the initial interview.

Besides being the first (and ideally the only) interview about the facts of a case, the initial interview is a time when everyone on my team, and the parents too, are assessing the credibility of the victim's report, digging for possible corroboration, thinking about other witnesses who may have information, drawing preliminary conclusions, and deciding how the entire case will proceed.

Meanwhile, the child is also making assessments, gauging who can be trusted as well as who believes her report, and trying to figure out a grown-up system she's likely too young to fully understand. But even if child victims don't fully understand the system, they always have a sense they have entered a process that will have great ramifications, not only for themselves but for their family, the suspect, the suspect's family, their friends, schoolmates, and so on. And that makes them scared.

Each interview presents its own unique challenges, but each also provides a unique learning experience. From each interview, my understanding of the new realities of children's lives deepens, I learn more of the diverse dynamics of the various cultures in our society, and I am continually pushed to find different ways to better handle the same types of crime.

One of the toughest challenges in the interview would seem to be the easiest: to just listen to what the victim has to say. But to accurately hear a victim, the whole team must own up to and deal with the fact that we—like everyone else in our society—have stereotypes, biases, and prejudices. If we let those attitudes filter what we hear from the victim, we will not hear her accurately.

I mentioned in the last chapter the need to stop thinking of all victims as angelic eight-year-old girls. Even prosecutors have to remind ourselves that there is no such thing as a "perfect victim." But even as we repeat that mantra, we still feel the tug of what we'd prefer to see in our victim, and at the very least what we'd like her to be able to tell us.

Victims come with all kinds of attitudes, problems, histories—all the standard human imperfections (and occasionally some not so standard). Here are a few behaviors that the members of our team are trained not to use in assessing the victim's credibility:

- manner of dress, whether sloppy or neat, filthy or clean, staid or scandalous
- voluntary use of drugs or alcohol
- how victim met suspect (e.g., bar, sex chat room)
- prior consensual sex
- prior record (e.g., prostitution)
- delayed report of the event
- failure to take a possible opportunity to escape
- lack of physical or other resistance, passivity
- absence of emotion

Oftentimes, the victim is the one who most keenly recognizes one or more of these imperfections in herself. She may blame herself for not trying to get away or not fighting back harder. She (and sometimes her family) may be quick to chastise her for dating someone she knew only through a chat room or a hangout. This kind of self-blaming attitude, often reinforced by many in our society, can prevent victims from ever coming forward and reporting a sex crime. These negative self-attitudes can even be recognized and taken advantage of by an abuser.

What do I mean by that? Simply put, kids who will make poor witnesses are natural targets for sexual assault. Why molest a confident kid who's well known and trusted in his school, who'll probably report you and be believed by all, when you can prey on a "black sheep" kid who doesn't have many friends, gets sent to detention a lot, and is already distrusted by his or her teachers, friends, and maybe even the authorities?

An unfortunate but understandable problem is that DAs and cops tend to run from cases where they know the victim's imperfections will make her vulnerable to attacks by the defense lawyer. After all, if the jury can be made to disbelieve the victim, the chances of conviction go out the door.

But I think the prosecutor's job is to *wrap the defendant's guilt around the victim's weakness*. That is, if the drug abuse, poor grades, or promiscuity is the elephant in the room, the DA must stop trying to ignore it and instead turn around, recognize it, and use it.

Perceived weaknesses are potential sexual assault case strengths. If we take weaknesses and acknowledge them up front, we can turn them into corroboration for how and why a particular child was raped. For example, as in Lucy's case, the young woman who got drunk at the Halloween party, an astute prosecutor should explain that of course a smart guy on the make who wasn't having any luck would take advantage of a drunk girl like Lucy rather than taking the risk of raping a sober girl.

It is my job to teach jurors, and through them society at large, how and why a particular child became a victim. If I fail to resolve questions in the jurors' minds raised by some imperfections of the victim, then I am not only risking the success of an individual case but I am also perpetrating society's implicit bias that a "true" victim must be pure or ideal. The jurors on any given case are not only sitting in judgment on the particulars of one case, but they are taking what they learn from that case outside the jury box and sharing it with parents, friends, educators, and others in society.

Remember Tina's story? "He grabbed me from behind, blindfolded me, pushed me into a van, pulled down my pants, and stuck it in." Violent crime is something that we hear about every day. It fills newspapers, radio waves, and television screens. It is not inconceivable that a thirteen-year-old middle school girl was snatched from a bus stop, pushed into a van, and raped.

Stories like this send parents abuzz with fear. Even thinking about a strange person grabbing a child is terrifying. As a prosecutor, I immediately want to identify and find this guy. As a mom, I want him off the streets for good.

But going back to Tina, something about her story just doesn't feel right, and it's not just the curt way she tells it. Something does not make sense. For one thing, I happen to know how hard it is to have a baby, even when you are trying. I can't help but wonder how it is that Tina's one-time rape resulted in a pregnancy.

As I ponder that question, others come to mind. How is it that Tina didn't even know she was pregnant until she had emergency appendix surgery? (The police report came in from the doctor who discovered the pregnancy. He was required to file a "suspected child abuse report" because a pregnant minor is per se child abuse.)

And why is Tina sitting next to me answering questions matter-of-factly, calmly, with no emotion? And why does she use precisely the same words when I ask her to tell me again what happened?

Is she lying?

After Tina's interview, the investigation continued with other interviews, sketches of the van, searches for similar suspects in the area, and repeated requests for the public's help. The investigation came up with no leads, no suspect, no description of the perpetrator, and seemingly no justice for a young girl we know was impregnated by *someone*.

The case was filed away and sat in my drawer. Six years later, I got a call from the receptionist that Tina was in the waiting room wanting to speak to me.

"Remember me?" Though she is now a nineteen-year-old woman, I could never forget those sad eyes with pools of secrets lying beneath them.

"Of course, how could I not?" I answer.

"I lied," Tina blurts out before I can even get her to sit down in the very room we met in six years earlier.

I stay standing too, looking straight at her. "I know," I say.

"I need to tell you what happened, the truth."

"Why now?"

"Because I have a sister, actually two, they are nine and eleven, and if I don't come forward they will, I mean, will . . ." The tears began streaming down Tina's face and she collapses into a chair.

"Okay, I am here," I say. "Let me reconvene the team."

And so the three additional years of continuous abuse at her father's hands is revealed—the times he raped her, orally copulated with her, and the time he impregnated her. She tells of the times he threatened her if she told and relates how he told her what to say to me six years earlier.

And so the case is reopened and a new investigation begins. We start by determining the whereabouts of the fetus (in politically correct terms, "the product of the conception") following the abortion Tina had six years ago. If we find it, we can do a DNA comparison to the father's. I am certain that there is no way it would still be around, even if it had been made available to us back then as evidence.

After dozens of calls and hours on hold with the crime lab, we get a break. The fetus is there, one jar sitting in line with the hundreds of other bits of evidence from backlogged cases waiting for analysis.

Tina's case is a good example of how when prosecuting sex crimes, the rug can suddenly be pulled out from under you and everything changes. Any criminal investigation can change direction, for example, when a different lead suspect emerges after some new evidence is found. But in Tina's case, it wasn't just the suspect that changed, it became a different crime at a different location with a radically different report by the victim of the crime.

On the first go-around, Tina's case was a crime of a vicious stranger snatching and raping an innocent school child. In my mind, I had to conjured up images of what the perpetrator looked like, where he might strike next, and what I could do to catch him. I had sketch artists lined up and police ride-a-longs scheduled with Tina to help locate the suspect.

But nothing I was thinking or planning was even remotely close to finding out what had in fact happened to Tina. The single instance of a man with a van snatching a little girl he didn't know off the street turned into the case of the father molester repeatedly raping his daughter in their home over the course of years. As if Tina had not been through enough, the scientific results not only confirmed that her father was the rapist but also revealed that he had intercourse with Tina on the very day of her abortion.

Tina has not been my only case involving a "phantom" stranger used to cover-up a different sex crime that the victim either refused to reveal or was too afraid to report. Tina's wasn't the first, and I am sure many more will come across my desk in the future.

So now what? What happens the next time I get a suspicious report of a "stranger" rape? Do I assume the victim is lying? What happens if I press the victim and finally get her to tell me the truth, but there isn't a jar with solid corroborating evidence to back up her change? A defense attorney would have a field day with that one.

Like the public misconception about "ideal" victims, the public tends to have an unrealistic understanding of the most common forms of rape. When most people hear the word *rape*, they picture a stranger with a knife at a woman's throat, or a man pulling a little girl into an alley, stuffing a rag into her mouth to muffle her cries, and doing with her what he wants. People expect screams, blood, ripped clothing, and settings like alleys and park bushes.

Well, it just ain't so, as I've said before. These images are the exceptions, the unusual cases, not the norm. The routine cases that fill a prosecutor's brief case and filing cabinets are cases where the victim knows the perpetrator very well, is raped in the family home (often the child's own bed), and threats are used to silence the victim rather than a rag stuffed in her mouth. When a pregnancy or report of suspected abuse from a doctor or school forces her to come up with a story, is it any wonder that she describes the perpetrator as a stranger? If she were emotionally or mentally able to tell the truth, she would have done so long ago.

And in a way, the report of a "stranger" rapist has a measure of truth to it. The molester is often someone the victim has long known in one capacity, such as being her "daddy." Yet her "daddy" becomes a stranger when no one else is watching, and he does to her what no "daddy" would ever do.

Of course, I am not suggesting that stranger rapes never occur. Rather, I am trying to point out the discrepancy between the public perception that most rapes are stranger rapes while intra-family rapes are the exception. The opposite is true. Reliable statistics confirm that approximately 76 percent of victims know their assailants—that's three out of every four.[1] And what about rape usually happening in dark alleys or under bushes? The numbers show that 50 percent of all rape/sexual assault incidents occur within a mile of the victim's home, and 40 percent occur *in* the victim's own home.

So, if the numbers show that most sexual assaults are perpetrated by people close to the victim, why is the public focus so heavily weighted toward the danger of strangers? Why do parents preach, "Don't talk to strangers" but shy away from lessons about "good touch and bad touch" by people the child knows?

Perhaps part of the answer is that none of us wants to accept the reality that a person we know, love, and trust—a family friend, an uncle, a teacher—might be a molester. And while it pains me to have to say this, from my experience, this reluctance is often due to the parents actually knowing (whether subconsciously or consciously) that a person they have allowed to have access to their child is a dangerous abuser. Time after time, the signs are there. The kids are tuned in to their parents' denial and know they'll get no support if they reveal the truth, so they too perpetuate the cycle of either not reporting or falsely reporting. It is often the child who tries to protect her parents from the upsetting reality of the abuse by hiding it.

Please do not misinterpret my position. Strangers do exist and there are perpetrators out there, but remember that three in four of all sexual assault victims know their attackers, and 93 *percent of juvenile sexual assault victims* know their attackers. This means that actual occurrence of "stranger danger" among kids is only 7 percent. So, instead of focusing on people who lurk in alleys and bushes, we all need to wake up and watch people who have access to our children.

MYTHS AND MISCONCEPTIONS

But the misconceptions that most child sexual assaults are made by strangers and take place in alleys and under park bushes are not the only myths about child sex crimes. Public and state legislatures need to understand the truth if they are to deal effectively with the problem. Victims also need the public to understand the reality. After all, they are part of our society and so share its misconceptions. A victim who thinks her abuse is rare and that people won't believe her if she reports it isn't likely to report it at all. Even those victims who have the courage to disclose often feel judged or disbelieved by others. Misconceptions and myths are truly harmful. So let's take a look at some additional common myths about child sexual abuse.

There are many myths and misconceptions about child protection agencies and other professionals dealing with child abuse. One is that they focus solely on the allegedly abused child. Social workers are expected to help keep children safe. However, to effectively do this they must deal with the entire family unit and rely not only on information from the child but also information from parents, family, friends, schoolteachers, and other members of the local community. Their objective is not only to protect the child but also to provide education and other resources that will help the family unit stay functional and together.

Another myth is that if a concerned person reports possible child abuse, it will automatically result in the child being taken from the home. This is not the main aim of child protection investigations, and it is rare when a neighbor's report of possible abuse causes removal of a child from a home. Removing a child from his or her home requires a court order, and to get one the social worker must demonstrate that there is serious and immediate risk to the child. However, police do have the authority in emergency situations to remove a child, but only for up to seventy-two hours.

In line with this myth, some people tend to believe that reporting suspected abuse may cause more harm than good: that the children may be negatively affected by their efforts, that there may be costly legal ramifications, or that the abuser may later "take it out" on the victim. However, survivors of abuse routinely say otherwise—continued abuse causes more harm than action taken to stop the abuse.

One of the most stubborn myths about child sexual abuse has to do with gender. Specifically, there is a common misconception that boys are rarely victims of sexual abuse. The numbers tell a different story, and the reality may be even worse than the numbers indicate. While the landmark 1994 Badgley Royal Commission Report out of Canada did estimate that one in two females are victims of unwanted sexual act before the age of nineteen, it also estimated that one in five males are similarly victimized before reaching nineteen years of age.[2] And there is evidence to suggest that sexual abuse of boys is not reported as readily as with girls, so the one-in-five number may actually be higher.

Certainly, half of our juvenile female population being sexually abused before nineteen is a horrible, tragic statistic, and I do not mean to suggest otherwise. But 20 percent of our juvenile male population being abused is also a number we all should find difficult to live with, and the public should be aware of both numbers to address the whole problem of child abuse properly.

Also, it is generally believed that child abuse doesn't happen in normal-appearing, well-educated, middle- and upper-class families. The truth is that child abuse happens in every type of family and socioeconomic condition. One of the public's most dangerous misconceptions is that a person who both appears and acts normal—particularly if the person is cultured, courteous, and well-off—could not be a child molester. Sex offenders are well aware that their public presentation can allay suspicion, and they use that misconception to gain access to their victims.

Another myth is that the culpability of an abusive parent is somehow less if the parent was himself or herself abused as a child. Adults who abuse or neglect children are responsible for their own behavior. Yes, they may be influenced in their actions by factors such as their own experiences as a child and how they learned to treat children. However, this must not be used as an excuse for their behavior, or to deny full protection and redress to the victim.

One of the most troubling and deeply rooted myths is that children are sometimes to blame for their abuse, or that they frequently make false accusations of abuse. Neither is true. Adults are responsible for their behavior with children, and children are never to blame for the adult's abusive behavior. This gets back to what I talked about earlier. Children simply do not have the capacity to make choices about sexual activity; the impression that they may try to do so and "invite" abuse is simply wrong.

Equally false is the idea that children often make false claims of abuse. Children rarely lie about abuse. Certainly, their descriptions of the abuse may not always be consistent, given their reluctance and fear to tell what has happened and how their juvenile mind has attempted to assimilate what has happened. Similarly, just because children may later retract their stories does not mean they were lying about the abuse. Children are usually very reluctant to disclose abuse in the first place, and when they do they are often exposed to parents who may be very upset or in conflict with each other about the accusations, exposed to the serious consequences that flow from the offense, and maybe even exposed to direct and intense pressure from the abuser. Children may fear that the parent whose abuse they have disclosed will be removed from the family, or that they will be taken away from their families. Even in adults, there is a measure of relative comfort in "the devil you know." For a child, the unknown of what may happen if a parent is put in jail or if the child is taken from her home can be terrifying.

People also tend to think that children exaggerate the abuse they have suffered. After all, children do tend to exaggerate minor things like a cough that might keep them out of school or a scrape from a fall. However, contrary to popular misconception, research shows that children are far more likely to minimize or deny a family member's or friend's abuse rather than embellish what has happened to them.

These myths and misconceptions about child abuse need to be replaced by knowledge and facts. In summary, here are some important points to remember.

- Reporting suspected child abuse will not automatically cause the child to be removed from the home. The proper agencies will investigate and must obtain a court order if they find removal is necessary.
- Abuse may be partially understood or explained by the abuser's own experiences with abuse as a child, but it cannot be excused. An adult is responsible for his or her actions.
- Abuse victims are not always model or ideal children, but their imperfections do not excuse an adult's abuse and should not be used as an excuse not to prosecute.
- Children rarely make false claims of abuse, or exaggerate the abuse they have suffered. In fact, the reverse is more often the case, that is, that they tend to deny or minimize the abuse.

CHAPTER FIVE

HELPING VICTIMS REMEMBER WHAT THEY WANT TO FORGET

Four-year-old Sarah came to the Center to talk about what the man who owns the house her mommy rents did. I introduce myself as I do with most very young children: "I'm Robin, the helping lady, whose job is to help families—mommies, daddies, and kids." "Hi, helping lady," she said. In the initial chit chat and small talk (the ice-breaking stage), I am not only trying to put the child at ease but also studying to determine what her level of understanding is, how mature she is, and how articulate she is. We talk about everyday things like our favorite colors, TV characters, and food (pizza is by far the number one answer, by the way).

One of the ways I try to determine how well children can separate fact from fiction (or, as I like to refer to it, "things that are 'so' and those that are not"), is by saying silly things to see if they will correct me or simply agree with what I am saying. For example, I will say, "I have a pizza on my head," to see if the child will correct me and say, "No you don't." Then we can engage in a conversation about things that are so (truths) versus things that are not (lies).

After I remind the child that this room is the place to discuss things that are "so," we can then begin to the move toward the purpose of the interview. Sarah spoke very clearly, corrected me in things that were not so (there was no pizza on my head, there was no elephant sitting on the chair next to me, and she did not drive herself to the Center that day). So far, so good. As the interview progressed closer to discussing the act, Sarah began telling me she was a fairy with magical powers. When I asked her if that was so, she immediately said yes. She then went into elaborate details of her fairy costume, fairy rituals, and magical powers.

The practical prosecutor in me wanted to simply turn off and end the interview right about there. I thought, "There is no way in hell that I am going to be able to convince a jury to believe a four-year-old who thinks she is fairy." But something told me to continue, to roll with this whole fairy notion for a bit and see where it takes us. And after she told me about her travels to faraway lands, she told me about the wizard who told her that she was a fairy because she has the magical seed. When I asked her to describe the magical seed, she told me that you can only get it from the most private place of the wizard and it is hidden in warm milk.

Sexual assaults are crimes that occur in privacy, rarely with eyewitnesses to substantiate or corroborate the crimes. Whether or not we like it, in a sex crimes case the victim's testimony is the core of the case. In my case, that victim is a child.

Is it fair that the criminal trial for a sex crime focuses so intently on the victim? Is it fair that the victim, her life, her past, her decisions—everything is put under a microscope? Believe me, it is extremely troubling to watch a child testify about sex abuse acts in front of her abuser and then have that abuser's lawyer confront and challenge her on cross-examination, throwing up every childhood misstep she has made, no matter how natural or normal, trying to undermine her credibility and convince the jury she is at best mistaken or at worst an outright liar.

And what's more challenging is that more than 85 percent of sex crimes against children are perpetrated by someone whom the victim knows; the perpetrator knows more about the victim than the prosecutor ever will. For example, take the biological father who is molesting his daughter. He knows every test she has cheated on, when she got caught for lying about hitting her brother, when she snuck out of the house in the middle of the night, and all of the normal kid behaviors that can be turned around to smear and discredit the victim. It's hard to believe a father would actually put his child through such hell on the stand, but I've seen it happen time and time again. It's the "blame the child to save one's own hide" defense. In *Conversations with a Pedophile: In the Interest of Our Children*, Dr. Amy Hammel-Zabin draws on her own experiences as a victim and her conversations with a pedophile she calls "Alan." She writes: "What is so distressing to me is that although the victim and the offenders with whom I've worked experience feelings of being 'different,' the victims feel ashamed and blame themselves for their different-ness, while the offenders feel they are different by chance, by default, or by circumstances out of their realm of reality."[1] She explains that the perpetrator feels he is different because of some external reason—the family he was brought up in, the experiences he had or didn't have, and so on—while the victim feels that the difference is internal, that she somehow did something to invite or deserve the abuse. In short, victims blame themselves and perpetrators blame others.

Child blaming and victim blaming is not new, Erna Olafson writes in *Sexualized Violence against Women and Children*. "For most of the 20th century, when child victims were not viewed as liars, they were labeled as sex delinquents." She goes on to explain that "When a man sexually assaulted a child (or woman), it was the victim, not the offender, who was blamed and held accountable for the crime."[2] I wish I could say that this is no longer true in our modern, enlightened society, but the fact is that very often children are blamed for the behavior of the accused perpetrator.

Perhaps the most poignant example I've ever witnessed was in a sexual assault case where the stepfather perpetrator was accused of molesting both of his stepdaughters. After the first victim (age thirteen) testified for about an hour during my direct examination about the sex acts she endured and the difficult and scary process of coming forward and disclosing the abuse. She then had to endure an entire day (six court hours) of cross-examination by the defense. Hour after hour, she was asked about things like the time she got caught cheating on her fourth grade spelling test, about how she never really wanted her mom to get remarried, and so on. When it was finally over, this thirteen-year-old abuse victim stepped down from the witness stand, walked to the defense table, and hugged the defendant—her stepdad—right in front of the judge, jury, and all of us. I have never seen a more dramatic example of the conflicts an abuse victim can feel when her abuser is a parent she loves.

The defense attorney, however, used this hug as another reason to continue blaming the child. In his closing argument, he used the hug as yet more proof that she was lying. He argued that the hug was a sign of apology for her false testimony, and the visual proof was right there in front of the jury.

Naturally, in my final rebuttal argument I suggested that the jury look at the hug as proof that you can still love someone who hurts you and as a demonstration of how conflicted and tormented this victim was. I got the conviction, but at what price? Yet another victim who was further victimized by a defense attorney whose only real defense was to discredit the victim.

Another tactic used by defense attorneys to discredit the victim's testimony is to blame the adults to whom the child disclosed the abuse, arguing they suggested, coached, or even coerced the child into claiming she had been abused.

I see accusations of coached testimony most often when there is a concurrent divorce or custody battle going on. In that situation it seems that no matter what, any accusation of sexual assault or abuse must be false, nothing more than a fabrication induced by one spouse as a tactic in the divorce or custody case. Sure, that happens sometimes, but no way is every abuse disclosure that comes while a divorce is going on false, and no way is my investigating and prosecuting it a "misuse of the criminal justice system," as I've been told on more than one occasion. In fact, I'm not at all surprised when the separation of a husband and a wife, which also separates the child from the abuser (at least for significant blocks of time), gives a child the comfort she needs to come forward and make a disclosure without fear of retribution by the abusing parent.

I am not suggesting there aren't situations when an adult coaches a child to claim abuse in order to get the criminal justice system to go after the alleged abuser. Of course it happens. There is nothing that drives me crazier than seeing people who are willing to induce a child to file a false police report. Think what that does to a kid! I have seen kids who, many years later, literally do not know whether they were really molested or not. Not to mention how false claims take investigators away from pursuing real cases, tie up prosecutors, social workers, courts, and so on. Just as my job is to protect and seek justice for victims, I think people targeted by deliberately fabricated claims of abuse should equally be protected, and those who fabricate the claims held accountable and punished. (It is often very hard to prosecute charges of coaching a child to make false abuse claims due to the high "beyond a reasonable doubt" standard of proof in criminal cases. I'd like to see the legislature pass a law that would let us send such people a bill for the costs of pursuing the false claim they coached, and sue them in civil court, with its lower "preponderance of the evidence standard," if they don't pay.)

The ease with which a jury can be persuaded that a child's description of abuse must have been suggested or coached by an adult is just one example of a bigger problem: how much do people trust a child's testimony? While some people feel that kids are guileless and so should be automatically trusted unless proven liars, more often I see the attitude that kids are to be automatically distrusted from the get-go. And it seems the way we value their ability to honestly disclose and describe the abuse that they have suffered is directly related to the value we put on children generally.

While kids do have some special considerations that must be weighed in evaluating their testimony, jurors (and people generally) should begin their analysis of a child's veracity like they would an adult. Some are honest and some are not. Some are "good" and some are "naughty." Usually, we're a mix. No one is perfect, so instead of holding kids to a different standard we should look at kids with the same lens that we look at all people—as humans who can and do err. The only way to evaluate a kid's testimony is to focus on that individual child and evaluate him or her for who he or she is.

Even though it's obvious, it bears reminding that not all kids are alike. Just as there are mature and immature adults, there are mature and immature children. There are children who can articulate well and others who cannot. There are kids who are academically or socially advanced and others who are academically or socially challenged. There are children who appear to be cognitively aware and really are not, and vice versa. The bottom line is that even within each of the various divisions of "kids" (preschoolers, young children, adolescents, and teenagers), there is a huge range of behavior, development, ability to articulate, and overall level of sophistication, almost all of which is considered normal.

And there's no way around it. Some children are warm and immediately grab our hearts. It's not difficult for the jury to warm up to a child who is reminiscent of Macaulay Culkin from *Home Alone*. He's cute and precocious and people are automatically on his side. But there are also children who aren't so endearing. There's the kid who's already been caught shoplifting three times, has a reputation for being obstreperous and mean, and shows it on the stand. Should the jury treat that child's claims of abuse any differently than if the claims came from a child with Shirley Temple's charm?

Of course the answer is no. But making that no a reality can be tough. It is my job to make sure the jury never forgets that we're dealing with a child, a child whose sexual innocence was stripped away, even if she isn't exactly innocent in other ways.

I see these issues of juries reacting differently to claims of abuse depending on whether they come from "good" versus "bad" kids most often when the victim is an adolescent. Adolescence isn't society's favorite age group. Adolescents are loud and cause trouble no matter what walk of life they're from. Plus, they tend to take on the worst adult traits—sarcasm, egotism, materialism. I have to remind juries that these dislikeable personality quirks are often just a mirror of adult behaviors, used to cover the insecurities of youth. I try to show that these quirks are not really signs of adult sophistication but instead how young and green the victim is. And, bottom line, no amount of disagreeable behavior is an excuse for what the defendant did to the victim.

As a prosecutor, it is my job to teach jurors about children, make sure they understand that different rates of development are perfectly normal, and that children naturally react differently not only to the abuse but also to the investigation and interview process. But I'm no a therapist, psychologist, or educator; and even if I were, the judge would never let me lecture the jury about these things. This means that most prosecutors must educate jurors via the testimony of expert witnesses: therapists, psychologists, or trained teachers.

An *expert* is defined as someone who has specialized knowledge in a particular area. That specialized knowledge need not only come from education; it can also be a result of one's background, experience, or hands-on training. Despite the problem with finding "paid" experts, prosecutors should find the experts that are available and free. These experts are other police officers from neighboring police agencies, prosecutors, or people who can testify to the intricasies of child sexual assaults. No child sexual assault case should be tried without an expert of some sort. But using an expert to educate the jury about what's going on inside a juvenile victim has its own problems. There are not many experts who are both available and affordable, and judges limit what the expert can actually say in court. For example, experts may be allowed to testify to the basic tenets of child development in general but not permitted to talk about how those basic tenets apply to the victim's particular development or psychology. So great—I get a generalized lecture as evidence in front of the jury, but jurors very often do not know what to do with this information.

For example, take my case with fifteen-year-old Dana. Dana was walking home from school when a "handsome" man pulled up "in a nice ride." Do you feel your attitude shift a little? Calling him "handsome" is a sexually mature comment; referring to his car as "a nice ride" is the materialistic vernacular of adolescents that oftentimes annoys adults. The man engaged in small talk, recited poetry, and asked Dana if she wanted to hop in his car. Without even a moment's thought, Dana got into the car. It took only a few minutes before the man began rubbing her legs, her thighs, and eventually her crotch area. She asked him to stop and let her go. But after driving her around for a while, he pulled into a small, quiet neighborhood street and raped her in the car. While we had a DNA match to link the defendant to the event, that didn't help with another big issue: that I had to explain how a fifteen-year-old who "consented" to get into the car with a stranger she found "handsome" did not consent to the sex act. (I charged this case as a forcible rape rather than a statutory rape because of the higher penalties available for forcible rape; as a result, her consent was a defense.)

I wanted to bring on a child development expert to present the scientific evidence that shows how the stage of development of a typical teenager's brain actually makes her have the least chance of using good judgment while engaging in the highest-risk behaviors. Another analogy I wanted the jury to understand is that kids may have a full-size toolbox (their brains), but they don't necessarily have all of the tools in there yet. This isn't made up; it's a biological/physiological reality that explains why kids make the worst judgment calls (like getting into a stranger's car) at the worst times (when the behavior is the most risky), and so Dana's bad decision to get into the car was a mistake, not consent to the rape. The judge, mindful of the need to have the ultimate issue in the case—the credibility of the victim—communicated to the jury, allowed me to ask only very general questions on the development of teenagers. I was not permitted to ask any questions that even resembled the facts of the case, even if they were asked as "What if?" hypotheticals. I spoke with the jury following the verdict (they did convict), and not surprisingly they said that the expert witness was not very helpful to them. I had been lucky. In my case, the jurors were smart enough to make the distinctions on their own. But the psychological realities of children in high-stress situations are what most jurors need help understanding, and I had not been able to get it admitted.

Even if the judge allows an expert to discuss more of the facts of the case as well as the scientific data, what often happens is that there is a "battle of the experts." Each side presents its own expert and guess what: They don't agree. The mere presence of two opposing opinions strikes many jurors as precisely the definition of reasonable doubt. So what's a prosecutor to do? Not use an expert and leave complex behaviors up to the jury, or use one and risk not getting enough of his testimony in to help the jury and also risk prompting the other side to hire its own expert whose contrary opinion creates the appearance of reasonable doubt? It's not an easy call, but a call that needs to be made.

If jurors were to keep their common sense intact, then most would realize that there are inherent differences between children and adults— that children react differently, do things differently, think differently, and feel differently than adults. Common sense tells us the first way to evaluate the reliability of a child's testimony (or the testimony of any other witness for that matter) is by what I call the "pee-yew" test. If what a child is saying smells rotten to me as a prosecutor, it will likely smell to the jury too.

Beyond that, I try to encourage jurors to see four differences between children and adults that are really important in understanding what goes on in child abuse cases:

1. Children are dependent on adults for all their needs—physical and emotional.

2. Children trust adults and are naturally curious.
3. Kids need attention and affection and will do almost anything to get them.
4. Adolescents are prone to take risks and to try to get attention by acting out and being defiant.

So, let's look at each of these as they affect child abuse victims, as well as my ability to convict their abusers.

CHILDREN ARE DEPENDENT ON ADULTS

There is the miracle of the dawn of life, which I don't claim to understand, but there's no mystery about our condition upon first entering the world— we're helpless. As babies, we can't satisfy any of our needs ourselves or even verbalize them with anything more than an all-purpose wail. It takes years and years of development, all guided by the adults we trust, to gradually learn life's self-sufficiency skills. It's easy for us—showering, cooking, driving, self-reliant adults—to look at situations and say, "Why on earth would that child go off with such a creepy-looking stranger?" But as a child whose life experiences to date have been dependent on adults to clean you, feed you, and transport you, all with the trust that adults will (and do) protect you from harm and with the desire to get all the adult attention you can, the creepiness of the adult stranger may never enter into the equation.

As adults, we've learned not to take people at face value. If someone offers to do us a favor, even our spouse (especially our spouse?), a part of us wonders, "Hmm, I wonder what he's up to?" Whether you consider that reaction cynicism, caution, or common sense, the fact is it's based on years of experience, often finding out the hard way, that people are not always what they seem and people are more likely to do something if there's something in it for them. A child hasn't had that life experience, but it's worse: a child has had years of the opposite. Their growing-up experiences have been filled with learning they must and can trust and depend on adults.

Even teenagers on the brink of adulthood, striving for independence and rebelling against the adults on whom they once depended, can fall into situations where their dependence on adults can create the potential for abuse. For example, high school students applying to college depend on adult teachers to write letters of recommendation on their behalf. Football players want playing time, which is controlled by the coach. And teachers control that all-important GPA. Fortunately, the vast majority of educators treat such dependent situations with professionalism. My point is that even teenagers can find themselves in the kind of powerless versus powerful relationships that abusers look for and take advantage of.

Here's another example, one I see way too often. A teenager needs permission to go out with his or her friends, say, and a stepfather or mother's boyfriend responds with "I'll tell your mom you can go out but only if you do me a favor." There's nothing wrong with teaching teenagers that freedom and independence come at the cost of showing responsible behavior, but not at the cost of providing sexual gratification to an abuser.

Dependency on adults is a gateway for perpetrators. A child may depend on adults for different things when he is sixteen than he did when he was six, but there is often still a need for adult assistance. For children, the dependence is inescapable. Even if we didn't understand why, most of us knew we had to do what our parents told us. (Eventually the "because I said so" reasoning becomes ineffective, but it generally works for a while.) Dependency is at the root of automatic response to obey. Adults are in charge. So, even though the child may be uncomfortable with the adult relative who's telling them to do strange and even painful things, the child feels powerless to say no. This deep-seated dependency and obedience are significant reasons why some abusive relationships go on for so long before they come to light.

It's especially difficult for me as a prosecutor to pull the whole story out of young children who have been victimized over an extended period of time. Children tend to live in the now. A child abused over a long period often loses track of how the abuse began and how it escalated. The child begins to block out the unpleasant experiences. She wants to continue to trust, depend on, and be loved by the abuser, and try to shut out "the bad things."

In order to get past these walls, I do what I call "honor the victim." I teach parents how to do this too. A simple example can illustrate this common scenario. Take the case of the fourteen-year-old Maggie who is active on Myspace, Facebook, and other social networking sites. One day she gets an instant message from someone she doesn't know. Knowing that she's supposed to "tell an adult" when that happens, Maggie runs into the kitchen saying "Mom, I just got a message from a someone I don't know saying that he wants to be my friend. He wants to know what I'm doing." The mom, in a panic, runs to the computer, looks at the message, and says, "Thanks, honey, for telling me. This is what Dad and I were afraid of. We just can't let you use Facebook anymore."

The parent feels she's taught the child safe practices—to report when she receives a strange or unwanted message—and also protected her child by taking her off the social networking site. But has she? The child did exactly what Mom wanted the child to do: recognize a red flag and tell a parent. But what happened, from the child's point of view? Instead of being praised, supported, or—as I call it, honored—the child was punished. At least that's how the child is likely to see it.

What happens if instead the child is honored? She is told, "You did the right thing and I am so proud of you!" And then you honor her by treating her as responsible enough to have a discussion about why she shouldn't respond to instant messages from strangers. Not in graphic details that'll give her nightmares, of course, but in terms that let her know she's safe at home and with people she knows, but she needs to be careful of people she doesn't know. Instead of merely obeying her parents, she's learning why, and so she is learning to make good choices. After all, isn't that what we are trying to teach children? To become responsible, independent adults who make good choices and decisions?

When I speak with children, I want them to feel that despite what happened to them, that the disclosure of the abuse they have made is brave, right, and will protect other children. I want them to feel safe and to always know that whatever the outcome of the case, an adult listened to them and cared about what they said.

CHILDREN ARE NATURALLY TRUSTING AND CURIOUS

Tied closely to a child's dependency on adults is their natural tendency to trust. As a child, everything you need in life is given to you by an adult. What else can you do but trust them? You obey what they say without thinking. Without knowing why, you just trust them. Dependency, obedience, and trust go hand in hand for children. Experience has told them that adults can be trusted and that they hold all the power. In fact, we train our children to trust adults and see them as authority figures.

This trust begins from the moment a child enters the world. From moment one, a child is dependent on someone for feeding, bathing, changing, and being put to bed. Think about how the dependence works. It's magical in a way. A baby cries and a bottle is placed in his mouth or he is breastfed; another cry and he gets a burp patted out of him; another cry and a diaper change. Children age, learn to feed themselves, and get potty trained, but their dependence on adults continues as adults enroll them in school, buy them clothes, take them to their doctors, and continue to be the people the children rely upon for their basic life needs.

Depending on the victim's age, life experience may have taught him very little about what qualifies as creepy or unsafe, and what information he does get may be inconsistent messages. For example, take the child who gets the standard "don't talk to strangers" admonition as mom is driving him into town for a little shopping. Then, just a few minutes later in the grocery store, his mom is telling him to be polite and "say hi to the nice grocery man," who is, up to then, a stranger. Have you ever asked your child what a "stranger" is? You might be surprised by the answer. Our confusing messages leave children still not knowing how to handle a specific situation and so they must continue to look to an adult for direction. This is especially true if the victim has led a happy, secure life, filled with trustworthy adults. Then the victim really has no bearings to guide him, no experiences to compare to, when a creepy stranger smiles at him or an uncle puts an overly friendly arm around his shoulders.

An outgrowth of trust—a very valuable outgrowth—is that it facilitates the child's natural curiosity. We encourage children to explore the world by assuring them nothing bad will happen. What do we say to our kids when something has frightened or upset them? We say in our most reassuring voice, "It will be okay." And we should. I'm not saying that we should bombard our children with images of bogeymen or even the harsh but true realities of the world. My point is we need to realize the effects of our reassurances, and not expect a child to suddenly be able to identify risky situations and treat them as dangerous if we haven't taught them how to do that.

In order to help jurors understand the behavior of a child victim, I need to remind them of the natural behaviors of kids, of their need to trust and rely on adults, their hunger to obey and be loved, of the instinctive curiosity we nurture in them by making them feel secure. Instead of penalizing the child for these natural behaviors, we must recognize they exist and remember this as we speak to him or her, especially on the witness stand. We need to recognize these elements are present in order to understand how an assault may have happened. Further, parents should make it a priority to help their kids learn how to listen to their instincts and recognize which situations may be safe and those that are unsafe.

KIDS HAVE A NEED FOR ATTENTION AND AFFECTION

Most kids today, even well-behaved kids, have a "gimmee" mentality. Kids want things. Kids want things now. Sometimes kids know exactly why they want things (candy tastes good). Other times they aren't so tuned-in. Children may not be able to articulate why they want to be held or cuddled, but they know when they want it. And their concentrated focus on what they want can cause them to overlook the risks involved in getting it.

Attention and affection are driving forces for children and are another easy opportunity for predators. Children, especially young children, live in the moment and are easily distracted. When a kid is sad, we make him laugh or offer him candy. When they're young, kids don't hold grudges, the same way we do as we get older. They can be upset one minute and happily playing with a new toy the next.

This kind of living in the moment means young children receiving the attention of an adult don't necessarily think about what the adult looks like or whether he's a stranger; they just know they like the attention they are receiving. And kids crave attention. They get a ton of attention as babies, and sometimes I think they spend the rest of their young lives trying to get all the attention back.

Predators count on this innate desire children have for attention. Perpetrators often prey on attention-starved children. They look for the child who sits alone or isn't the center of attention because they know that particular child will be more susceptible to letting them in. Introverted children are easy targets.

The perpetrator will find some excuse to start up a conversation with his target and give his undivided attention to the child while having the conversation. He asks questions, sympathizes with the child's concerns, gives advice, and shows genuine interest. He has also prepared for this moment, taking the time to learn what kids like—the movies they enjoy, the hip bands, and the new trends.

It's not that hard to figure out what kids of a particular age group like in this Internet age. In fact, a perpetrator gets most of his information straight from the conversations he has with the child, from a Facebook page or just by knowing the child's daily schedule.

So, does this give you any ideas about who is in the best position to groom a child into accepting a relationship, one that will soon turn sexual? Someone who has access to and the time to get to know the child—a family member, neighbor, mom's boyfriend, and so on. And don't forget as I have mentioned before, an abuser gets additional leverage if he "knows the dirt" in the child's background and can use it to black-mail, hurt, or scare the child.

Kids don't just crave attention; they crave affection. Perpetrators know this, count on it, and use it. Kids need to be physically touched in a loving and understanding way from the time they're babies, even into adulthood (although we don't always admit it). Kids also need emotional affection—simply to feel loved. When kids are missing affection in their lives, they are more vulnerable to someone who seems to offer to replace it.

I know how difficult it is to give your children all the attention they want. I have three kids and a husband, I work full-time at more than one job, I travel, and so on. So I get it, trust me. But affection is a common gateway for starting an abusive relationship, and it can also be an effective cover for sexual assault. Our society sees some affection between certain adults and children as normal and acceptable, for example, with a relative, a close family friend, a babysitter or a teacher. In these circumstances, the affection may hide the sexual assault because no one perceives the interaction as inappropriate and so are slow to pick up on when normal affection grows into abnormal behavior.

I had a case in which a baseball coach often squeezed his team members' shoulders as a sign of approval and encouragement. The kids were nine years old and the squeezes all occurred in front of parents at the baseball games. Once, when one of the kids struck out, the "nice coach" came over and hugged him. No one thought anything of it. It all seemed perfectly appropriate. Then the coach went from squeezing shoulders and hugging to patting the boys' buttocks. Well, don't we see football players and such giving each other a swat on the behind now and then? But the coach started doing it every time he was close to a boy. Still, there was nothing secretive about it. It would happen right in front of the whole team and all the parents. As a matter of fact, parents who were videotaping the games had his behavior right on tape. And no one said anything.

It was only after the coach grabbed a child's groin area that the *child* (not even the parent) said the coach was making him uncomfortable. After he made the disclosure, it dawned on the parents that maybe the coach's constant shoulder-squeezing and bottom-patting were inappropriate. After interviewing the entire team of boys and parents, everyone independently said they thought the coach's behavior was inappropriate, and each of the kids said the coach made them uncomfortable when he touched them on the shoulders or on the buttocks. Yet it took eight weeks of this behavior and a groin touch before anyone stepped forward and said anything. As a side note, in the interviews four other boys said the coach had grabbed their groin areas during practices when no other adults were around.

I'm not saying that every time a coach puts his arm around a player, it's sex abuse. My point is that affection is an easy and frequently used road for a perpetrator to groom a victim for a sexual assault. Children accept attention and affection readily and trust quickly, so this foundation can be quickly accelerated into sexual assault. This happens with older children as well as young ones because they don't see what's coming.

As a parent, don't be alarmed at the normal physical contacts prevalent and acceptable in our society. However, pay attention to anyone expressing affection to your child, notice if it expands into something that isn't normal, and listen to your *and your child's* gut feelings about when the affection makes him or her feel uncomfortable.

ADOLESCENTS ARE UNIQUE

We probably all agree that adolescence is one of the most challenging, difficult, and exciting periods in life, whether you're the adolescent or the parent. This is a time of body changes, hormonal changes, school changes, and relationship changes. Kids who were once "our babies" are now acutely aware of even being seen in our presence and of any suggestion they are not ready for full adulthood. What was once a child's testing of the boundaries may turn in to full-fledged teenage defiance. What was once a child's body now looks like an adult's. The kid who was once eager to learn is now the kid who is eager to prove what she knows. All of these changes make adolescents unique sexual assault victims.

When the victim is not the innocent, pig-tailed six-year-old girl most people imagine, the playing field changes. Or perhaps I should say that lots of playing fields change, because:

1. The perpetrators who assault teenagers aren't the same perpetrators who assault toddlers, and they don't necessarily see their crimes as crimes against children because the victims don't look or act like children.
2. The statutes defining sex crimes are often different for adolescents. As I discussed in greater deal in chapter 2, the law recognizes that the natural developmental changes as a child ages may require differences in punishment.
3. Finally, the trials of adolescent victim cases are quite different. Juries feel differently about adolescent victims than they do about the "typical" innocent six-year-old, and the adolescent makes a far different kind of victim witness.

But just because adolescents look like adults or act like big pains in the butt, this doesn't make a perpetrator's sexual abuse of them any less of a crime, or does it?

It is my job to get through to teenage victims. It is my job to let them feel heard, understood, and believed. With adolescence, they are facing probably the most challenging times of their lives, and on top of that they have to deal with an adult's sexual abuse, and on top of that they have to deal with a criminal trial where they'll be given the third degree by defense attorneys (and often by their parents).

Luckily for me, I have two boys who have taught me a lot about teenagers, and lucky for me, I remember what a pain in the butt I was as a teenager. I'm not so sure I've left that entirely behind, which I think gives me a natural gift for this age group. But mainly I've learned to say it like it is. No games, no innuendos, no beating around the bush. Here I am in an interview with a teenager and I need and expect that teenager to be completely honest with me. So I need to be the same.

This is really the same as what I said before—honor the victim. I say it like it is. I give victims the respect they deserve. I don't talk down to them, I don't judge them, and when I ask them questions, I shut my mouth and listen to their answers.

But I also don't back down. If a child has attitude, I make it clear that I am being respectful and expect the same. Kids of all ages want rules and boundaries, so I provide them. I tell kids what the rules of talking to me are and I make sure they follow them. But I do it with respect and I treat them with dignity, like the young adults they are.

In the end, I can't win my case unless I get the jury to understand and see the adolescent victim as I see the victim—a child. This means seeing beyond the attitude and through the teenage bravado; but bottom line, it means they need to understand why I believe the victim. Sometimes this is an uphill battle. Scared or sullen victims, awkward testimony, combativeness during cross-examination, and defense counsel accusations and attempts to blame the witness—these all can present challenges. But if I can get the jury to focus on the perpetrator rather than the victim, I've gained serious ground. If I can get the jury to understand that the victim is a child despite age and/or attitude, then I've gained even more ground.

What this all really boils down to is the most important thing that I have learned about being a prosecutor. *A DA can't win a case she doesn't believe in.* If I have doubts about the veracity of my victim, then I simply cannot file that case. In order to convince the jury to believe the victim, I must believe the victim. Only then will my passionate belief in the truth of the victim's story come through.

Perhaps this explains more than anything else why I chose to be a prosecutor rather than some other kind of lawyer. The best part about my job is that I have the ability each and every day to make the right decision, for every case that comes across my desk. I don't get paid by the number of times I file charges or take a case to trial. If I think a case stinks, I am lucky enough to have the autonomy to do what I feel is right and not file it. On the other hand, if a case looks weak but I truly believe the victim, I also have the authority to do the right thing there, too. What a job!

CHAPTER SIX
PROFILE OF A PREDATOR

It's a Sunday in October and this year's annual Rape Treatment Center fund-raiser brunch is being hosted by Ron Burkle at his posh Bel Air estate. Those in attendance are impeccably dressed—men sporting either brunch-appropriate chinos or light-weight suits, women in bedazzling and bejeweled outfits they try to pretend are understated and subtle. Each year there's a different celebrity host, or even better yet, a full celebrity cast. Of course all the local politico celebrities are there as well—the mayor, the chief of police, the district attorney, judges, and state legislators. And while the well-heeled donors and supporters of the fantastic institution that is the Center hobnob with each other, there is a small cluster in the back of people like me who sit and watch as selected reports of our daily work in the trenches are used to encourage donors to write big, fat checks.

So what is the best way to get a big, fat check? To share the most horrific, mind-blowing, heart-wrenching cases? And which are those? The stranger who picks up the girl and so brutally attacks her that she has no recollection of what happened, but the authorities manage to piece it together from her broken bones, vaginal tears, and DNA evidence? Or the case where a concerned citizen (God bless him!) calls 911 because he sees "a man take a girl into the back of a van" and the police arrive moments later to catch the girl's father in the act of raping his daughter?

Yup, these cases have the "Oh my God" factor. But the reality is that my whole caseload has the "Oh my God" factor. The awful truth is that sexual assault of children happens every day, and in large numbers. If that's not worth an "Oh my God!" I don't know what is.

So as I sit there at the brunch listening and watching as these good people shake their heads and mutter appalled reactions to what they hear, I wonder what their mental image of a predator is. I fear they think the people who commit these horrible acts all look like our stereotypical portraits of perverts. That kind of thinking—that it is only a handful of trench-coated perverts who do this kind of thing—keeps people from understanding the full breadth of the problem. In fact, the perpetrators are more likely to be hiding behind a veneer of normalcy, a veneer that is undetectable to the generous donors enjoying this brunch.

So let me ask, what do you think predators look like? What characteristics do they have? Do they all jump out of dark alleys when they want to snatch a kid?

In my experience, the general image people have of predators is one that is a whole lot more comfortable for them than the truth. Maybe that's why the false impression is so persistent. People's image of a sex crime perpetrator is some shady stranger who nabs a kid who is walking home from school. That happens, to be sure. I'm not saying there's no "stranger danger" out there. Especially for children old enough to flirt but young and naive enough not to have the tools or confidence to protect themselves.

But for children of all ages, the real danger comes far more often from someone within the family and social circle. The "stranger" is the strange dark side lurking within someone they know and trust.

You may have seen from some of the high-profile media cases that investigators typically start with the victim's inner circle of family and acquaintances in a child abduction case before widening the scope of the search. Look at the Caylee Anthony and Haleigh Cummings cases, for example. In these instances, the investigators looked first to those closest to the child and for Caylee's murder found their lead suspects there. As I write this, a lead suspect in the Haleigh Cummings case has yet to be identified.

I know it is a sickening thought that those closest to the child should be the ones the detectives focus on first. A sexual assault of a child is terrible enough, but for her father to be the one doing it, or her teacher, coach, or preacher, this is inconceivable for most of us. But our disbelief is not only wrong, it is dangerous. A parent's intuitive belief that such people would never commit these crimes can cloud judgment and even lead the parent to disbelieve the child's first timid, frightened disclosure.

The fact is that these "inner circle" sexual assaults make up most of my cases. I am still sickened but no longer surprised by the inner circle offenders I see. The only thing that may be "new" is that as I work with more and more abused children, I am finding the range of people within that inner circle, those who have access to them, is growing. For example, just last week I got calls from three different county health departments, all telling me about different doctors who have been molesting their children patients.

Doctor offenders are a good way to illustrate why many kids don't disclose abuse, or when they do they seem reticent or uncertain about what they are saying. Imagine a young child with little or no concept of sexual activity who is fondled and finger penetrated by a doctor. The doctor explains to her that it is all part of the normal examination procedure and should be kept private, between doctor and patient. Can you see why she might never disclose what happened to her in the privacy of the doctor's examination room? The variety of reasons why kids may be reluctant to disclose abuse is one thing investigators need to understand when they investigate child sex crimes cases.

Let me give another very troubling statistic about the prevalence of inner circle offenders versus stranger offenders. Among my cases where the victim initially reports a "stranger" assault, it has been my experience that at least 50 percent end up with the perpetrator being someone the victim knew. The perpetrator had been able to use his relationship with the victim to force, coerce, threaten, or persuade the victim to withhold the suspect's identity and to blame an unknown and fictitious stranger.

Along with all the other traumatic emotions that come from being a victim of sexual assault, one of the most damaging is the shattered trust and belief in love that comes from being assaulted by someone you know. Seeing an adult a child knows and trusts become an entirely different person can rock a child's stability and cripple the ability to trust and love for the rest of her life.

So who are these wolves in sheep's clothing? How can you identify them, if they look just like you and me? I wish I knew. Sadly, there's real no way to predict whether some adult in a child's life is a sicko. And it's made even tougher by there being so many different kinds of sickos to watch out for.

Sociologists and psychologists define a *predator* in lots of different ways. Some terminology focuses on the psychological characteristics of the perpetrator, and others look primarily to the nature of their actions. Some of the main terms used to categorize perpetrators are *pedophile, predator, opportunist, molester, sex offender*, and *incest offenders*. Having so many terms can be confusing for not only victims and parents but also for lawyers, judges, and juries.

The terminology can also factor into the reluctance of a victim or her parents to disclose suspected abuse. It's a big deal to accuse someone, and what should you accuse him of being? A pedophile? A molester? Parents can be uncertain whether an actual crime has been committed because there are so many definitions. And that doubt can piggy-back on their preference to believe the inappropriate behavior didn't happen or was a naive misunderstanding of their young child, which again leads to nondisclosure.

Even when parents feel confident about the people they allow their child to have contact with, they need to keep their parental "antennae" attuned for something that just feels wrong. Parents can tell when their child starts acting differently, particularly when these behaviors happen most around a specific adult. And they must have the courage to alert the authorities and let them investigate what, if anything, is happening.

When parents try to handle the situation on their own, say, by taking a child off a sports team when he or she has bad feelings about one of the coaches, the only person well served is the perpetrator. The perpetrator gets off and remains free to find another way to access the child or to abuse some other child. Even if the parents succeed in protecting their child from future contact with the suspect, the child can end up haunted by what already happened and was never rightfully addressed.

Sammy loved being a Cub Scout in a troop with Dave as the scoutmaster. Dave was kind, enthusiastic, and had a special talent for making ten-year-old boys feel comfortable, confident, and like they had a safe place to go have fun. Sammy's parents were thrilled to see him thrive, finally coming out of his shell and feeling comfortable around other kids. And they were very, very thankful to Dave for all of the personal growth Sammy had achieved over the past year.

So when another kid's mom told them Dave was talking to some of the boys about sex and teaching them how to masturbate, it was very hard for them to accept, especially since Sammy hadn't said anything about it to them. They were, of course, concerned about the allegation and Sammy's safety, but they were also concerned about making a police report that would subject Dave to being labeled a predator, a pedophile, a child molester, when maybe none of that was true. These are damning labels to put on anyone and can ruin someone's life even if it is later determined to be wrong. And besides, did they want to deprive Sammy of an activity that was helping him so much, on such thin evidence?

So Sammy's parents did nothing, said nothing, and allowed Sammy to stay in the Cub Scout troop. Six more weeks went by before another family finally reported Dave's behavior to the police. All of the children were interviewed, and it came out in Sammy's interview that Dave not only talked about sex and taught them how to masturbate, but only two days prior Dave had showed Sammy how to masturbate someone else.

When I spoke to Sammy's parents, they were upset about the abuse and saddened that Sammy hadn't felt comfortable enough to disclose it to them. But what really devastated them was that they had been alerted to the abuse yet allowed it to continue for six more weeks, all out of concern for embarrassing the pedophile predator.

So who are these people who commit these crimes? While psychologists have one set of criteria based on academic research for classifying types of child sexual abuse, based on my firsthand experience, I would define the profiles of predators as follows:

- the sickos,
- the Peter Pan types,
- the all-powerful authority figures,
- the control freaks, and lastly,
- the plain dumb ones.

Of course, classification of most perpetrators isn't so neat and tidy. They do not fit precisely into one category or another. Some fit mostly into one group but also spill over a little into another, and some fit into multiple categories. The bottom line for me is that anyone who sexually touches a kid is a pedophile, with the possible exception of the nineteen-year-old who has consensual sex with his sixteen- or seventeen-year-old girlfriend.

Let's take a closer look at my categories of offenders.

THE SICKOS

Lulu had had enough of her mom. She hated Las Vegas and everything about living there—she hated the city, hated how there was nothing for kids to do, and worse, she couldn't stand her mom's work. Mom was a casino showgirl, which meant she was absent most evenings.

But even more than hating Vegas or her mom's job, she hated the constant arguments. She and her mom argued about what clothes Lulu could wear, where she could go at night, when she had to be home, how long before she could get her driver's permit, and so on. Losing patience one night, Lulu's mom said, "If I'm so terrible, why don't you go live with your dad in LA?"

Lulu jumped on the suggestion and excitedly arranged her move to LA. At last, she was going to have the relationship with her father she had dreamed of. When she got to LA, everything started out swimmingly. Her dad was so the opposite of her mom. He included her in activities, treated her like an adult, and they never fought. He bought her the sexy clothes she wanted to wear and not only let her do what she wanted but always included her in the activities he and his friends did. She was invited to parties, allowed to drink alcohol, and even smoked pot for the first time, with her dad. And what was best was that Lulu's dad never embarrassed her by introducing her as his kid and instead referred to her with the grown-up term "my lady friend."

Little did Lulu know that calling her his "lady friend" was part of her father's process of grooming his daughter to become his

125

wife. Yup, you read correctly, his wife. After three months in LA, Lulu's dad told her to "call me Jim," bought her a ring she was to wear on her wedding finger, and said she was to become the "woman of the house." While she had freedom to act as she wished during the day, she had responsibilities in the evening, including tending to the sexual desires of the "man of the house."

Lulu loved her father and loved being treated like a desirable adult woman. She had the choice to go to school but decided against that and instead socialized with only Jim and his friends. Fortunately, one of those friends sensed that something wasn't quite right and put in a call to the Department of Children and Family Services. When DCFS responded and met Lulu, she claimed she was Jim's wife, she lied about her age, and she vehemently protested that nothing was wrong. She told them that whoever made the call was mistaken and must not have realized she was Jim's wife.

But investigators contacted Lulu's mom, and she confirmed that Lulu was Jim's blood daughter, not his wife. Jim was arrested and Lulu returned to Las Vegas to her mom. For a time, she screamed and railed at the system, her mom, and everyone who had ruined the wonderful, loving relationship she had with her dad. It took nearly one year of intense therapy before Lulu could even acknowledge she was a victim and that what Jim had done was not only criminal but also sickly deranged.

In my mind, the sickos are the worst of the awful. That a pedophile is turned on by children is bad enough, but sickos have no problem victimizing their own daughters, nieces, students—in other words, the kids who most depend upon and trust that they will take loving good care of them. Sickos are the people who see children as sexual objects to play with, and who understand children's vulnerability as something to be taken advantage of to satisfy their own desires.

I confess that with all my experience, I still don't get these people. How can one take sexual advantage of the trust and vulnerability of a child, especially *one's own* child? If the general idea is there's some sort of sickness that makes these people unable to resist their sexual attraction to children, then why not do the decent thing and avoid contact with kids? And why would such a person ever let himself become a father?

Sickos don't have a particular look, are not a particular age, and don't live in any particular kind of neighborhood. They are everywhere and could be anyone. Sometimes they're not so good at concealing themselves and give off a vibe that gives you the willies. But most the time, and always for the ones who are good at it, they carefully cultivate an image that makes them the last people you'd suspect.

For me and the trained detectives I work with, it's easy to know if we are dealing with a sicko. Sickos are plain and simply gross. They are the ones who turn your stomach. Fortunately, that also makes them the ones who are easiest to prosecute and convict if I can get a jury to see through their veneer of normalcy to the sickness within. If I can, the chills that will run down the jurors' spines will leave not the slightest doubt that this perpetrator belongs in jail for a very long time, hopefully forever.

When I train police officers, I tell them to pay attention to this same feeling. If they feel in their gut that a suspect belongs in jail for a very long time, they are probably dealing with a sicko. I don't care if the formal definition of a pedophile in the *Diagnostic and Statistical Manual of Mental Disorders IV* requires a prior conviction for a child sexual assault to classify the behavior. In my mind, someone's a pedophile and a sicko the very first time he molests a kid under twelve, diddles a family member, or seeks out a prepubescent minor to have sexual relationships with.

THE PETER PANS

He was handsome, charismatic, kind, and totally fun to be around. He always knew where the party was and always had a connection to get into the latest hot spot. His Blackberry had the cell phone numbers of A-listers like Britney Spears, Rihanna, and Lindsay Lohan. He drove a hundred-thousand-dollar car and claimed "music producer" was his career. His charm and wit attracted the interests of all sorts, but he was particularly a hit among the ladies. The thing is that thirty-eight-year-old Brandon preferred the girls—little girls.

Peter Pan types are the guys who plain and simple never grow up. They don't see themselves as adults, so they can't even imagine that the sex acts they commit with children could be crimes or even wrong. Their growth is so developmentally stunted that they cannot relate to people their own age and have trouble holding a conversation with another adult. They feel out of place in the adult world, like they don't fit in.

They seek out children for their sexual needs because their trouble relating to adults extends to sexual relations. They feel children are their peers, and they are insecure and uncomfortable with adult sex partners. This is why they molest children. They are unable to direct their sexual energy toward people their own age. Oftentimes, their stunted emotional growth stems from being abused as children themselves.

THE CONTROL FREAKS

Fourteen-year-old Amy was gradually pulled into an Internet friendship with a boy named Billy on the social networking site urbanchat.com. Unfortunately, Billy was a thirty-year-old pimp. He coaxed her into meeting him in person and then used his senior prostitute—a twenty-year-old woman—to gain Amy's trust. Billy and his prostitute convinced Amy they could set her up with a glamorous career in modeling, using their contacts in a city in a near-by state. Amy ran away from home and the three of them hit the road.

Once they were well on their way, Billy revealed to Amy his real plans. He was going to turn her into a prostitute. When she protested, he slapped her until she shut up. After a tense drive, Amy managed to slip away, borrow a cell phone from a kind stranger, and call her mother and the police. The investigation uncovered that Billy, in addition to trolling urbanchat.com for victims, also had a MySpace page promoting his "escort" service and a page on the social networking site blackplanet.com saying he was "looking for girls who want to make money!!"

Control freaks who use physical abuse to get sex are called "sexually violent predators." Their methods are very much like those we see in domestic abuse, gang violence, and the like. They enjoy the feeling of completely controlling another person and also get turned on by it. The following case illustrates the close relation between a sexually violent predator and a domestic abuser.

Cindi was sixteen when she began dating twenty-one-year-old Matthew. He seemed beyond charming and doted on her, showered her with compliments and gifts, and was always eager to spend time with her. But after only two weeks of dating, the kinds of questions her new boyfriend kept barraging her with started to make her uncomfortable. He repeatedly asked questions like "Where are you?" "Who are you with?" and "How long have you been out?" With the questions came accusations of being untrustworthy, flirty, and lying about where she was and whom she was with.

While Cindi was uncomfortable with and a little scared by the questioning, she was also flattered. "He must really love me if he cares this much about me," she thought. But there was more than overly possessive affection behind Matthew's conduct. He was going to great lengths to isolate Cindi from her family and friends. As time went by, the questions and accusations increased. Sweet talking turned into foul-mouthed arguments. Soon the accusations and arguments escalated to pushes and punches.

Just days before Cindi and Matthew's three-month anniversary, Matthew wanted to have sex but Cindi declined because she had just finished menstruating. That did not stop Matthew. He pushed her on the bed, pulled down her panties, and forced his penis inside her. Cindi whimpered, "Stop, please don't" in between cries of pain. Afterward, Matthew kicked Cindi, saying that her crying "ruined it for him" and he stormed out of the house. Six hours later, he was back with roses, a card, and an apology.

Many people think of sexual assault and domestic violence as distinct and different kinds of behavior, but the fact is they are not, particularly when you are dealing with sexual assault of older children who may have romantic relationships with their abusers, like Cindi. Both are crimes of control, whether the victim is a child or an adult. The only differences with children is that they fall prey more easily to the controlling types and find it harder to break away because children seek and need adults to care for them, and will cling to a care provider even when the "caring" turns hurtful and manipulative.

THE ALL-POWERFUL ONES—PEOPLE IN POSITIONS OF AUTHORITY

David's family were Orthodox Jews. They lived in the Orthodox section of Los Angeles, which allowed them to easily walk to shul, walk to kosher restaurants, and socialize among other Orthodox Jews. Eleven-year-old David lived like many other Orthodox kids. His was a kosher home and he went to an Orthodox Jewish day school, walked to shul on the Shabbos, and spent most of his social time playing with his four brothers and two sisters. While he enjoyed his siblings, he also sought friendships outside of his family.

One day at the temple he met Moshe. Moshe was also eleven-years-old and lived only a few blocks away. Because Moshe was a "member of the tribe" and his father was one of the esteemed rabbis in town, David's family felt comfortable with David spending time playing over at Moshe's house and eventually allowed him to go to sleepover there.

On the night of the sleepover, David and Moshe turned in, sharing Moshe's bed. At about 3 a.m., David woke up to find Moshe's dad touching his private parts. Alarmed, David sat up but Moshe's dad said very firmly, "Sheket," which in Hebrew means quiet. David obeyed and remained quiet that night. But he told his parents when he got home, and they immediately reported it to the police.

The reaction in the Jewish community was typical for cases where the alleged perpetrator is someone in a position of authority. The reporting caused an uproar. Many people rallied around the rabbi and the rest of Moshe's family and shunned David's family for the accusation and for turning to the secular authorities rather than keeping it within their community.

Clergy in our society, especially Catholic priests, have gotten a bad rap because of the sins of a few. But people who use their position of authority to force sex on children—the category of offenders I call "the all-powerful ones"—include more than just the priests, rabbis, and other members of the clergy. The all-powerful ones are in all kinds of positions of authority, from teachers to coaches, rabbis to priests, doctors to school bus drivers. These are people we should hold to a higher standard because they have been entrusted with a measure of power over our children.

The all-powerful ones are especially prone to committing repeated acts of child molestation on multiple victims. They have ready access to many children in ways other offenders don't. They can hide behind the strong presumption of responsibility that comes from their positions with highly professional and upstanding institutions. They count on parents focusing most on the respectability of the institution and missing clues that otherwise might raise suspicions and lead to investigations.

The fact is that while the virtues of the institution are in fact reflected in most of its members, those virtues are unfortunately and definitely not reflected in *all* of their members. If parents assume all share the virtue of the institution, parents' guards will be lowered and their protection of their children undermined.

Clergy in just about every denomination have faced sex scandals. The media have naturally jumped on the revelations about sex abuse among those working for the Catholic Church, and the revelations are truly dismaying. But the media's emphasis should not blind us to the fact that Catholic priests aren't the only ones using their positions of authority to abuse children.

The vast majority of persons in positions of authority over children have those jobs because they love children, and they find child sexual abuse as abhorrent and incomprehensible as the rest of us. They are rightfully revered as models of virtue. But just as it is unfair to assume that because a handful of priests or teachers or coaches are bad, all are, it is equally wrong to assume that *all* people in positions of respect are virtuous just because most are.

HOW TO SPOT A PEDOPHILE

There are no common physical or psychological signs that someone is a perpetrator. Perps come in all kinds and from all sorts of ethnic and socioeconomic backgrounds. There are, however, some fairly reliable, telltale clues that savvy parents can pick up on. Let me help make you a savvy parent.

For starters, remember that sexual abusers generally have a *preexisting relationship* with a child or children. They have access, authority, and trust of both the parent and the child. If you see one such person spending an unusual amount of time with kids rather than adults, this should raise a red flag that they may be a Peter Pan type. If your child seems intimidated or overly compliant around a particular adult, find out why. You may be dealing with a control freak type.

Second, these sickos like kids and want access to them. So they often take jobs that provide that access. (Remember John Wayne Gacey, the "Killer Clown," who was convicted and executed for raping and murdering thirty-three boys? He drew kids to his block parties by dressing up in a clown suit and makeup to entertain them with the comical actions of "Pogo the Clown.") Whether it's the priest or the coach who has daily access or someone working at the videogame center, child sex abusers seek out situations where they can more easily get kids alone. Be especially alert if someone in such a position pays particular attention to your child or to someone else's child. They may be grooming the child for abuse.

A third red flag is someone who gives gifts to children or does favors for them. I'm not talking about a Mrs. Wilson who shares a cookie with Dennis the Menace out of the batch she's just baked for George. I'm talking gifts that surprise you, that seem excessive, that might be a sign of grooming, bribes for silence, or atonements for guilt. It's always a good idea for kids to ask their parents before accepting any gift, and not just gifts from strangers. Remember that an abuser is far more likely to be someone you and your child know than a stranger.

The fourth red flag is the most important, and the one I always advocate parents fall back on: the "pee-yew" test. If you get bad vibes about someone, your child feels uncomfortable, or your child starts acting differently with someone, don't ignore your intuitive sense that something is wrong. Don't be fooled by the person's charm, by his position of authority, by how unthinkable it is that he could be an abuser. Trust your instincts and keep your eyes open. And especially realize it doesn't make you a bad person to put your child's safety above your concern for a suspect's reputation. Reporting your suspicion is not the same as making an accusation. You are just asking the authorities to investigate the possibility that there may be a problem.

Although I talk a lot about the pee-yew test and following your gut instinct, I have to emphasize too that most molesters are adept at preventing such feelings. Most don't look creepy or scary. They can seem like the caring and loving type of person you want around your child. But abusers know how to use this persona to cover up their crimes, and most have good qualities mixed in with the evil.

So much for my experience-based opinions; it's time I gave you some science. Studies have found common qualities for molesters:

- depression,
- social isolation,
- a rigid religious background,
- inability to relate to adults,
- a sense they have special rights or privileges with children in their care, and
- a history of having been abused themselves (neglect or physical and/or sexual assaults).

So, while there isn't any sure-fire way to tell if an individual will molest, some of the things to watch out for are whether the person has a history of sexually abusive behavior or being abused, if the person has special access to children, and if the person has the ability to isolate the child in one-on-one situations.

But trying to identify possible predators is only one way for parents to help protect their children. Certainly, keeping their eyes open and knowing exactly who is in their child's life is extremely important. But it's also important to lessen your child's attractiveness to a molester, and believe me I'm not talking about looks.

A strong child is less appealing to a molester. Molesters generally want to feel powerful and in control. So they are more likely to go after children who are from dysfunctional homes, have few friends, aren't doing well in school, or have other circumstances that erode their self-confidence and make them more vulnerable. Molesters also like vulnerable children because such victims are easier to intimidate into silence, and so make the molester more confident that he will get away with his crimes. Parents can make it less likely that a molester will target their children by fostering confidence and self-esteem in them, which is a good idea anyway.

After the molester gets his claws into a vulnerable child, he or she will go to great lengths to keep the ongoing criminal relationship under wraps. Above all else, the molester is focused on keeping a "good thing" going. So he might promise gifts, explain away the molestation as normal behavior, make the victim feel responsible for the molestation, threaten to harm the child or her parents, or describe how lonely the child will be without the relationship. All of these actions are meant to keep the molester in control and the child feeling helpless.

Just as there are certain characteristics common among molesters, there are a few characteristics that can point to a likelihood of reoffending—that is, that an offender is likely to continue his criminal sexual assaults repeatedly, even after serving prison terms for them.

Generally, the younger the molester is when he starts sexually offending, the more likely he is to continue offending. Also, offenders who target male victims are more likely to reoffend. So are those who assault unrelated and unknown victims as opposed to family members. Being unmarried and/or having an antisocial personality disorder also are linked to reoffending.

So, history shows that many offenders have a likelihood of reoffending. Can't we prevent that with therapy? Can't perps be cured? I hear these questions a lot. But, as surely you are aware by now, I'm no shrink. I am, however, very familiar with the data and information available in government crime statistics and from the research of those who work with offenders. These sources show that the rate of recidivism among those who sexually assault children is extremely high. Plus we know the rate of repeat offenses is probably even higher than these studies can measure, since we know that for every victim who reports an assault there are usually more victims who don't. But what does this prove? That sex offenders cannot be cured and we shouldn't bother trying? Or that we just haven't figured out how yet and must keep looking?

One of the problems I see in how the criminal justice system treats recidivism in sex crimes is there is no real "halfway house" for sex crime perpetrators. Perps released from prison go straight back into the community. While they may be subject to registering as sex offenders and the terms of their probation, they are for all intents and purposes back on the street.

We know how to do better, and we are already doing better with drug offenders and other categories of criminals. We need live-in, lockdown facilities with staff members who are equipped and trained to handle offenders with the moral, mental, physical, or whatever disease it is that causes them to molest children. We need places where people with the expertise and training (continued training that stays up to date with the changes and research that are constantly going on in this area) to address the real issues behind molestation and pedophilia. Only if we look at the sickos as being sick will we be able to hope for and find ways to treat their illness.

PART II

BEHIND COUNSEL TABLE

Time for Court

CHAPTER SEVEN

CORROBORATING A CHILD'S WORD

Other Evidence

Not more than fourteen hours after the rape, sixteen-year-old Lizzie comes to the Center to tell me what happened. She's already had a rape kit done, the medical exam performed down the street at the clinic part of the Center. It's not uncommon for a victim to come in within hours of an assault, not having stopped anywhere before, not even having taken a shower. Some victims seem to know that their bodies bear evidence.

She not only tells me beginning to end the details of how her date turned into rape, but she is forthright, direct, and articulate. She talks in complete narrative detail, with almost no questioning by me. She tells how she met Shawn, why she was attracted to him, and how one thing led to another until she said no and he went ahead anyway. It's a story I've heard dozens of times before.

He met her at a party and seemed nice enough that after a few minutes Lizzie gave him her e-mail address and cell number. The next day, Lizzie couldn't stop thinking about him. He seemed perfect. He was handsome, seemed so much more mature than high school boys, was in the know—he even had Lindsay Lohan's number in his speed dial. When Lizzie checked his

MySpace and Facebook, he had pictures with other A-listers—Britney and Paris.

So you can imagine how thrilled a high school junior like Lizzie was when HE started instant messaging and e-mailing her just a few days after they met. Soon, Shawn suggested they go out. Why not meet at his house (he still lived with his folks) then go out on a date from there? So Lizzie drove over just in time to grab dinner before the 6:30 movie. The "house" was an apartment at the foot of the hill, but even though his parents' pad didn't seem as magical as she had hoped, Lizzie was happy to hang with him.

After about a half hour at the apartment, Lizzie suggested that they head out for the dinner and movie. But Shawn said they should watch a movie on television and order pizza instead. Lizzie wasn't crazy about the idea but she acquiesced. As they waited for the pizza, they spoke of school, friends, and life. Lizzie was honest about who she was, a sixteen-year-old junior at the local high school. Shawn also told Lizzie the truth. He wasn't exactly a college student. He worked at the local city college as a janitor because, he said, he couldn't afford school. Lizzie also learned that while Shawn looked nineteen, he was in fact twenty-five.

As they hung out, Shawn began kissing Lizzie, with which she was totally comfortable and fine. Lizzie explained to Shawn that she was a virgin and did not want to lose her virginity until she got married. Shawn was not only understanding, but he even commended her for this.

As Lizzie and Shawn watched the movie, Shawn began rubbing Lizzie's leg, inner thigh, and eventually her genital area. Again, Lizzie was comfortable with and enjoyed the petting, but she repeated that she would not have sex with him. The sexual petting continued through the evening. Shawn offered to give Lizzie a massage, which she accepted. During the massage, Shawn slipped Lizzie's pants down past her knees and thrust his penis into her vagina. Lizzie screamed, jumped up, pulled up her pants, grabbed her stuff, and fled.

While in her car driving away, she could not believe what had just happened. "Wasn't I clear?" Lizzie even had to ask herself, "Did he just . . . rape me? What do I do?" Lizzie did the right thing. She drove to the sheriff's department, where she gave a full report. And the sheriff's office did everything right. They took the report and brought her straight away to the Center, for an acute medical exam (an exam conducted within forty-eight hours of the assault) and the interview with me. The medical result came back quickly: seminal fluid that would undoubtedly match my suspect, Shawn.

The sheriff immediately went to Shawn's apartment and arrested him. He said sure they had sex, but it was absolutely consensual. He doesn't say anything else other than "I cannot imagine why Lizzie would have made up these allegations." I ran Shawn's rap sheet (criminal record) and it came back clean, not so much as a speeding ticket.

So, I know what you are thinking. What a great case, right? I've got an immediate disclosure, a credible victim, a DNA match on the sperm, and a defendant who doesn't even deny the sex? You are not going to like what I am going to tell you, but I have vowed to be honest, so here it is.

I believe Lizzie. She is credible. But there is no corroboration and without corroboration I cannot file rape charges. I believe there was a rape and I believe that everything she told me happened just as she said it did. But there's no evidence other than her word.

No evidence, you ask? The DNA evidence from the medical exam nailed the guy, didn't it? Well yes, but . . . the DNA does corroborate that

Shawn had intercourse with Lizzie, and that's enough for a statutory rape charge. But that's not a registerable sex offense (meaning he won't have to register as a sex offender), doesn't count toward the California Three Strikes law, and is generally not taken very seriously by judges when it comes to sentencing.

I have one other option, and it's the one I really want to file: rape— nonconsensual intercourse. A rape charge is a serious and violent felony, so it is a registerable offense, counts toward Three Strikes, and generally draws heavy sentences. But the DNA evidence isn't going to do squat so far as proving lack of consent. That's an essential element of a rape charge, and all I've got is Lizzie's word against Shawn's.

Don't get me wrong: a statutory rape charge is better than nothing. However, I believe this guy raped Lizzie and should be charged for that crime. But I can't file rape charges on nothing more than he said/she said evidence. And what's worse is if I file the statutory rape charge, I'll be forever barred from filing the nonconsensual rape charge for this act, even if some corroborating evidence later drops in my lap, such as Shawn doing this kind of thing again with some other girl. The Constitution bars filing twice on the same act—it's called double jeopardy.

So what to do? File the statutory rape charge, or wait in hopes we'll find some corroborating evidence to prove nonconsensual rape? How do I explain either of these less-than-optimum choices to Lizzie while at the same time making sure she understands how much I believe her, sympathize with her, and appreciate her strength and bravery in coming forward immediately?

Again, the only way is to be straight with her. I always start by explaining the legal basis for why things happen they way they do. But I also try to go deeper and explain why the law is the way it is.

So here it goes. Under the US Constitution there is the fundamental right known as the presumption of innocence. This means that as the prosecutor, I must prove each and every element of the crime beyond a reasonable doubt. So in the case of rape, while proving that the sex occurred does prove one element of the rape—intercourse—it's not enough on its own. I also have to prove the additional element of the crime of rape: lack of consent.

One of the jury instructions given in almost every criminal case basically says, "When there are two reasonable interpretations of the evidence, the jury must adopt the one that points toward innocence." Basically, this means a "tie" goes to the defendant. That is what the presumption of innocence is. I don't make this stuff up. It's the law, it's the Constitution, it's what it is.

So in Lizzie's case, while the DNA corroborates the fact that the sex occurred, it doesn't help me prove the sex was accomplished by force, violence, fear, duress, or undue influence. I have no corroborating evidence for this element of the crime, and so I cannot file the rape charge.

How bad a situation is this? Here I have a case where, hands-down, I believe my victim. I can tell that she is being absolutely open and forthright. She is a straight-shooter who recounts everything from the consensual touching to the fact that she lied to her mom about where she was going when she went to Shawn's house to begin with. But while I know that she's telling it straight, what is my jury going to see, after the defense attorney has at her in cross-examination? Jurors are likely to see a star-struck kid who lied to her mom to go on a date then either had buyer's remorse about the sex, was afraid of getting into trouble for coming home so late, or some other version of events that casts reasonable doubt on my victim's story.

Here I am in a situation where I wholeheartedly believe Lizzie, but given the burden of proof and that pesky constitutional presumption of innocence, I cannot in good faith file rape charges. I need corroboration.

That's the problem with sexual assault. Most of the time, there are no witnesses, there is more than one way to interpret what little evidence there is, and any form of corroboration is hard to come by. Plus, let's not forget what we're talking about here—we're talking about sex, just about the most taboo talk-out-loud-about subject out there. If you think we've moved beyond such puritanical self-consciousness about sex, remember how discreet most people try to be when discussing sex, especially when they don't know each other very well.

Now think about a young child who doesn't understand sex at all, probably can't even define *consent*, and has just been sexually victimized. How talkative can we expect the child victim to be? Now add that the child may be terrified of the perpetrator's threats of what will happen if she tells, or be horribly embarrassed, or even feel somehow to blame for the "bad touching" done to her?

A scenario that I see happen over and over again is that a child will come to the Center and be happy to talk about anything but the "act" or the "abuse" or the "thing that maybe made them uncomfortable" or the "thing that hurt" or "when someone touched a place they weren't supposed to." This is especially true with young kids.

For example, take five- and six-year-olds. These are kids who tend to be chatty if you speak their language. Lucky for me, I have a six-year-old who keeps me updated on kindergarten slang and what's hot and what's not among first graders. For example, I just love it when kids tell you how "over princesses" they are and who is who in *High School Musical*. They can sing all the lyrics to the Miley Cyrus/Hannah Montana songs and proudly tell you the names of their nonprivate body parts (arm, leg, eyes, tummy, etc.) as readily as naming all the crayon colors.

But what happens countless times is that when you move into the "other stuff," the kid can't give you a detail, a sentence, or anything that would confirm the prior statement the kid apparently made to his teacher about how "Uncle Davey touches my pee-pee." Why would we expect anything different? For all the reasons I went through above, anyone with a basic understanding of children is not surprised by this reluctance to talk about what even adults consider taboo, especially if "Uncle Davey" said something awful would happen if the kid ever told anyone.

This type of situation is exactly why I start off in my jury trials by illustrating how child sex assault is almost always a very private crime.

Usually, there is no evidence at all beyond what the two persons involved say happened. Corroborating evidence is especially important but also especially tough to come by in child sex crimes cases. Also, I have to make the jury understand how difficult it is for the child to talk about what happened. This introduction prepares the jury for the child's halting testimony, as well as sets the stage for whatever evidence I'll use to creatively corroborate the child's story.

CORROBORATION FROM THE VICTIM

Sometimes the child victim's ability to accurately describe what happened can offer corroboration, especially if it includes details a child would know only because of the abuse. The classic example of this kind of corroboration is when a five-, four-, or even three-year-old says that when Uncle Davey touched his "pee-pee," white milk came out of Uncle Davey's privates. That, ladies and gentleman, is corroboration because a young child would never know about ejaculation or semen or be able to accurately describe it unless it actually occurred.

A lot of people think you need medical or DNA evidence for corroboration, but you don't. Sure, DNA evidence is great for proving the sex act occurred and that the defendant did it, if those are disputed issues in the case. But as I discussed in Lizzie's case above, the DNA evidence does not prove anything about consent.

Moreover, often there simply isn't medical evidence. There are several reasons. One is that many sexual acts that are criminal do not, in and of themselves, necessarily cause injuries. Take oral copulation or fondling. These are acts that may not be forceful or harsh and so naturally don't always leave marks or scars.

Another reason is that with postpubescent girls, their vaginas accommodate a penis. Imagine a stretchy rubber band that a girl uses to tie up her hair in a ponytail. The rubber band can stretch to accommodate a lot of area then shrink down to hold the hair. That is what a vagina is supposed to do. It is meant to stretch and retract, and therefore injuries from penetration by a penis are not necessarily expected.

And then there are the many cases where the report of the abuse has been delayed. It's unlikely there will be any physical evidence if the exam is done more than seventy-two hours after an assault. There are some cases where the force of the attack has left injuries that do not heal within seventy-two hours, but evidence such as sperm or pubic hair from the perpetrator will likely be gone.

> No matter how little hope we may have of finding any medical evidence from a physical exam, we often have one done anyway. Juries expect a "no stone unturned" approach during the investigation, and so want to hear evidence that the investigators did all they could to try to find physical or medical evidence of the assault. Sometimes, we need to bring in an expert to explain why we found no medical evidence, for example, because of the passage of time.

There is another way a medical exam can provide corroboration, even if no medical evidence is found during the exam. Often a nurse will take a medical history of the victim, including the circumstances of the attack, and write that history into the medical chart. If the account given in the doctor's office matches the victim's later account to investigators, there may be corroboration from the consistency between the statements. Plus, the willingness of the victim to undergo a medical exam may provide some corroboration: it's not something a person falsely claiming sexual abuse is likely to go through.

Apart from DNA, the kinds of medical findings that can provide corroboration of a sexual attack include pregnancy, genital injuries, nongenital injuries (like scratch marks on the back), and sexually transmitted diseases. The younger the child is, the easier it is to sway the jury that this evidence corroborates the sex crime. This is because the younger the kid is, the less likely there is some other explanation for the medical finding. Claiming a six-year-old got the injuries through intercourse with someone else probably won't get the defendant too far.

CORROBORATION FROM THE PERPETRATOR

Besides the victim, corroborating evidence can come from many places you might not realize. Sometimes I can get the defendant to provide my corroboration.

I love it when a defendant thinks that consent is somehow a defense. Let them rattle on and on about how the kid wanted it, how it was consensual, blah, blah, blah, and so on. The reality is that consent doesn't matter at all in cases where the victim is very young (under fourteen in most states) or statutory rape, and consent has a very limited role in other sex crime cases involving minors. Similarly, for very young victims, a perpetrator's mistaken belief that the child was older, even if victim told the perpetrator she was, is no defense.

So one of the techniques that I train law enforcement officers to use is a strategy to encourage the suspect to make the argument that the victim consented or said she was over eighteen. One classic ruse is for a detective to show a defendant DNA results that are not really his and challenge the suspect to explain how his DNA came to be in the victim's vagina. "See," the officer says, holding up the fake test result, "I have the proof of the DNA right here." The suspect feels he cannot claim he wasn't there or that he didn't have sex with the victim, so often he falls back on a claim that the victim consented. If the victim is under fourteen, bingo! I've got a rape conviction. Even if she's older, the officer has gotten the defendant to admit the element of having had sex with the victim.

Sure, ruses like these are good ole' fashioned trickery. But before you get too concerned for the suspects who walk right into our little traps, think about this: there's nothing illegal about them, they're extremely effective, and we only lay the trap—the suspect is the one who "walks into it" by making a confession.

Another ruse that I like cops to use when interviewing a suspect is for the detective to talk about how old the victim looks, as if it matters. I've seen skilled detectives say to a suspect, "Gee, that victim looked old. I mean I would have easily thought she was eighteen or nineteen. Did she tell you how old she was?" The detective goes on and on about that and— boom—the defendant admits, "Well, yeah, that's right. She swore she was eighteen and she sure looks it, doesn't she? Anybody'd think she was eighteen, at least." Again, at least I've got a confession to the act, and that's enough for a rape conviction if the kid was under fourteen. This type of situation is very common.

If the defendant has been charged with a prior act similar to what he's charged in my current case, I can use that prior charge as corroboration. I don't even need a prior conviction. I'm using the prior act evidence to show a pattern of sexual behavior. Basically, I'm telling the jury, "Look— you know this guy has done this kind of thing before. The kid described that he did exactly the same thing here. How likely is it that's totally a coincidence?"

Another favorite of mine is using the suspect's own words against him. Statements made by the defendant that have been videotaped, recorded, or sworn can be used against him. Having this kind of evidence can be legally corroborative even if it's not an actual admission. For example, if the suspect describes all the details surrounding the crime in the same way as the victim, except when it comes to the sex part, that's a huge red flag. Why would that be the only difference?

And then there are the times when we use another ruse called *pretext calls* to get the perpetrator to give me the corroboration I need. One common kind of pretext call is to have the victim call the suspect. The entire call is recorded. (Pretext calls are often the only way we can get the suspect's words on record.) The point is to get the suspect to spit out some sort of information about the crime, maybe an apology, words of remorse, or even fear. Having the victim's family call the suspect often works, too. Bash this trickery all you want, but there's no denying how effective it can be.

One of my favorite techniques is to have the victim call the suspect and tell him that she is pregnant. The suspect's response can be very telling, and often solid corroboration. For example, responses like "Damn it, I thought you were on the pill!" or "Oh my God, don't tell anyone. I'll pay for the abortion!" are quite different from a response, "Holy cow, who's the dad?" The first two get me my corroboration.

CORROBORATION BY PHYSICAL EVIDENCE

Physical evidence can also be great corroboration. The usual kinds of physical evidence we see are clothes with bodily fluids on them, a collection of pornography, items on a computer, guns, keys to secret rooms or hotel rooms, items in a car, or anything else that supports the account the victim gives.

Creative corroboration can be found in the little things, the details. Just proving that the defendant had possession of a particular item can be a huge break because it corroborates the victim's account of what occurred and how. For example, I had a case where a child said that it always smelled like vanilla when she was raped by her uncle, yet he never put lotion or cream on her. Upon searching the house, vanilla oils, candles, and lotions were found under the bed where she had been raped.

Evidence that only a victim would recognize is corroborative. In a stranger abduction case, if a victim can describe a room (the scene of the crime) and has never been to that location before, I've got my corroboration. Or, if the child can describe things on the suspect's body, such as a tattoo or birthmark that's only visible when the suspect is naked, I've got my corroboration. Or sometimes, the child uses terminology that is beyond her years. Most six-year-olds are completely unfamiliar with the term *blow job*. When a child uses this terminology to describe the sexual act she was forced into, it becomes pretty clear that someone has taught her this term. That someone is most likely the suspect. Once again, I've got my corroboration.

Even things that may seem really negative—things we shy away from as poor evidence—may turn into corroboration. For example, my favorite clichéd story of the scantily clad, completely inebriated fifteen-year-old girl at Halloween party who is raped. At trial, the jurors may be focused on what she was drinking, what she was wearing, and what were her expectations about what was going to happen.

But all of those negatives can be turned into positives as corroborating evidence. During testimony, I'll ask the victim, "So, how drunk were you?" I'm not trying to destroy this girl's reputation but rather to show what an easy target she was for the rapist. Out of all of the people at the party that the defendant could have chosen to have sex with, he went after the most wasted girl with the shortest skirt. He wasn't going to try to rape the person in the full-length bunny outfit or nun outfit. He needed easy access and someone too drunk to know what was happening. That's my corroboration.

Another example is when the rape victim is a prostitute. You can't imagine a worse case to prosecute, right? After all, how do you convince a jury that a woman who has sex for money didn't want to have sex with this particular guy? I don't hide the fact that she's a prostitute. I put it right out there, then turn it to my advantage. I ask her, "How many people have you had sex with voluntarily? Three hundred? Five hundred?

And how many times have you gone to the police before?" None. A woman who frequently has voluntary sex with strangers doesn't just up and go to the police, because if she does, she knows it will be all but impossible to get anyone to believe her. Nonetheless, here she is, in public, owning up to the fact that she's a prostitute in order to go after the perpetrator. That's my corroboration.

These are the kinds of things that can really turn the tide in one of my cases—if I can be creative enough to figure out how to use them.

CORROBORATION FROM STILL OTHER PLACES

Witnesses are a good source of corroborative evidence for obvious reasons: They saw what went down. They can add details. They can confirm facts in the child's story. And they can dispute the story told by the defendant and attack his credibility. Witnesses are great—if you can find one. There's the big problem. For the most part, perpetrators of sex crimes, especially of child sex crimes, do not commit the crimes where a witness might see them.

But even if there aren't witnesses to the crime, there still may be witnesses who can corroborate other parts of the victim's story, which can be a huge help. For example, if a rape defendant made sexual advances to the victim multiple times at a party to only be rebuked, and a witness can testify to seeing the defendant being repeatedly shot down, there's some serious corroboration of the victim's story.

Statistically and unfortunately, perpetrators of child sex crimes are often repeat offenders. That's why we make them register. This also gives us an ugly potential source of corroborating evidence—multiple victims. When multiple victims accuse the same suspect of the same kind of sex act, there's generally one of two things going on: either you've got some vindictive kids who hate their new stepdad, or you've got corroboration. Sometimes it's easy to tell, like when two children, unbeknownst to each other, recount very similar stories of a suspect's behavior. That's very powerful corroboration. For example, take the Beltran case from Lincoln Middle School. In that case, fourteen victims over a span of thirteen years described almost the exact same behavior of sexual abuse. The preabuse grooming was the same, the comments were the same, and the assaults were the same. While many people hung on for a while to the belief that it was all a plan cooked up to oust a teacher, the individual and multiple disclosures became overwhelming corroboration when it was determined that most of the victims did not know each other and were so far apart in age that they wouldn't have heard of each other or had access to each other. In contrast, two sisters who accuse Mommy's new live-in boyfriend (whom they don't like) of sexual assault are not nearly as likely to provide reliable proof and this may not be enough for corroboration.

The bottom line is that sex crime prosecutors have to be creative when looking for corroborating evidence, especially when a child is the victim. If anything, corroboration is even more important in child sex crime prosecutions. There are so many more unknowns when dealing with children. Do they know what they're talking about when they say that? Do they even understand what sex is? How well do they separate fact from fantasy? Is shame keeping them from telling the whole truth? Combine all these reasons for needing corroboration with crimes that are usually kept very carefully behind closed doors, and I've got my work cut out for me.

CHAPTER EIGHT
KIDS ON THE STAND

It has been six months of continuances requested by the defense and granted by the judge before Enid's case has even made it to a preliminary hearing. (A preliminary hearing is also known as a "probable cause" hearing, or a mini trial where the judge determines if there is sufficient evidence to proceed to trial.) And despite the passage of time since Enid finally disclosed that the apartment manager was touching her privates and penetrating her with his finger, she still felt nervous, fragile, and scared to even see the defendant in court. To help her, I'd met with her for court school, a time to learn about court, to know what to expect, and to ask me any questions that may be on her mind. Still, despite careful description of the process and other preparations, I know Enid is trembling at the notion of actually confronting (let alone being in the same room with) the manager who used his keys to enter her apartment when her mom was gone and abused her more than seven times.

SHOULD WE EVEN ASK A CHILD VICTIM OF SEXUAL ABUSE TO TAKE THE WITNESS STAND?

"Will my child have to testify?" is a question every child sex crimes prosecutor has heard hundreds of times. Child testimony is a great source of dread and angst for parents. They are already carrying guilt over the assault their child suffered, and they feel helpless to fix what's happened. The prospect of making their child describe the abuse on the witness stand is always in the forefront of parents' minds.

Their distress is understandable, but "protecting" their child from testifying can destroy a criminal case. The child victim's testimony is pivotal in sexual assault cases, and, to put it bluntly, there are times when it isn't up to the parents (or the child) whether the child victim will testify. My job is to get the sexual predator/defendant off the streets so others aren't at risk and to deter would-be predators. Of course, I do that with as much sensitivity for the victim as humanly possible, but if a child receives a subpoena to testify, then he or she is legally required to appear and testify in court. That is not to say that I don't take a victim's wishes and desires into account, much less the child's parents, because I do. Not just because I care about the victim's opinion, but also because the law in California does give the victim a say in whether he or she wants to participate in the criminal prosecution of a sex crimes case (which is much different from how we handle domestic violence cases, by the way).

So, how does this all work? How can I listen to the victims' wishes yet slap them with subpoenas? I have found in my career that while no one wants to come to court, children victims and their parents generally agree—sooner or later—that it is the best thing to do. They know that their children's safety and the safety of other potential victims depends on them. And so, while they still dread walking into that courtroom, they realize it is something they must do.

I can hear you wondering, How does this "conviction at all costs" Sax woman live with herself? First, because I believe in what I do, but there's something that makes this part of my job a whole lot easier: for most child abuse victims, testifying is a cathartic, healing, and occasionally even enjoyable experience. You may have trouble believing that, but it's true. I have literally had kids get off the witness stand and say, "That was fun." More often than you would imagine, children leave the witness stand astonished how much better the experience was than they thought it was going to be.

Well, at least that's the case when they testify at preliminary hearings. Recall that these are hearings done in front of a judge, not a jury, to see if there is enough evidence to go forward with the prosecution. The defendant almost never testifies at these, and defense attorneys tend to hold back some during the cross-examination of the victim, saving their best for the trial.

Fortunately, the preliminary hearing is often the only testifying the child victim will have to do. Ninety percent or so of my cases settle via plea bargain before ever getting to trial. But more than half of my cases still require the child's testimony at the "prelim," as it's informally referred to. The child's testimony there is often key to not only showing there is enough evidence to go forward with the prosecution of the defendant, but it is also an important step toward getting the defendant to accept as stiff a plea bargain as I feel is warranted.

The unavoidable truth is that the judge, the lawyers, and the jurors (if the case goes to trial) at the preliminary hearing all want to hear from the victim. They expect to hear from the victim. And nine times out of ten, hearing the victim's words and seeing his or her emotions makes my case infinitely stronger. The victim's testimony reaches jurors in a way no other evidence can. They see the victim as a real child, not as an abstract "six-year-old female Caucasian," and hear her describe what the defendant allegedly did and its effects on her brings the crime into the courtroom and makes it real as well. There's very little if anything the defendant can do to overcome that. For these reasons, I tell parents, "Yes, if the case goes to trial, your child will need to testify."

Having the child give testimony at a preliminary hearing is also a dress rehearsal. Later, when the child testifies at trial, she will likely be much more comfortable with the situation, and therefore, even more believable. It's also a dress rehearsal for the trial director, the prosecutor. This way, the prosecutor has a preview of what the child will be like on the stand and how he or she will hold up to being cross-examined. Plus, hearing what the defense brings up in cross-examination gives the prosecutor advance notice of at least some of what the defense will try to do at trial.

Last but far from least, there is another important reason for the child to testify, and it's one that has nothing to do with winning the case. Whether the testimony is made at trial or at a preliminary hearing, the act of testifying lets child victims realize their ability to confront their perpetrators. The empowerment that comes from such a confrontation can do a tremendous amount for the child on his or her path toward healing.

ALTERNATIVES TO LIVE TESTIMONY BY THE CHILD VICTIM

Daesha was fourteen when she was pulled into a van by a stranger. He covered her eyes with a towel, put a knife to her neck, warned her not to make a noise, and raped her. Afterward, he drove her about forty-five minutes away from where he picked her up and pushed her out the back of the van.

Daesha reported the rape, and the investigators moved with incredible speed. Within forty-eight hours, the perpetrator and his street address were identified along with a lengthy record, including prior rape charges that had not produced convictions.

When Daesha came to the courthouse to testify at the preliminary hearing, she was so shaken at the prospect of facing her attacker that she threw up before even stepping into the courtroom. She was physically unable to testify. I made a motion asking the court to allow Daesha to testify via closed-circuit tele-vision. For the first time in ten years, the court actually allowed me to do this.

Many states permit children to testify through a closed-circuit television if the child would be traumatized by being in the same room as the defendant. If the main source of anxiety for the child comes from the courtroom setting and not the defendant, however, then closed-circuit testimony won't be allowed.

Closed-circuit testimony may seem like a much better route, especially to parents, but to a prosecutor its benefits are out weighed by its disadvantages. The reality is that watching the child testify on television just doesn't have the same emotional impact on a jury as having the child testifying live in front of them. In Daesha's case, her testimony was presented just to a judge since it was the preliminary hearing. Had her case gone to trial, I would have done everything I possibly could to prepare her so she could testify live for the jury. (In fact, I got a plea bargain that sent the defendant to prison for eighteen years. I told him if Daesha threw up like that in front of the jury he wouldn't have a prayer.) And, where there is electronic equipment, there is the possibility of malfunction, which can be grounds for a mistrial.

PREPARING THE CHILD WITNESS FOR WALKING INTO THE COURTROOM

A lot of people feel they're familiar with criminal prosecutions and what goes on in the courtroom from watching shows like *CSI* and *Law & Order*. But when they step into a real courtroom, it takes just minutes for them to realize that the carefully edited TV shows and movies don't really prepare anyone for what's involved in a criminal trial. Even after I went to law school, where I studied criminal law, criminal procedure, and evidence, I still didn't know how a real case played out, how lawyers really acted, or how close the defendant's chair would be to mine while I was prosecuting him. I still remember like it was yesterday how intimidated I felt the first time I entered a courtroom. So, clearly it's going to be tough for a child to come into a courtroom and testify. We are all afraid of the unknown, and a child witness who hasn't been properly prepared has no conception of what lies ahead, or even what they don't know.

I am a firm believer that knowledge is power. Therefore, before any child witness of mine ever steps into a courtroom, I've scheduled time for me to take her to what I call "court school." In court school, I show the child witness pictures of the courtroom and point out where she will sit, where the judge sits, where the courtroom reporter is, where I'll be, and, of course, the dreaded one—where the defendant will sit. I talk about why the different players are there and what they will be doing. For example, I explain that the bailiff is like a policeman, will have a gun, and is there to maintain order and make sure everybody is safe. The court reporter needs to write down everything that anyone says, so we need to speak clearly and not just nod our heads or mumble some uh-huhs or unh-unhs. The judge will run things in the courtroom, will wear a black robe, and should be listened to very carefully. I talk about the court clerk, who will ask the victim to state her name and if she promises to tell the truth.

And we go over the process—who will ask her questions and in what order, why lawyers make objections, and what the judge means when he says "sustained" or "overruled." Plus, there's a lot I do to prepare the child witness for her actual testimony, her examination and cross-examination, but I'll cover that a little later in this chapter.

The more about the process the victim and the family knows, the more at ease they tend to be. Probably the biggest and most frustrating piece of information that I have to convey to them is how the criminal justice system sometimes moves at a snail's pace. What I say to prepare them for that is the subject of the next section.

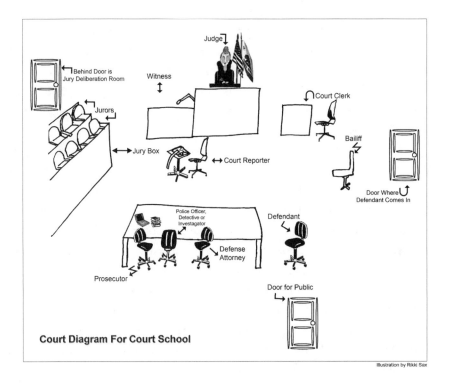

Court Diagram For Court School

Illustration by Rikki Sax

PREPARING THE CHILD WITNESS (AND THE FAMILY) FOR DELAY

The time a case is filed until when it comes to a conclusion can seem like an eternity. For me, the average time between filing and trial (assuming no settlement via plea bargain) is over a year—about fourteen months. Cases usually don't make it even to the preliminary hearing for at least two to three months after filing.

What about the right to a speedy trial, you may ask? Well, that is in the Constitution, but both the prosecution and the defense often waive this right and ask for more time. A few continuances in the early stages of a case are normal and expected. But once cases start getting five, six, or seven months old, it's a different story.

As a prosecutor, I know only the defendant benefits from delays that long, so I try to get my cases to trial as fast as possible. The longer the delay, the more memories fade, the greater the chance a witness or the victim will move, the higher the probability that evidence will be lost, and so on. And the longer the case is drawn out, the more people tend to lose interest. Making the bad guy pay becomes less and less motivating and less and less realistic.

If I had my druthers, child sexual assault cases would go to trial as soon as possible, and definitely within six months of when the case was filed. These cases should not be continued, delayed, or trailed for any prolonged period of time. This means prosecutors should oppose and judges should carefully examine the defense's requests for delay. When a continuance is requested that would bring a case near the six-month mark, I'd like to see the judge deny it or grant it only with the condition that the defendant agrees there will be no more continuances.

While I think it is detrimental to delay going to trial, that's not to say I prefer rushing recklessly and ill prepared into the courtroom. No kind of lawyer should go to trial until the case is fully prepared, but this is especially true for criminal courts. Most of the time, prosecutors get only one shot at a defendant, which is a great motivator to do it right the first time. So, if there are good reasons, I will sometimes ask the judge to allow more time to prepare for trial. Oftentimes those reasons are things beyond my control. DNA analysis, forensic lab work, physical and psychological testing, and other methods of evidence gathering can often be time consuming. But having that painstakingly collected evidence can make the difference between winning and losing.

Speaking of things beyond my control, the backlog of DNA tests and other scientific evidence preparation is shocking. I mean truly unbelievable. There is a ridiculous number of specimen jars sitting untested in labs throughout the country, potentially for years, that are linked to cases in which there is not enough evidence (maybe because the science work hasn't been done). But there are also countless cases for which we do have a suspect and do have a victim witness but still can't get the lab evidence done in time to use it in court.

Hard to believe? Where are all those "get tough on crime" politicians when lack of lab funding keeps us from the evidence we need to put offenders behind bars?

This isn't just me, one prosecutor, griping. In 2003 the National Institute of Justice collected data from a sampling of local law enforcement agencies across the country and prepared a National Forensic DNA Study Report. Based on all the data collected, the report estimated:

- The number of rape cases with possible biological evidence that local law enforcement agencies have not yet submitted to a laboratory for analysis is more than 169,000.
- The backlog of unanalyzed DNA cases reported by state and local crime laboratories is more than 57,000.
- More than half a million (542,700) criminal cases have biological evidence either waiting to be submitted or backlogged at forensic laboratories.

The practical reality is that it comes down to a balancing act for a prosecutor, weighing the pros of going forward without delay and the cons of going to trial without evidence that might or might not, depending on lab work that hasn't been done, help get a conviction.

PREPARING THE CHILD WITNESS TO FOLLOW THE RULES OF THE COURTROOM

So what else do I have to prepare the victim and the family for, besides doing my best to explain the frustrating delays? I try to give them as much instruction as they can handle so that they can deal with the whole process with as few bumps in the road as possible. By the end of court school, the child witness and the parents are able to "talk the talk" with the rest of the multidisciplinary team for the rest of the process. This sense of being keyed into what everyone else is doing and saying empowers the parents, who otherwise may feel like clueless, helpless bystanders.

There are special rules for trials that the parents and the child need to know. For example, they should not speak to other witnesses. They should always be careful of what they say in the hallway outside of court, in the elevator, even in the bathrooms or anywhere else they might be overheard. They should behave as they would in church: wear nice but not fancy clothes, keep quiet, and so on. I have attached an appendix to this book that is my standard witness preparation outline. Every time I use this, I tweak it for what the individual witness needs, but the basics stay the same.

My number one rule for victims or any other witness I'm preparing for court is "Always tell the truth." I don't care if they think the truth is going to hurt us or help us. I don't care if the truth is that they don't know and can't answer the question. I don't care if the truth is that they simply don't remember. Sticking with the truth means the jury gets genuine testimony they can believe. If the victim is worrying about whether what he or she is saying is helpful or damaging to our case, the jury will pick up on that. In the eyes of jurors, the victim's only job is to give them a straight, unembellished description of what he or she experienced.

Interestingly, most courts make the determination of whether a child is competent to testify based not on age but rather on the witness's ability to participate in the court process. The judge must feel the child knows the difference between right and wrong, understands the difference between telling the truth and telling a lie, and recognizes and agrees to tell the truth in court.

Here's a typical line of questioning a lawyer might use to show that a three-year-old is competent to testify:

> Q: How old are you?
> A: Three.
> Q: If I said you were ten, would that be the truth or a lie?

A: You're silly. That would be a lie.

Q: Do you know your colors?

A: Yes.

Q: What color marker is this?

A: Red. (correct answer)

Q: What color marker is this?

A: Blue. (correct answer)

Q: If I said this marker was yellow, would that be the truth or a lie? (marker held up is red.)

A: A lie.

Q: Have you ever told a lie?

A: Yes.

Q: What happened?

A: I got in trouble.

Q: What was the lie?

A: I told my mommy I brushed my teeth when I didn't.

Q: When you are in court, you are going to always need to tell the truth. Is that something you can promise to do?

A: I promise.

This child would likely qualify as a witness because she was able to give answers, could identify the difference between the truth and a lie, and promised to tell the truth.

I also emphasize to the victim that above all else (besides telling the truth), they should take their time. Listen to the question—the whole question. If the victim doesn't understand what is being asked, then she should say so. You can't give a truthful answer to a question you don't understand. Think through your answer before saying it. The court reporter will take down whatever you say. Are you sure this is how you want to say it? A witness should not fall for the standard lawyer gambit of pausing after the witness gives an answer, staring expectantly and hoping the witness will blurt out something he didn't want to say. The witness doesn't have to fill any silences that come up. When I sum up, I keep it simple—listen, think, and tell the truth.

Another of my basic rules for witnesses is to be calm, courteous, and respectful—*especially* if the witness becomes pissed off at the defense attorney. Cross-examination is a part of trial just like taxes are a part of life. If the prosecuting lawyer objects, wait for the judge to sustain or overrule it. Mistakes made during testimony aren't the end of the world; you can ask to go back and clarify. If you get tired or need to go to the bathroom, request a break.

In the end, it just takes time for the witness to realize she is just having a conversation and answering questions on a subject she knows. After a bit, her nerves usually calm down and she can focus on answering the questions calmly and directly.

Even though the witness and the family need basically the same information in preparation for their testimony, I find it's always better for the family to go through court school separately from the child. This way, both the parents and the children can feel free to ask questions they might not ask in front of each other. Plus, I give parents additional information on how to support their child through the process.

PRO PER DEFENDANTS

There's one type of case that probably won't leave a child with the feelings of strength and empowerment that testifying should and normally does. This is the situation when the defendant decides that his lawyer just isn't cutting it for him anymore and so he decides to represent himself. This doesn't happen very often, but it occurs enough to warrant mention.

Defendants have a constitutional right to represent themselves, just like they have the right to an attorney, so long as the court finds that they know and understand the risks of doing so. This is known as being in *pro per*, or in some jurisdictions, *pro se*. While this right exists, courts try to discourage the practice because pro per defendants are often their own worst enemies, are rarely as effective as trained defense counsel, and make it very difficult for the jury, the judge, and the lawyers. The judge spends much extra time educating the lawyer/defendant, and both the judge and the prosecutor have to make sure that the defendant is doing a sufficient job so as not to invite some prejudicial error that can result in a mistrial or later be grounds for reversing a conviction on appeal.

With this in mind, I am a firm believer in the old saying that "anyone who represents himself in court has a fool for a client and an ass for an attorney." Everyone is better protected—including the defendant—by going through the normal channels and having a trained, licensed lawyer represent him. No matter how smart a defendant may be (and even if he is a lawyer himself), independent counsel has the objectivity, skill, and resources to do a much better and more effective job.

There is another reason I discourage pro per cases. I have found that the kind of sexual assault perpetrators who want to represent themselves are often doing it to feed the narcissistic pleasure they get out of exercising power over their victims. By representing himself, the perpetrator gets to confront the victim during cross-examination, as well as her family or anyone else who takes the witness stand on her behalf. And the pro per defendant gets access to all the discovery. I once had to sit through a viewing of the victim's rape exams with the pro per perpetrator, and it made me physically ill to watch him smirk and practically get off on watching the twelve-year-old being examined.

What to do about it? I believe there should be a total ban, or at least limitations, on what a child sexual assault defendant is allowed to do in the criminal process. For example, he should not be able to personally conduct the cross-examination of the child victim. He should not personally have access to private and confidential information about the victim, such as her school records, rape exam photos, the records of doctors who have examined her bodily injuries from the assault, and so on.

WHAT IS THE DEFENDANT GOING TO SAY?

While it's true that allegations of a child sexual assault can be very challenging to prove—largely due to the lack of witnesses, as I've talked a lot about—it is also true that there aren't many defenses that the defendant can turn to.

One defense is to claim "it wasn't me." My first and best line of attack for such a defense is DNA evidence. If I can show the defendant's DNA was on the child's body or clothing on the day of the attack, then the defense fails. Also, I'll use the testimony of people who can place the defendant at the scene of the crime, or I'll point out the defendant's prior similar acts. Sometimes, if I'm lucky, I can even use some of the defendant's own statements against him, such as what we sometimes get through pretext calls like I described in chapter 7. I'll use whatever evidence I can find to show the defendant is lying about not knowing the victim or about not being near the child around the time of the crime.

The "it wasn't me" defense is used less frequently than you might think, and for a tragic reason: in most child sexual assault cases, the child and the perpetrator have some kind of preexisting relationship. Imagine you are on trial and the victim is your daughter, the kid of a girlfriend you're living with, your niece, or your student. It's hard to argue she mistakenly identified you.

While consent is often used as a defense in adult sexual assault cases, it is used much less in child sexual assault cases because the law says most "consents" by minors are not a defense. Most states have laws stating that victims under a certain age are incapable of giving what amounts to legally effective consent to sex because they are emotionally and intellectually unable to exercise the judgment of whether or not to have sex. In such cases, it doesn't matter if the child did give his or her consent. A defense simply isn't available.

By far the most common defense (and the safest because the defendant doesn't have to take the stand) is to try to raise a reasonable doubt about the prosecutor's case. I talked a lot about what a slippery concept reasonable doubt is back in chapter 7, with its clear-as-mud definition in California's jury instructions: proof beyond reasonable doubt is that which leaves in the minds of the jurors an "abiding conviction" of the truth of the charges. *What does that mean?* Once I had a juror come up to me and say, "I'm reasonable and I have doubts about all DNA evidence, so that's reasonable doubt." I felt like saying, "Yes, and I suppose Martians could have come from outer space, stolen the defendant's semen, and then placed it in the victim's vagina, too." Fortunately, I bit my tongue. My sarcasm probably wouldn't have gone over very well.

So reasonable doubt is a very big target for the defense to shoot at, and that's usually where they aim. As long as the defense attorney can raise a reasonable doubt in the jurors' minds about a single element of the prosecution's case, then their defense is made. And if they can raise even the teensiest doubt at all, they'll try to argue that doubt is reasonable.

To raise these doubts, the defense strategy is to take the prosecutor's theory of the case and show the jury how it's not as straightforward as the prosecutor says it is. The defense will question every bit of evidence (recall the O. J. Simpson trial), attack the credibility of every witness, and try to distract the jury with red herrings.

Unfortunately, this often means trashing the victim. This is done to impeach the victim's credibility; in fact, it is more often to raise the red herring of a victim who "ain't no angel herself." The defense will use anything it can find that makes the victim look like a troubled, defiant, unlikeable youth, from her sexual history to drug use to mental health issues to getting caught cheating on a spelling test in the third grade.

For obvious reasons, no one likes disclosing bad things about oneself, and so victims may not tell prosecutors about every negative thing in their personal histories. In addition to the embarrassment, victims often think these negative things can hurt the case, so they try to keep them under wraps.

If there's one thing you learn as a prosecutor, it's that the dirty laundry always comes out. There's no such thing as a secret past. And in my experience with child sexual assault cases, the defendant usually knows more about the victim than I do, so a victim who holds out on me puts me at an immediate disadvantage. Prosecutors need to know everything so that they can develop a successful case strategy. This is why it's important for the prosecutor to build a comfortable and trusting relationship with the victim.

To err is human, which jurors not only can swallow but probably have learned the hard way themselves. So if I know all the bad stuff about the victim, I can get it out there early and minimize the shock value that the defense might be hoping for. One of my law school professors called this "pricking the boil."

But more than just minimizing the shock value, I have found that almost any negative can be turned into a positive if you know about and take control of the information. If the victim was drunk and drugged up the night of the assault, that can look bad if the jury first hears about it from the defense. But if I know in advance, then I can use this information to say, "Of course the defendant had planned it as a sexual assault—he picked the most inebriated girl in the place." I use the negatives to show how calculating the perpetrator was in committing the crime.

Trying to discredit the victim is such a common defense that there are really no arguments that come as a surprise. Here's a concise list of the most common accusations the defense makes against the victim.

- The child's delay in reporting shows she is lying.
- The child's disclosing more and more as time has passed shows she is lying.
- The child's minimizing, initially denying, or recanting the allegations shows she is lying.
- The child misperceived or misinterpreted the defendant's behavior/actions.
- The child has a history of poor behavior and therefore cannot be trusted or believed.

- The child's lies were coached by the other parent, as there is a divorce/custody case going on.
- The child's lies were coached or bullied by overzealous prosecutors, police, advocates, or other members of the multidisciplinary team.
- The child fantasized or dreamed about what happened.
- The defendant is a good guy—an upstanding member of the community, an involved parent, has no record, and so on—so the victim must by lying.
- The child is lying to get attention or because the rules of the house are too strict.

These arguments are no mystery, so I can start preparing to overcome them way in advance if I know what facts in the victim's past the defense will use to establish them.

So what does a good prosecutor do to shoot down these defenses? Sometimes I'll call an expert witness and have him explain the *child accommodation syndrome* to the jury, which affects how, when, to whom, and so on a child sexual assault victim discloses what happened. This way, I'm not only shooting down the defense's use of things like delay in disclosure, disclosing more as time goes on, and even recanting, but also I'm appealing to the jury's common sense and having them at least try to put themselves in the shoes of a child trying to figure out how on earth she's going to disclose the awful things that have happened to her.

KID'S COURT

Everybody understands that children are vulnerable and can be easily scared and intimidated by adults. For that reason, courts make accommodations for kids who have to testify. These accommodations vary from state to state and even courtroom to courtroom. Here are some examples of typical ways the courtroom and what happens in it are made more kid friendly.

One of the most important courtroom accommodations is to adapt the timing of the proceedings. A child's attention span is short. A traumatized child's attention span is even shorter. Children don't have the mental strength or stamina of an adult. So, just like we have restrictions on how many hours per day a child can work, many courts limit the number of hours the child must be in court. A typical restriction, especially if the child is under eleven years old, is to limit the testimony to what would otherwise be his or her normal school hours.

Courts will also accommodate child witnesses by letting them bring certain items into the courtroom that make them feel more at home. Normally, no one can take items with them to the witness stand during testimony, but a child's blankie or favorite stuffed animal from home can mean the world to her while going through examination and cross-examination. And, as a general rule, a glass of water and tissues should also be there for the children during testimony.

Another big concern about the court proceedings, especially for parents, is how to protect a child's privacy. We don't want her having to go through life stigmatized by this court case, nor do we want the media dragging her name through the mud with daily reports during trial. So, for these and other reasons, court documents and proceedings never use a minor child's first and last name (just like I've used no real names in this book). Sometimes the court may use the victim's first name and last initial, or just John Doe or Jane Doe.

The court may also accommodate the child aesthetically by rearranging the courtroom layout to make it less formal and imposing. The courtroom personnel may sit around a table, and the judge may come off the bench or even take off his or her robe.

Another accommodation of child witnesses in some states relates to the procedure of the testimony. There are laws that dictate how questions to a minor are asked, how the child should be told to respond, and how objections should be dealt with, all of which make the questioning easier for children. As a prosecutor in a child sexual assault case, I can ask the judge to allow me to ask questions in a more sensitive way, even though it might be outside the usual rules for gathering evidence. And there are objections that can be made when questions contain words a child can't understand or are deemed harassment.

So what more would I do if I were queen of the world? Or even a state legislator? For one, it's an unfortunate fact that most major cities have enough of these cases that specific courtrooms are designated for child sexual assault (and child abuse) cases. But it's good these cities do have courtrooms that are 100 percent designed and equipped for the needs and realities of kids who testify. For example, some courtrooms are painted in kid-friendly colors like pastels and are decorated with posters and pictures so they look more like classrooms than formal, intimidating adults-only places. The chairs on the witness stand should be adjustable so that both a four-year-old and a fourteen-year-old can sit with their feet reaching the floor.

Photo Illustration by Rikki Sax / Photo by Glenn Campbell

Perhaps most important, judges should be provided special training in understanding the psychology of child sex assault victims and the ways to help them give their evidence with a minimum of additional trauma. They should be allowed to remain assigned to these kinds of cases so they become familiar with matters like the laws pertaining to child testimony, the circumstances for when testimony by close-circuit television is permitted, the areas of expert testimony with sufficient peer-acceptance to be admitted into evidence, and so on. This child sexual assault court system can be modeled after the drug courts that are in place in many jurisdictions and have become well equipped in addressing the issues and the needs of addicts and how and when to use treatment as opposed to prison.

There should be limits to an attorney's ability to badger kids during cross-examination. Attempts to impeach a child's credibility should be limited so that a defense attorney can't bring out every misdeed he or she has ever done, similar to the way we limit the defendant's ability to use the sexual history of a rape victim.

Fortunately, there exists today significant procedural leeway in child cases that doesn't exist elsewhere in the criminal justice system. The end goal is always full, truthful evidence, and that can best be achieved by understanding and accommodating a child's needs. I once had a judge tell me I should reimburse the county for all the tissues my child victim used while crying on the stand. We can do better than that.

CHAPTER NINE

IT NEVER HAPPENED

Uncooperative Victims
and Unsupportive Moms

Detective Rojas called me and said that she and Shaina were on their way to court. "Where's Shaina's mom?" I asked. "Too much to explain," the detective answered. "We'll see you there." And so a half hour later they met me outside Division 129 of the Criminal Court. Thankfully Tanya, the victim advocate, came walking down the hall to meet us too. At least Shaina wouldn't have to sit alone outside the courtroom, waiting for her turn to testify. Thirty minutes later, I'd finished the testimony of one of the first responding police officers. Now I had only ten minutes before I had to call my next witness, Shaina. I stepped out into the hall.

Shaina was sitting on one of the hard wooden benches. She was quiet, withdrawn, and all I wanted to do was to wrap her up in my arms and tell her it was all going to be over in a few hours. I asked her if she was okay, if she needed anything. She simply shrugged her thin shoulders and said no.

Shaina took the stand. She testified with practically no affect or emotion at all, not even anger, just the clear recollection of that awful day she was kidnapped by a strange man and raped in multiple locations around Los Angeles. The defendant sat and stared at her throughout. The defense tried to paint her as the one to blame, saying it was her fault for getting into the car with a stranger. After her testimony, the trial lasted a few more days with police officers, psychologists, doctors, and DNA analysts, then the defense put on its case.

Following closing arguments, the jury deliberated for two days. What was taking so long? Could some jurors really be buying the defense's argument that it was all Shaina's fault? Finally, the jury filed back into the courtroom and announced its verdict: guilty on all counts, guilty on all sentence enhancement factors, and guilty on all special enhancement factors. The jury had seen right through the narcissistic, sweet-talking defendant and his "I'm not to blame" argument.

After the jury was discharged, the jurors and the lawyers got the chance to ask each other questions. The lawyers wanted to know things like what the jurors thought of the case, what they thought about certain witnesses, and so on. The jurors had only one question for us: Where was Shaina's family?

I get that question often and I still can't answer it. Every time it happens, I find myself thinking, "How can a child possibly heal in a family where she gets no support?" Not surprisingly, there were no family members there for the defendant either. It never ceases to amaze me, day after day, how many courtrooms are empty except for the lawyers, the witnesses, the defendant, the jury, and the courtroom staff. No one at all sitting in the rows of observer benches behind the attorneys' tables. Empty courtrooms are so symbolic for me—they are the visual proof of the voids that sexual abuse leaves in the victim, in the family, and in our society.

There's no question that sexual assault is an emotional train wreck for a child, one that will leave scars well into adulthood, if not for a lifetime. What many people do not realize is that there is a tremendous impact on the family of the victim as well. An attack on one's child can provoke a slew of intense emotions in parents, from guilt to denial, outrage to despair, frustration to vigilantism. Over the years, my experience has taught me to expect family members to be deeply affected by a child's abuse, but there are still times that some of the ways these feelings play out are beyond anything I could imagine.

The behaviors of the parents have run the gamut. I've had a mother tell me that she would just put a lock on the door to her daughter's bedroom so that her husband couldn't get in there anymore—that'd keep her safe from molestation (so instead the dad would just take her to the car and rape her there). I've had mothers break down into sobs so severe the children try to comfort them, reassuringly saying, "I'll be okay, Mommy." I've had parents who were abused themselves as children become so fearful of their children becoming victims. One mother checked her child's vagina every day for any signs of semen or abuse, which itself provoked an investigation into the appropriateness of the mother's behavior. I have met parents so convinced they are not fit parents because their child did not disclose the abuse to them first that they were ready to give up all of their children for adoption. And perhaps most difficult of all, I've had cases where I have never met the parents because they never bothered to come in.

THE OVERLY INVOLVED PARENT

Many times, parents are so overwhelmed with the fact that their child has been sexually assaulted that they do not use their better judgment in trying to deal with it. Understandably, parents often feel outrage, and some are overtaken by guilt and self-blame for not better protecting their kids. They want to *do* something: help the police catch the offender, help me convict him, or even confront the offender themselves. Or they may become obsessed with helping their child recover from the abuse, trying everything and anything to make things better, ultimately making it even more traumatic for the child as they push him or her way too hard.

I recall the case of thirteen-year-old Willie, whose mother who was adamant that she must sit in on the interview. She explained to me over and over again that her son would not open up to me unless she was there. I explained to Willie's mom that her presence would jeopardize the case; her presence during the interview would be a departure from protocol that would undoubtedly become the focus of the case should it go to trial. I asked her if I could just speak to Willie for a moment to get to know him—not talk about the case—just get an idea of how comfortable he would be with me. Reluctantly, she agreed.

When Willie sat down, the first thing he said to me was "Thank God you got my mom out of here. I really don't want her to hear everything." After a few minutes, I got up and as I opened the door I found the mother's ear pressed against the door. She said she heard through the door what he had said. "Go ahead, do the interview without me," she said.

As the well-known expression goes, "The road to hell is paved with good intentions," and I can't tell parents any single "right way" to channel those good intentions. First, I'm no shrink, and second, what an abused kid needs from her parents varies according to the kid, her age, the circumstances of the assault, whether a family member was involved, and probably a dozen or so other factors. But my experiences have taught me some things parents definitely should not do. So let me at least try to help families avoid the "road to hell" part.

1. PARENTS SHOULD NEVER CALL THE SUSPECT, THREATEN HIM, OR DEMAND ANSWERS FROM HIM.

As a matter of fact, any calls or interrogations done by the parent tend to backfire. First, they can tip the suspect off that an official investigation is coming, giving him the chance to triple-clean the site of the abuse, lawyer-up, work on the story he'll use as an excuse or defense, and so on.

Or, these often heated conversations can turn a perfectly good case into a one that looks like the parent had some vendetta or axe to grind with the suspect and may have coached the victim into making the accusations as part of that.

2. PARENTS SHOULD NEVER CONDUCT THEIR OWN INVESTIGATION.

Whom do you go to when you have a cavity? The dentist, right? Even dentists don't fill their own cavities. There are experts and professionals who are part of the investigative team. These are the people, like me, who have made a career and a life out of investigating and prosecuting crimes dealing with sexual abuse. There is no good that can come from family members conducting their own investigations. I am not suggesting family members shouldn't be fully involved in the investigation, but they should do so through the professional investigators and the prosecutor, not on their own. As a prosecutor, what I most want from the parents is their support of their child. I need them to be focused on their child and themselves.

I want them to feel confident that law enforcement is doing its job, but if the professionals don't, parents should advocate and pursue change or even bring in other professionals—but parents should not conduct an investigation themselves. Parents who begin investigating put tremendous pressure on the child and subject him or her to duplicative interviews, which will probably lead to inconsistent statements whose discrepancies can be used to challenge the victim's credibility.

Participating in the investigation of a case may feel like it is being supportive, but it is not. It switches the parent's focus away from the child onto the criminal case, puts extra pressure on the child, often undermines the case, and takes time away from the entire family's healing, recovery, and survival. I tell parents to not even talk about the facts of the case with their child unless the child brings it up, and in that case don't ask questions. Just listen and let the child talk in a free-flowing, natural way. Let her say what she wants or needs to say, not what she thinks you want to hear.

3. Parents Should Not Show Their Own Feelings of Anger, Frustration, Hurt, or Despair to the Child.

As I discussed before, it is clearly natural for parents to have their own feelings of guilt, shame, disbelief, frustration, and sadness. But venting or even showing those feelings in front of the child can put a crushing burden on her. Of course no parent means to do that; the parent is just being emotionally honest, right? Go be "emotionally honest" on your own time.

For kids, the line between a parent being upset because of *what happened*, on the one hand, and being upset *because of* the kid on the other, is often too fine and too emotionally sophisticated a line for them to draw. Especially when the parent doesn't bother to explain the distinction, and sometimes doesn't even see it himself.

The result? The kid feels the parent is upset *because of* the kid. She feels she is the cause of the parent's pain and therefore responsible for it. A child trying to deal with abuse needs that kind of additional self-blame like a hole in the head. More on this in the next section.

A couple years ago I had a case involving a teenager who had extremely conscientious parents. They did all of the "parentally appropriate things": attended school activities, participated in family activities, read to their children when they were young, monitored their TV watching, eating, and so on. And as much as they wanted to control their fifteen-year-old Britney, her parents knew that they needed to allow her freedom and time to hang with her friends.

One Saturday night, one of their worst fears came to pass. Britney, with five other girls, decided to go to a college fraternity party. They thought it would be fun to hang with the college boys, and in order to fit in she drank alcohol and smoked dope. Though all the girls were pretty loaded, Britney was by far the most affected by the drug/alcohol combination and has no recollection of leaving with the twenty-one-year-old college boy. She also had no recollection of how her clothes were removed, nor did she know in whose apartment she was when she woke up.

She did know, however, that she needed get home immediately and be honest with her parents about what had happened. So, despite her fear of getting in trouble, Britney went home and told her parents everything—the drinking, the drugs, and the aftermath. Her parents took her to the Center, where I conducted an interview with the team. Although we were not able to find corroborating evidence and therefore were unable to file a case, I did have the opportunity to speak often with Britney, as she called me on a weekly basis.

Three weeks after the incident, Britney's parents pulled her out of school, began home-schooling her, made her cut off all communications with her friends, barred her from accessing the computer or even using the phone, and completely isolated her. At first I thought this was some sort of lesson or temporary punishment. What amazed me was that even six weeks later, Britney's parents kept it up. It was for real. It was her new way of life. I can see that her parents had good intentions, but pulling in the reins as tight as this after an assault was, in my mind, going to backfire, and it did. About six months after my interview, I found out Britney ran away from home. When she was found, she was on Sunset Boulevard, selling her body in order to stay on the streets and escape the prison her parents created for her after she was victimized.

THE OVERLY DISTRAUGHT PARENT

When Anastasia came into the interview the first thing she asked me was, "Are you going to tell my mom what I say?" This question comes up in some form or another in about 90 percent of my interviews. It comes up so often that I've added a comment to my pre-interview, ice-breaking spiel, explaining how I don't tell parents about what is said by the victim or anyone in the DA interview.

But you know what? Kids don't ask this question because they're afraid they'll get into trouble if I do tell their parents. Most of the time, they are trying to protect the parent. What they are afraid of is that the full details of the abuse will get to their parents and upset them even more. Mental health professionals have a name for this—*parentification*—the child is taking on the parent's role of protector. Not only is this way too much for such young shoulders to bear, but it can lead to the child never telling the full story of the abuse—to me or anyone—for fear of what it will provoke in the parent.

Children are unbelievably aware of their parents' emotional states. We were all children once. Remember how upset you got by seeing one of your parents cry? When parents are upset, children will either hide from the situation or actively do just about anything to make their parents happy or calm again. I see children exhibit these responses all the time in sexual assault cases when their parents can't hold back their distress in front of the child (or don't even try). The child, instead of focusing on her own healing, takes on the burden of calming her hysterical parent. Or, as I think happened with Anastasia, the child just shuts down emotionally in an attempt to remove herself from yet another painful situation that is beyond her ability to fix or bear.

I once had a mom sob so uncontrollably that the victimized daughter ended up patting her mom's eyes with a Kleenex, stroking her hair, and saying over and over into her ear, "It's okay, Mommy, I'll be okay."

Another time, I had just finished an interview with Bryan, a four-year-old boy, and was taking him back to his mommy in the waiting area. The instant the mother saw Bryan she broke down sobbing. I don't mean sniffles, I mean hysterical, heaving sobs broken only by gasps for air and attempts to mumble words of love to Bryan. Bryan looked up at me and said, "Robin, why is mommy crying?" Then he started talking about how much he loved the Center and didn't want to leave. I asked why he didn't want to leave, afraid he'd say he didn't want to go home with his sobbing mommy—something I could totally understand. But that wasn't it. He answered, "Well, Robin, you are a helping lady and see, my mommy needs help. I don't need help. She does." *This four-year-old boy was trying to get help for his mother.*

This is not how things are supposed to work. Our children count on us to be strong. We are the adults. We are the ones who have dealt with the bad crap in life before. We're experienced. We're toughened. But I'll tell you, nothing upsets me more than a parent who allows the focus to turn onto him or herself. Note that I didn't say "who deliberately shifts the focus to him or herself." Very few do it deliberately, but many, many *allow* it to happen. Parents who are overly distraught in front of their kids do far more damage than good. But getting them to understand that is never easy.

THE PARENT IN DENIAL

Overly involved and overly distraught parents can be unbelievably detrimental to the case and the child. Still, it never fails to amaze me how many parents simply turn their backs on their kids when claims of sexual abuse surface. I don't know whether they are blinded by guilt at failing to protect the child, can't accept the idea that their boyfriend is a child molester, or are just plain in shock. And the way the parent's denial gets expressed most often is the most poisonous—the parent refuses to believe her child.

There have been an unbelievable amount of times when I've had cases where the perpetrator was the mother's boyfriend and she either decided not to believe the victim or, even worse and even more common, blamed the child for being a flirt, having a crush, or even being a "whore."

Disbelieving a child who finally musters the courage to disclose sexual abuse is the most harmful reaction a parent can have. Can you imagine how devastating it is then when the most important people in your life don't believe you? Don't forget the power that adults have over children—children depend on adults, trust adults, and look to adults for attention, affection, and even for the roof over their heads. Denial of the child's report of abuse turns all of that upside down. How can a child count anymore on a mommy who doesn't believe her? Does mommy still love her? Will she even still be her mommy?

Disbelief is a very common defense mechanism. We all suffer from it.

We all have a lot invested in believing that the stuff we hear about in the news won't happen to our children. I see denial at work in parents even *before* there is any abuse: when parents teach their kids only about stranger danger, they are implicitly denying the far more prevalent danger that a child molester can be among the people we know, love, and trust.

I see this kind of denial and disbelief all the time. I speak all over the country and am constantly amazed at how few parents even attend classes, programs, seminars—anything to educate themselves about sexual assault and abuse. It seems the taboo isn't just the abuse itself, but talking about it as well. I recall a school I spoke at that got eight hundred of the thousand parents to turn out for a school auction, but could only get twelve parents to show up for a free program on protecting kids from predators.

Denial is an effective defense mechanism. It is a mechanism that is used to protect ourselves from emotional pain. When someone we love— a child—tells us that someone else we love—a husband, boyfriend, brother, or someone else close—is abusing her, there's going to be serious emotional pain one way or the other. It's a lot easier to disbelieve and deny than it is to accept and deal with the awful truth.

Well, I am here to tell you that children rarely lie about the disclosure of child sexual abuse, as I discuss in greater detail in chapter 5. If the parent chooses denial or disbelief, she will almost always be wrong, and the effect on the child can be devastating.

I am not saying that children don't lie. What I am saying is that there's a big difference between lying about sneaking a cookie before dinner and lying about being sexually abused. I'm certainly not naive to kids lying. Just last week my six-year-old adamantly assured me she had brushed her teeth when I knew she hadn't. A simple touch of the bone-dry toothbrush proved it.

But children rarely lie about being sexually abused. I am not just saying this because I'm a prosecutor. Yes, I see this confirmed every day in my practice, but this is also backed by evidence from sociologists, criminalists, and professional forensic interviewers. As Kathryn Brohl explains in *When Your Child Has Been Molested*, "Children seldom lie about being molested. Most of the time they have no reason to lie or lack the intellectual capability to do so."[1]

Just like overly emotional parents, parents who deny or disbelieve their children cause the child to shut down and withdraw into themselves, confused and afraid to trust anyone. It is impossible to support a child you disbelieve. If you want to be there for your child, you have to move beyond denial and into belief.

If a parent won't or can't believe the child's report of abuse, my ability to do my job and the child's healing are hindered and, even worse, the abuse will probably continue.

THE JUST PLAIN AWKWARD PARENT

Then there are those parents who make it abundantly clear that they have no idea what to do with the situation at hand. They don't know whether or not to talk about it, or what to say if they do try to talk. The result tends to be a permanent, awkward silence that effectively ignores the abuse. This too is an incredibly harmful situation for the child. The assault has already caused feelings in the child of alienation from the adults the child formerly trusted and depended upon. But now, treating that assault as the elephant in the room no one wants to talk about pushes the alienated child even further into isolation.

As I said, children are keenly aware when something is up with their parents. They know when their parents avoid looking at them directly, paste false smiles on their faces, talk to and treat them differently. When this happens, the child's hope for support from her parents disappears. It feels like her real parents aren't there anymore. Now all the child knows is that her disclosure of the horrifying events has changed the whole family, and the parents' awkward ignoring of it means there's no chance of returning to a normal life.

It is hard enough for children to learn to cope with their abuse, even when they have people there to support them along the way. Awkward parents make the child feel even more uncomfortable with themselves and far more alone in their struggle.

So, what to do with an awkward parent? When I encounter an awkward parent, I try to encourage the parent to pursue his or her own counseling and help. It's no easy job to understand and support an abused child, and there is absolutely nothing wrong with asking for some expert help. Awkward parents need to get comfortable in their skin before they can provide a comfortable environment their child can count on.

HOW TO TALK TO YOUR KID ABOUT THE ABUSE

So what should parents do? How should they react if a child comes to them and discloses some abuse? Here are some guidelines that come straight from my experience with sexually abused kids, plus all the parents I've seen get it right and get it wrong.

Stay calm. As I mentioned, the best first reaction is to under-react. The child has just done what is for her a terrifying thing: told you that an adult is making her do something very wrong. The last thing she needs is to see her terror reflected in the eyes of the one she is turning to for support.

Believe your child. Affirm the child's disclosure, but also listen carefully to what the child is saying and trust your instincts. I'm not suggesting blind belief here. No one knows your child better than you do, so is what she's telling you possible? Has she lied about anything like this before? Are there any marks or indications that would corroborate what the child is saying? Marks that should be there if what she says is true, but aren't? Does your child have any motive to lie about this? And, what's your child's demeanor as she's making the disclosure? Knowing your child and thinking about these questions should immediately give you a gut reaction about her disclosure.

Go slow. Things happen to all of us that we don't want to talk about right away. It takes us a while to process what's happened before we can bring it to the surface and talk about it. Children are no different. Many times, they need space to come to grips with what's been done to them, before they feel comfortable talking about it. It will come out when the child is ready to talk—sometimes everything, sometimes just little parts of things. Pushing a child into talking when he isn't ready can cause him to shut down or refuse to deal with his emotions in positive ways. The child may start exhibiting more negative outlets for her emotions, such as substance abuse or suicidal tendencies, or she may suffer from post-traumatic stress disorder.

Make the child feel safe. The best rule of thumb is to focus on making the child feel as safe as possible. Safe to talk or not talk. Safe from making mommy cry. Safe from any repercussions of disclosing the abuse. Safe from feelings of embarrassment, shame, or feeling it was the child's fault. Safe from having to worry about anyone else's feelings but the child's own.

Here are some other great ideas from the Warren Washington CARE Center to tell your child to help him or her deal with what's going on:

- I believe you.
- I know it's not your fault.
- I am so proud that you told me, that was very brave.
- I am sorry that this happened to you.
- I am not sure what will happen next.
- I am upset, but NOT at you.
- I am angry with the person who did this.
- I am sad and you may see me cry. That's all right. I will be able to take care of you. I am not mad at you.[2]

In order to help the child cope with the situation, the Warren Washington CARE Center also suggests doing the following things:

- Return to a normal routine as soon as possible.
- See that your child receives therapy as soon as possible.
- Find help, counseling, for yourself and your family.
- Teach your child the rules of personal safety.
- Be careful not to question your child about the abuse.
- Avoid discussing the case with other victims or their families.
- Never coach or advise your child on how to act or what to say to professionals or investigators.
- Avoid the suspect.[3]

Even when the parent reacts in the most supportive and appropriate way, there is still much that the child needs, including to be free of the emotional state of the parents.

IT'S NOT YOUR FAULT, EITHER

It is important for parents to know that it is not their fault if their child was molested. Parents of sexually assaulted victims often blame themselves for the abuse. Their guilt is focused on their inability to recognize signs and clues that indicated sexual abuse was occurring.

Given statistics like one in five girls and one in six boys will be sexually abused before their eighteenth birthday, it should surprise no one that a parent of an abused child may have also been abused. The abuse of the child may well stir up traumatic and unresolved issues relating to the parent's past sexual abuse. In these situations, the sexually abused parent—whether the abuse occurred as an adult or as a child—should seek professional help to understand her feelings and how they are affecting her response to her own abused child.

Also, parents need to remember that it was the molester's choice, not theirs, that resulted in the child's abuse. The act committed against their child was done without their permission. Although this is no exhaustive way to assuage a parent's guilt, it can help the parent realize he or she did not make the abuse happen. And as big an advocate as I am of educating parents in steps to take to help keep their children safe from abuse, even I recognize that it is impossible to make any child 100 percent safe.

WHEN IT IS THE PARENT'S FAULT

However, in some cases, a parent *is* at fault. This includes, of course, a parent who actually performs a sexual act with the child. But it also includes a spouse who sits silently by, pretending not to know what is happening out in her husband's truck or in her daughter's bedroom upstairs. It also includes a parent who helps hide the abuse from others like teachers, child protective services, medical professionals, neighbors, and the police.

Parents have a duty to protect their children once they learn or suspect that a child has experienced some form of sexual abuse. And that means reporting these acts to local law enforcement, even if the offender is a husband or a boyfriend. Although this is not a parenting book, it seems a simple truth that a parent's obligation to protect a child's health and safety should always take precedence over protecting an abuser from exposure or prosecution, no matter who it is.

Let me also stress that if you believe the abuse will stop or believe the abuser when he tells you he will stop, *trust me, you're making a mistake.* Abuse is rarely a one-time thing. It will almost certainly keep on happening until you act and help the authorities stop it.

Children represent what is innocent and pure in this world. When a molester takes away a child's innocence, he is taking away what a child believes is good about himself. Parents must remember that oftentimes children do not have the strength to say no to adults and are unable to recognize what is proper and what is improper behavior. By allowing such perverse acts to continue, the parent may lead a child to believe that such behavior is "normal" or that the child deserved it, ideas that will affect the child throughout his life, corrode his self-respect, and increase the likelihood he'll commit similar acts himself.

MAKING THE SYSTEM WORK BETTER

If I had my way, I'd borrow a couple of pages from the family law courts, where things like divorce cases, custody battles, and decisions whether to remove children from their parents and place them in foster care are handled. The overriding principle that guides the family court is clear: do what is in the "best interest" of the child.

That's one page I'd borrow. The other is the family court's power to make orders or set requirements not only on a defendant, but also on family members and anyone else who has caregiving responsibilities for the child. In family courts, judges constantly make determinations as to who is most fit to have primary physical and legal custody of a child, be it one parent, both parents, a grandparent, an aunt, a foster parent, and so on. The goal is whatever is in the child's best interest.

While each state has a slightly different definition of "best interest," many state courts use a welfare checklist that pretty well sums up the main factors for determining how to best ensure a child's safety:

1. The child's physical, emotional, and/or educational needs now and in the future,
2. The likely effect on the child of any change in the child's circumstances now and in the future,
3. The age, sex, background, and any other characteristics of the child the court considers relevant,
4. Any harm suffered by the child or the risk of potential future harm,

5. How capable a parent is to take care of the child (in comparison to the other parent or other potential caregiver),

6. The wishes and feelings of the child, taking into account age, developmental abilities to make decisions, and so on.

The welfare checklist helps the family court safeguard children caught up in divorce, custody, and parental rights cases. Clearly it makes sense to consider the best interests of the child when deciding whom a kid should live with. Of course, that's not the issue being decided in a child sex crime prosecution, but I still think we can and should pay much more attention in child sex assault cases to the best interests of the child victim.

I know the answer the court and legislatures would give—the goal of the criminal court is to provide a fair trial to the accused. Sure, this places the focus more on the accused than on the victim, but still that's not as inconsistent with protecting the best interests of the victims as it may seem. For example, restitution is often ordered to pay for the victim's therapy if the defendant is found guilty. How about ordering restitution to pay for parents' therapy or family/group sessions when those may be the best ways to restore the secure family environment the child victim so desperately needs?

We can send wife beaters to anger management classes, drug addicts to treatment programs, pedophiles to sex therapy. So why can't we send victims of child sexual assault—and by "victims" here I mean the whole family unit—to rehab and therapy? I'll bet if we did, we'd increase our understanding of the factors that lead to abuse, how to encourage a child to disclose it, and what parents can do to better to prevent it. It's time that prosecutors, courts, and legislatures all think harder about what is in the child sex victim's best interest and about how to make that happen.

CHAPTER 10

THE REAL-LIFE EFFECT OF *CSI*

In this chapter we will look at using DNA evidence in court. Juries now tend to expect DNA evidence, whether or not there is DNA. Thanks to shows like *CSI*, jurors expect that crime scene analysts go out and "light up" crime scenes in order to find evidence of wrongdoing.

In my view, every case should include testimony about DNA, even if there are no DNA findings in the case. Because jurors expect to hear about it, the district attorney owes it to the jury to explain why (or why not) there is DNA, explain why (or why not) there should be DNA, and show that a DNA test was at least part of the investigatory process.

> *Avery was home alone, sitting on her couch and watching television when suddenly she was attacked from behind. A men's necktie was shoved into her mouth and the attacker—a man she'd never seen before—tugged at her blouse, trying to lift it up. Avery fought back, managed to get the tie loose, and bit the man's hand. With that he ran out of the house. Avery jumped to her feet, called 911, and the defendant was apprehended just down the street.*
>
> *Avery was lucky, in my opinion. It turned out the man was*

the prime suspect in four other adult rapes, as well as the rape of a sixteen-year-old girl. The police found items in his backpack that linked him to each of these attacks, and he'd used exactly the same MO in each. (MO is modus operandi, which means the way the person committed the crime.)

At trial, Avery described the attack and identified the defendant as her attacker. The arresting officer testified to apprehending the defendant just down the street from Avery's house. The police detective testified to the items found in the defendant's backpack and how they linked the defendant to the other rapes, all committed the same way.

On cross-examination, the defendant's lawyer spent most his time asking the detective at length why there was no fingerprint evidence and why the cops hadn't even bothered to dust for fingerprints at Avery's house. As I sat in court listening to the defense attorney go on and on, I couldn't help wondering, "Dusting for fingerprints? We've got an eyewitness, an arrest just yards from the scene of the crime, items in his backpack linking him to other sexual assaults, and all of them done with exactly the same MO as here. Who needs fingerprints?"

The defense attorney was trying to take advantage of what is known as the *CSI* effect. It's a consequence of highly popular TV shows such as *Law & Order*, *CSI*, and all their offshoots. These shows have shaped jurors' expectations of what happens in real-life crime and real-life investigations, resulting in the expectation that scientific evidence be included in every case—evidence like fingerprints, DNA, fiber analysis, and so on. When there isn't such evidence, they question the thoroughness of the police investigation, and defense attorneys like the one in Avery's case try to turn that question into a reasonable doubt as to the defendant's guilt. I'm not making this up. The *CSI* effect is a known fact of life in my world. It was actually studied from a sociological perspective by the Honorable Judge Donald E. Shelton, Young S. Kim, and Gregg Barak in 2006, resulting in a paper titled, "A Study of Juror Expectations and Demands concerning Scientific Evidence: Does the '*CSI* Effect' Exist?" The study surveyed people who had been summoned for jury duty and gathered information about their demographics, television viewing habits, expectations that the prosecutor would produce scientific evidence, and whether they felt scientific evidence was necessary before they could find a defendant's guilt had been proven beyond a reasonable doubt.

While some of the study's results were a bit mixed, it did confirm my experience with the *CSI* effect in cases involving serious violent crimes: 46 percent of the summoned jurors expected DNA or other scientific evidence in murder or attempted murder cases, and 73 percent of those surveyed expected it in rape cases.

Even more telling is what the surveyed potential jurors said about how the *CSI* effect would influence their decision to convict or acquit. The Shelton et al. study found that "in 'any criminal case' where the prosecution relied on circumstantial evidence without scientific evidence, 41.7 percent of respondents said they would probably acquit." Even if the alleged victim of a rape or other sexual offense testified to the assault and identified the defendant, like Avery had, still "a significant number of respondents (26.5 percent) stated that they would find the defendant not guilty if there is no scientific evidence."[1]

So how does a sex crimes DA deal with this *CSI* effect in the real world of a courtroom? First, dealing with juror expectations is nothing new for me. Every time I'm in a jury trial, I am keenly aware of what jurors expect from me. For example, I know that jurors expect for prosecutors to be dressed conservatively and simply. So what do I do? I stick to the safe, monochromatic, usually dark (gray, navy, black) suits. For opening statements and closing arguments, it's always a navy blue skirt suit.

Actually, I only wear pant suits if a trial is more than two weeks long, and even then, only once or twice a week, max. Why? Because almost every jury is going to have an older juror or two—often several—who still believe the only "proper" way for a lady to dress in a formal setting like a courtroom is a skirt suit. And I know the impressions jurors have of me will color not only what they think of me but what they think of my witnesses, my arguments, my whole case. Do I like it? No. I'd like to wear what I want to wear. But my job is to convince a jury to convict, and I'm not going to blow a case because I woke up one morning and felt it was a tight pants, open-toe high heels kind of day.

The second thing that the *CSI* effect imposes on me is more problematic than my wardrobe choices. I have to ask law enforcement personnel to investigate and attempt to collect scientific evidence, even in places where we don't expect to find any and even in cases where there is no need for it, like in Avery's case. What's worse is that when it comes to trial, I have to make some overworked, backlogged criminalist leave his lab to come to court and explain to the jury why there was no scientific evidence found, and why there was no reason on earth to expect there would be any.

Remember my discussion about all the backlogged DNA cases where evidence is still sitting in storage lockers waiting to be analyzed? Those are cases where there probably *is* scientific evidence, but the lab doesn't have the manpower to analyze it. So it's pretty easy to understand the push back I get from law enforcement and criminalists about spending time in court explaining the nonexistence of evidence. And while the investigators and criminalists are well aware of the *CSI* effect, no one wants to be the one subpoenaed for trial when there is so much other work to be done.

One suggestion people have made to me is to have a "nonevidence" expert stationed at the lab or at the police station to handle explaining the absence of physical or scientific evidence in cases. But to do that effectively, he'd have to be an expert criminalist, that is, someone who could be in the lab doing the real work that will result in real convictions. Having a designated "nonevidence" specialist wouldn't do anything to lessen the burden on the law enforcement personnel who still have to be at the crime scene, combing for scientific evidence they have no expectation of finding.

But there is something we can do to lessen the impact of the *CSI* effect on overworked cops and criminalists, and the fact we're not doing a better job of it is another pet peeve of mine. Actually, there are two pet peeves. First are the lawyers who are so scared or intimidated by DNA that they don't bother to learn the science involved. How can you explain something you don't understand yourself? Second are lawyers who let scientists drone on and on, speaking in scientific mumbo-jumbo terminology that confuses and ultimately ends up boring the jurors to tears.

There are solutions, from my experience, for both of these issues. The first is that prosecutors (and preferably their detectives) need to learn DNA from the inside out, which means a lot more than reading a textbook. Prosecutors and detectives MUST go visit the crime labs, make friends with criminalists, and see exactly what they do. Attorneys need to have a picture in their minds of what a DNA test procedure looks like so they can explain it to a jury. And speaking of pictures, if there are no crime scene photos or medical exam photos, it's not a bad idea to take some pictures of the crime lab so the prosecutor can re-create her experience with the jury. Since juries are fascinated by this stuff, lawyers need to learn it to feed the jurors' appetites.

The second thing prosecutors need to do is to prepare the DNA expert to explain DNA evidence to the jury as the nonscientists they are. This doesn't mean dumbing it down. It means getting rid of the fancy scientific terminology, speaking in short sentences rather than mile-long ones that sound like they are from a scholarly article, and cutting out what the jury doesn't need to know. In a case where the DNA testing doesn't have any complex issues like contamination, false positives, or other problems, the expert's direct examination should be thirty to forty-five minutes, max. All that needs to be covered is:

1. What DNA is,
2. Which testing methods and quality assurances are possible and which were used in this case specifically,
3. What the results are, and
4. What the results mean.

To illustrate how shorter versus longer works better, compare the eight days of DNA testimony during the O. J. Simpson trial to this simple statement of the actual results:

> [DNA analysis] showed that blood found at the scene of Brown's murder was likely O. J. Simpson's. The odds it could have come from anyone but Simpson were about one in 170 million. DNA analysis of blood found on one of Simpson's socks identified [the blood] as Nicole Brown's. The blood had DNA characteristics matched by approximately only one in 9.7 billion. DNA analysis of the blood found in, on, and near Simpson's Bronco revealed traces of Simpson's, Brown's, and Goldman's blood.[2]

MEDICAL EXAMINATIONS OF THE VICTIM AND THE SUSPECT

Perhaps the best tools I have for combating the *CSI* effect are medical exams of both the victim and the suspect. Since juries are so conditioned to expect scientific and physical evidence, I think an investigative team would be remiss in not pursuing medical exams to try and get it. The medical exam of the victim may reveal some sort of physical injury that corroborates the victim's description of the attack. It can also lead to finding hairs, fibers, DNA, or other scientific evidence that was left on the victim or her clothing by the attacker. And even if it doesn't, it shows how seriously both the investigative team and the victim took the assault and the investigation.

The suspect's medical exam can also provide corroboration of the victim's description. As with the victim exam, there may be hair, fibers, or DNA of the victim still on the suspect. There may be physical signs that back up the victim's story, like scratches or other wounds on the perpetrator. There may be identifying marks (like scars, birthmarks, moles) described by the victim in places the victim could not have seen but for the attack.

The suspect exam is also an opportunity to look for any sexually transmitted diseases, which may make for enhancements to the charge and the sentence. For example, if a suspect is HIV positive, he may be further penalized for committing a sexual assault while knowing he was HIV positive. And perhaps the best thing about a suspect exam is that the perpetrator is put through the same experience as the victim, subjected to swabs of the genital areas, inspections and pictures of private parts with the colposcope (see page 32), and collection of any potential biological evidence.

Ironically, one *benefit* of the *CSI* effect is that it is now widely known how important it is for a victim not to bathe, shower, douche, or even use the toilet if avoidable before an exam, because evidence of the assault and the perpetrator's identity (hair, seminal fluids, bits of skin, etc.) may be left on the victim's body. If the victim was assaulted orally, drinking prior to an exam should be avoided. Victims should not straighten up the scene of the incident and should take a change of clothes to the hospital rather than changing at home. If the victim must change clothes, put the items that were worn at the time of the attack in a paper bag (not plastic) and bring them to the hospital. (Plastic traps moisture, which can increase the risk of contamination by bacteria; paper allows the evidence to air dry.)

Unfortunately, police do not always like the idea of suspect exams. There is always a question of whether they are too invasive plus, frankly, they're a pain in the butt. First the suspect and the victim are transported to a medical facility that is equipped to conduct the exam. Once at the medical facility, the attending officers need to make sure the victim and the suspect get their exams in separate areas so there is no chance a hair, fiber, or other potential evidence will get transferred between them at the hospital rather than at the crime scene. I have heard that some officers think the law requires the victim and the suspect be examined at separate hospitals, but having separate areas with separate nurses and doctors will suffice. The gold standard is for there to be a specialized clinic specifically designed for rape and sexual assault cases, made to look as "un-hospital" like as possible to help make young victims feel more at ease.

One thing cops seem to have down pat is how to use the *CSI* effect against a suspect. Here's how it works. The officer strikes up a little chat with the suspect and mentions that there has been a thorough medical exam done on the victim, looking for DNA, fibers, hair, and so on. How the suspect reacts to just that much news can show a lot—he's seen such tests on *CSI* and knows they can be really bad news for a defendant. But then the cop pulls out some official medical report (perhaps from a previous case) and shows the defendant that the test reports showed a positive DNA match—can he explain how that could have happened? I have seen it time again where suspects start spewing all types of helpful statements when they think there are medical/scientific results. Even if they don't make a full confession (which they seldom do), their efforts to explain the test results can lead to some useful admissions. For example, "Okay, I was at her house and maybe I sneezed on her but we didn't have sex" or "Sure we had sex but it was only because she wanted to."

Generally, medical exams are not painful because the procedures physicians use to examine child patients are safe and noninvasive. For example, the colposcope is a binocular optical instrument used to magnify the genital area to assess the extent of the damage caused by the child's abuser. The colposcope does not touch the child but is equipped with a light and a camera to record any injury.

Use of the colposcope and the medical exam findings in court can be a source of conflict for a prosecutor. On the one hand, prosecutors want to show the jury what a traumatic experience both the assault as well as its aftermath were for the victim, including an invasive and embarrassing medical exam. That not only builds sympathy for the victim but also builds her credibility—who would go through all this if it weren't true? On the other hand, we as prosecutors want to make the victim's exam as painless and noninvasive as possible. These are children we are dealing with—who wouldn't want to ease their pain? We explain the colposcope in the most basic terms, telling children that it is basically a super magnifying glass that doesn't need to actually touch their private parts. Nurse examiners try to alleviate kids' fears by letting them put something like a stuffed animal on the exam table and then showing them how the fibers of the stuffed animal can be magnified via the colposcope, and maybe then showing the child how her own toe or finger can be magnified and portrayed on a computer screen.

Another misconception that needs to be put to rest is that even a small delay between the assault and the exam means no evidence can be found. While the less delay the better, it is surprising how long biological evidence can actually remain on the human body. I've had cases where useful biological evidence was collected in medical exams that took place forty-eight or even seventy-six hours after the assault. And the exam of the suspect may yield evidence that may never go away, like tattoos, abnormalities, or distinguishing marks that only a child who has been assaulted would recognize.

It was a big case. Three victims, ten counts for each, meant there were thirty counts charged against the defendant. He had a lot at stake—multiple life sentences were on the table. I had a fairly strong case, but I knew the jury was going to have problems liking two of my victims. Plus I had a battle of the experts about one key piece of evidence. My expert was a nurse, while the defense had hired an MD.

The disputed evidence was a finding my nurse examiner put on her OCJP form (the standardized form in California that all forensic exams are recorded on). She had found a vaginal injury she termed a "cleft," which she noted as "consistent with the reported history" the victim had given in describing the assault. Not surprisingly, the defense's doctor claimed the cleft was not an injury at all and was instead a vaginal abnormality that had probably been there since birth. So I had at best a tie—even assuming the jury would give equal weight to my nurse and their doctor—and as we know, any tie goes to the defendant. If there are two reasonable interpretations of the evidence, then there is reasonable doubt and I haven't proven my case.

So I needed a way to break the tie. I took the information to the head of the medical practitioners who oversees all the nurse practitioners and is himself a specialist in pediatric gynecology. And before we even began talking about the medical findings, he suggested we dig into the qualifications of the defense's expert. With the guidance of a doctor who knew how to carefully read another doctor's curriculum vitae (resume), I found that the defense expert was really an ER doc who had no specialized training in gynecology, let alone pediatric gynecology. I'd found my tie-breaker—this was going to be a fun cross-examination!

A continuing theme throughout this book is that child sexual assault requires specialized knowledge and skill. This applies just as much to the medical personnel who do examinations of child sexual assault victims as to law enforcement, prosecutors, social workers, and so on. The medical personnel should be specifically trained to conduct the medical exams of sexually assaulted children, trained not only in what to look for and how to handle traumatized kids with sensitivity but also so their results are in a form that can be used as part of the child sexual assault prosecution.

SANE and SART are examples of what I'm talking about. SANE stands for Sexual Assault Nurse Examiners and SART stands for Sexual Assault Response Team. These are teams that are set up with people who have the medical knowledge, skill, and training to conduct these unique kinds of examinations but who are also trained about the inner workings of the team approach and are familiar with the criminal justice process. As my case example above pointed out, some "experts" who are called in to testify on behalf of the defense are not trained or experienced in examining child victims of sexual assault, may have no specialization in pediatric gynecology, and sometimes aren't even pediatricians.

The reason pediatricians exist is because children are different biologically and physiologically, as well as emotionally and intellectually. They have different care and development requirements. Beyond these basic differences, there are specific legal requirements for how examinations of child victims of sexual assault are conducted and how the results are used and interpreted. Child abuse pediatrics, and specifically sexually abuse, are fairly new areas of study. Prosecutors working in this area must be aware of the unique nuances of child sexual assault medical issues in order to uncover for the jury the weaknesses in the opinions of defense "experts" that result from their lack of specialized qualifications in child sexual abuse pediatrics.

Speaking of the need for specialized knowledge, let's spend a moment or two on female anatomy. I know this is a subject that is tough for even women and girls to feel comfortable with. Many times adult women cannot distinguish one orifice from another. And if reading about this subject matter gives you the heebie jeebies, imagine what it is like for me and my young victims to talk about penises and vaginas in courtrooms in front of strangers. But not talking about it openly is what lets myths, misconceptions, and other fallacies grow and eventually make their way into jury rooms and factor into jurors' decisions.

I figure you, my reader, are one of my future jurors (or at least someone's future juror), and so I want to knock out as many misconceptions and myths as possible. There's probably none bigger than the confusion surrounding the hymen. As Andi Taroli said when discussing medical findings and the hymen in "Medical Examination of Sexually Abused Children":

> Any discussion of exam findings [relating to the hymen] is useless until a few matters are cleared up:
> - Every female has one.
> - It is not an impenetrable membrane; it does not break, rupture, burst, pop, or provide proof of virtue (or lack thereof).
> - From birth, the hymen has an opening in it. The hymenal membrane has a sort of donut-shaped appearance; only rarely is a female infant born without any opening in her hymen.
> - The hymen is an internal structure; it is recessed in between the labia majora and labia minora, at the very entrance of the vagina. It is NOT injured or affected by horseback riding, gymnastics, bicycling, or like activities.
> - Being an internal structure, there is no "causal" way to come in contact with the hymen (no matter what perpetrators may try to tell you).
> - Measuring the opening in the hymen cannot distinguish between abused or nonabused girls.[3]

Here's another myth: child sexual assaults always leave physical evidence of injury. The fact is that most don't. I know this is hard to accept, even troubling. After all, how could a five- or six-year-old be raped by an adult man and there not be any physical injury?

Well, the doctors and those in the medical profession can get into all the medical terminology, but what I have found helpful in explaining this to juries is something that most people can readily understand: vaginas are built to accommodate a penis. More so the vaginas of postpubescent girls, certainly, but the vaginal lining of all females is quite elastic. So it is only logical that not every penetration will cause an injury, at least one that will show up during a medical examination. In addition, the tissue in the genital area heals extremely quickly. Unless a medical exam was conducted acutely (within twenty-four hours of an assault), any abrasions or findings may have already healed.

Like "missing" DNA evidence, "missing" medical evidence doesn't mean the investigation was slipshod or that there was no assault. Such evidence is important when it is available, but it should not be elevated to a level of being all that matters. Other kinds of evidence can prove defendants' guilt beyond a reasonable doubt, as they have been used for centuries. In particular, prosecutors, investigators, and those involved in handling these cases must come to court prepared to deal with the *CSI* effect. A finding of normal after a medical examination does not mean nothing happened.

There are more reasons to pursue proper medical examinations than just to help prove a child sexual assault case. Sexual assault is often accompanied by other forms of assault including physical abuse, neglect, parental substance abuse, and so on. A medical exam can reveal information that will ultimately shed light on a child's complete circumstances.

Consider the case of Lily. When she came to America from Sri Lanka, she was mesmerized by a life of plentiful food, new clothing, and education, all graciously provided to her by her uncle. When she came in to the Center, all she could describe were fuzzy recollections of her uncle massaging her and then waking up with pain in her vaginal area. She came in because she wanted to know what had happened to her.

Upon completion of her medical exam, we figured it out. Large amounts of sedatives were found in Lily's blood. The exam couldn't tell us how the sedatives got into Lily's bloodstream, but that's where Lily cleared up the picture. Lily described how in Sri Lanka, she'd never had soda pop. She first tried it when she came to the United States and found she loved it, couldn't get enough of it. And Lily's uncle was more than happy to provide it for her, in large gallon bottles into which he could easily slip a sedative.

The best evidence in the world—DNA, medical reports, photos of injuries—does me no good at all if I can't get it admitted into evidence. Therefore, there needs to be care taken in collecting the evidence properly and in carefully storing it until trial to avoid any claim of contamination or alteration.

This is a "no brainer" type of issue, but it goes wrong often enough to be worth mentioning. Proper collection, identification, packaging, and storing of evidence in sexual assault investigations will greatly improve the chances for a successful prosecution. Also important is good communication between the investigating officer who brings evidence to the lab for analysis and the laboratory criminalist who will do the examination. The evidence should be accompanied by a transmittal letter that completely describes the facts of the crime, the evidence seized, and the scientific examinations requested. Under most circumstances, other examination reports such as by the initial examining physician should be included along with the evidence.

As I close this chapter, I need to address one final myth. At least *I* think it's a myth, and one of the most distressing ones out there for victims. One question I get time and time again is "Am I still a virgin?" Now, I know the dictionary says a virgin is someone who has not had sexual intercourse. And some define sexual intercourse as any penetration of a penis into a vagina.

If I were rewriting dictionaries, I'd bring a little human reality into the definitions of these terms. Virginity is not just a technical term. It's a word that carries much emotional and psychological significance. The definition I propose for virginity is someone who has not had *consensual* sexual intercourse. A person is a virgin until she chooses not to be. For us as a society to harbor the attitude that a rapist can take a woman's virginity away from her against her will is simply wrong, in my not so humble opinion.

Virginity is not something that can be "taken," but something you share with another person, like a once-in-a-lifetime sunset. If you haven't given it, it is still yours.

I think we need to do everything we can to help people who are raped or molested to still think of themselves as virgins, in the emotional sense, the psychological sense, and even the physical sense. Their attackers may have had sex, but they didn't. They were assaulted. They had something done to them; they didn't do something.

I think it is unfair to say a child sexual assault victim is no longer a virgin. Being victimized should not force a young person to live with a label he or she did nothing to earn.

With this in mind, parents, prosecutors, medical personnel, police officers, and therapists should feel comfortable doing what Dr. Elliott Schulman does at the Rape Treatment Center at UCLA Hospital. He gives children Certificates of Virginity, regardless of the specific nature of the abuse they've suffered. I think this adds a thin silver lining to a medical exam and is the least we can do to put victims' minds more at ease.

CHAPTER ELEVEN

DOING TIME FOR THE CRIME

Sentencing and Plea Bargaining

I enter the courthouse tugging my trusty wheeled brief case, which is stuffed to the brim. On my calendar for the day are first appearances in court for six new cases, jury trials in another two, and four probationers due for progress checks. Working the probationers in will be easy. It's juggling the six new case court appearances and the two jury trials that may be a challenge.

The six new cases are a slice of my everyday DA life:

- *Two involve protracted sexual abuse over many years, biological fathers molesting and raping their daughters.*
- *One is a thirteen-year-old girl in love with her thirty-six-year-old biological uncle and having "consensual" sex with him.*
- *Another is a concerned citizen who witnessed a man who turned out to be a registered sex offender pinching an unknown seven-year-old's butt at a Christmas Day parade.*
- *One involves a defendant who came into the police station and confessed that, ten years ago, he orally copulated his own niece. Unfortunately, the victim is uncooperative.*
- *The last one is a twenty-one-year-old who fathered a now two-year-old daughter with a now fifteen-year-old girl.*

My first stop is Department 100, the courtroom where cases ready for trial are scheduled and sent out. I peruse my files for the two jury cases. For each I have long since prepared a short summary of the facts, along with a mini-list of aggravating and mitigating factors to jog my memory as I walk into court. I have to smile as I remember how much I groan about writing those darn internal memos, but thank goodness I do. On a day like today I wouldn't be able to keep my cases straight in my head, otherwise.

I wonder which of my cases will be going to trial first. Both are more than a year old, but I can only be in one courtroom doing one trial at a time. If I had my choice, it would be the strongest—the case where we have DNA and a confession. Maybe a conviction in the first case will encourage the other guy to take the plea bargain I offered.

Once I figure out where I am going to trial, I can then report to the third floor, where I will deal with the six new cases. One thing I'll be trying to figure out is which ones have a chance of settling without a formal court hearing. In other words, which cases can be plea bargained?

PLEA BARGAINING: IS IT A BAD THING?

Many courts have an EDP (Early Disposition Program), where the lawyers try to settle a case without subpoenaing witnesses and going to trial. I know that words like *plea bargaining* and *settling* a criminal case make victims and victim advocates cringe, and many in the general public, too. These words carry ugly connotations of prosecutor, defense counsel, and judge conspiring to simply give a case away, to let the defendant off with a slap on the wrist instead of the serious prison time he might get if convicted. As with many other myths I've tried to debunk in this book, this view of plea bargaining goes way overboard. Sure, there are problems with plea bargaining, but there are benefits from it as well that go far beyond just reducing the case load of an overburdened justice system.

So what exactly is plea bargaining? A plea bargain is an agreement struck between a criminal defendant and a prosecutor. In exchange for a guilty (or no-contest) plea from the defendant, the prosecutor will do one of the following: 1) lower the crime charged, 2) drop some charges, and/or 3) recommend a reduced sentence to the judge. Ninety percent of criminal convictions are based on plea bargains, so why do victims and the public have such a lousy opinion about the practice?

Basically because people outside the justice system have a hard time understanding that there are no slam dunks in the courtroom. No conviction is a sure thing. And no sentence, even so-called mandatory sentences, can be counted on until the judge orders it.

In the eyes of a victim who can positively indentify the perpetrator in court and the public that knows only what is written in often one-sided news reports, a case can look pretty open and shut. Believe me, if any case is that close to certain, the only plea bargaining that'll be going on is something like James Earl Ray's, who plea bargained for a life sentence without parole in order to avoid possible execution for his assassination of Dr. Martin Luther King Jr.

The practical reality is that both the prosecutor and the defense face risks if they go to trial, and it is this parity of risks that makes plea bargaining work. The risks in a criminal trial can be grouped into two major hurdles, which both sides face. The first hurdle is the jury: will it convict or acquit? The second is the judge: if the jury convicts, will he or she impose a harsh sentence or a light one? Let's take a closer look at both hurdles.

WILL THE JURY CONVICT OR ACQUIT?

No matter what you think personally of the jury system (and I am a huge proponent of professional juries), there are risks and unpredictability when the outcome of a case is put in the hands of twelve randomly chosen members of a community who have no experience with the case and generally no experience with the criminal law they will apply to it.

In my opinion, the complexities, nuances, and intricacies involved in a child sexual assault warrant a professional jury. But not just because of the difficulty of the cases. We also need professional juries because of what is at stake if the jury makes a mistake: either the great danger of releasing a sexual predator back into society, or the great wrong of sending an innocent person to prison with the "sex offender" brand. There are no such things as professional juries right now, of course—it's just a dream of mine.

> What do I mean by *professional juries*? I'm thinking of a jury made up of people educated for the task, fairly compensated for doing it, and with no motivation other than following their instructions with complete objectivity. These people would have a complete understanding of typical court language like *beyond a reasonable doubt* and the different levels of criminal intent. They would know that their job is to follow the law, to not discuss the case outside of the jury room, and to avoid all media reports of a case they're sitting in on. There could even be professional jurors with particular scientific backgrounds who could be matched with cases involving that expertise, such as DNA matching, chemical analysis, or the psychology of children.

By randomly chosen, I don't mean literally pulled off the streets, but that's pretty close. Jury pools are drawn from voter and motor vehicle registration lists. So having a car and filling out a voter registration card are all it takes to be placed in the position of deciding a case where someone's life and liberty is at stake, or whether a child victim of a horrific sexual assault will get justice. Ask yourself: do you remember that jerk who cut you off on the freeway and laughed at you about it in his rearview mirror? Would you trust that guy to carefully and impartially weigh the evidence in a week-long abuse trial and make the right call on whether a man accused of being a violent child molester should be locked away or put back on the streets? What about someone who, in the last election, hand-wrote in Charlton Heston's name for every possible elected position? For those of you who still may not be convinced that juries inject a wild-card element into our justice system, I remind you of the jury verdict in the O. J. Simpson double-murder trial.

Here are some of the specific risks in a jury trial that, for a prosecutor, could turn a strong case into a bust. One is that someone in the jury will take a dislike to the victim or a key law enforcement witness or simply disbelieve one of them and convince the rest of the jurors during deliberations to go along. Another is the risk (actually a common occurrence) that not all jurors will understand the beyond a reasonable doubt standard of proof and mistakenly treat every conceivable possibility as a reasonable doubt. Another risk is the media. How will they report the cases? Will jurors truly be able to avoid hearing and being influenced by those reports? Haven't we all been drawing impressions in part from what we read or see on TV for our whole lives? Is it realistic to think the members of the jury can just turn off this lifelong habit?

Don't get me wrong, not every instance of media attention causes an unfair trial, and potential media coverage shouldn't cause a case to be settled for anything less than what it deserves. As a matter of fact, media coverage can be good for the prosecutor. Look at the Caylee Anthony case as an example. In that case, Nancy Grace's amazing coverage of the story showed the public how much effort and work a diligent police department puts into a case. Likewise, in-depth coverage of investigations and gavel-to-gavel coverage of trials show people the reality that a lot of the "evidence" that makes it into the newspapers never makes it to jury, and that difference can transform a case. Media coverage can show and explain things that occur behind the scenes—that is, out of the presence of the jury—and so increase their understanding of our system of justice.

Media coverage often affects the defense attorney's position on the case as well. In fact, many defense attorneys will ask the judge to transfer the trial to a different county (called a request for change of venue), citing pretrial publicity that the attorney feels has prejudiced potential jurors in the community against his or her client. Sometimes a denial of this motion might factor into the defendant's decision of whether to go to trial or settle the case early.

So far, I've talked about jury risks that apply to all criminal trials. However, child sex crime prosecutions have some additional risks all their own. Two prime examples are a couple of cases whose potential impact on juries I still, even though the cases are well over, have to factor into my plea-bargaining assessments.

One is the decades-old McMartin case from the 1980s. In that case, several members of the McMartin family, who operated a preschool in California, were charged with numerous acts of sexual abuse of children in their care. The accusations were made in 1983; the arrests and pretrial investigation extended all the way to 1987. The trial began in 1987 and continued to 1990. After more than six years of investigation and trials, all extensively covered in the media and avidly followed by the public, not a single conviction was obtained and all charges were dropped in 1990.

You may have your own opinion about that heavily covered, controversial case. As a sex crimes prosecutor I must know and be prepared to deal with the fact that many people recall the case as having the appearance of witch hunt that, in the end, found no substance to any of the charges. The case called into question the entire course of how child sexual assault charges are investigated, including how kids are interviewed, their vulnerability to implied suggestions from others (including police, parents, prosecutors, friends, etc.), as well as the credibility of parents and anyone else who makes claims of child sexual assault.

Unfortunately, few people realize the amazing progress the entire system has experienced as a result of the case. In the years following, federal funds went into training law enforcement and prosecutors how to investigate and prosecute child sexual assault cases. More and more prosecutor's offices developed written guidelines for filing these cases, including the requirement of corroboration. Programs have been set up to teach people the proper way of interviewing children so as not to be suggestive or leading. For example, Tom Lyon's ten steps for interviewing children have become widely accepted and used by prosecutors and others who conduct such interviews (see chapter 1). The system isn't perfect, but in most jurisdictions it has progressed well beyond what happened in the McMartin case.

While the prosecution of child abuse claims may be regaining some of the aura of respectability it deserves, it would be naive and foolish for a prosecutor to ignore when evaluating how a case should settle the traces of the "McMartin effect" that virtually every juror will bring into the courtroom with him or her. This is particularly true in cases that involve issues similar to those in the McMartin case—such as teachers, daycare, or multiple kids in a camp, school, and so on—and that therefore tend to stir memories of that case.

The Duke lacrosse team case also captures a negative public perception of sex crime prosecutions that I have to deal with every day: that overzealous (and possibly publicity-seeking) prosecutors file iffy cases and then relentlessly pursue convictions at all costs. That case began in March 2006 when Crystal Gail Mangum, an African American stripper/escort and a student at North Carolina Central University, accused three white members of Duke University's men's lacrosse team of raping her at a party held at the house of two of the team's captains. Many involved in the case, including prosecutor Mike Nifong, claimed or implied that the alleged assault was a racially motivated hate crime. Despite mounting evidence that Ms. Mangum's claims were false, the prosecution would not relent and sensational media coverage continued unabated for weeks. Eventually, the charges proved false and all charges were dropped.

Another case that had no direct relationship to sexual assault but still tends to play a role in the jury trials I face occurred in the early 2000s when the Los Angeles Police Department Rampart Division scandal broke. The stunning evidence of widespread police corruption (including framing suspects, planting evidence, robbery, drug dealing, and even shootings) continues to have lingering effects in the minds of jurors weighing the credibility of police officer testimony. And since virtually every case I prosecute relies to some degree on police officers investigating cases, taking reports, and gathering other evidence, any question about the integrity of law enforcement is crucial. Particularly, if a case involves an at least arguable instance of a police officer doing less than a great job, or using any possibly questionable police tactics, the "Rampart effect" could have an impact on the prosecutor's assessment of the likelihood of a conviction and so affect her decision of whether to go to trial.

While victims might be outraged that I am even suggesting their case is in any way similar to these, I would be a lousy prosecutor if I didn't explain to the victim and acknowledge to myself that these cases can and do affect jurors and jury decisions, whether we like it or not. The best way to avoid the jurors thinking that the case before them might be meritless and brought by an overzealous prosecutor is to be sure that there is independent corroboration for the victim's allegations. I discussed what constitutes corroboration in great detail in chapter 6, where we saw there were different kinds of corroborating evidence and that the jury will take into consideration how strong or weak it is. For example, take a victim whose friend corroborates her description of the crime versus a victim whose description is corroborated by the defendant's confession. While the victim and her friend might argue the point, most jurors are going to consider the defendant's confession stronger corroboration than the friend's agreement with the victim's story—the two of them may have an axe to grind, an agenda, or any number of other personal reasons for telling the same story. Don't misunderstand me. A witness backing up the victim's report of a crime is significant corroborating evidence, even if the witness is a friend or a relative. It's a matter of degree. A witness corroboration would be stronger if the witness were a stranger instead of a friend. A confession would be stronger still, and forensic evidence such as DNA matching may be even stronger. My point is that the strength of the corroborating evidence affects the likelihood the jury will convict, which in turn affects what type of plea bargain will be offered.

We cannot evaluate what a jury is likely to decide without being bluntly honest with ourselves, with the victim, and with the others involved in a sexual assault case. This means we don't have the luxury of relying on what an ideal, impartial jury *should* do. We must evaluate a case by what an actual jury will probably do. We are by nature a society that draws conclusions and makes judgments about people and things based on preconceived ideas, first impressions, prejudices, and stereotypes. We've talked about this before, but let me give you another example to try on yourself. If I were to ask you to imagine a person pushing a shopping cart, wearing tattered clothes, and smelling like booze, you would most likely suspect that I am talking about a homeless derelict. That suspicion, coupled with street-people stereotypes and your own preconceived notions about them, would in turn make it far easier for a defense attorney to prove that this person was mentally ill, an alcoholic, or both, and hence an unreliable witness. If this person is to provide corroboration of the victim's account of the crime, I have to take the possible impact of these preconceived notions into account, whether or not I like it.

If you are a woman reading this book, you know that some women can merely look at another woman and almost immediately know if you hate her guts or if you like her. In my experience, I have found this carries over into the courtroom. Women tend to easily judge while men tend to pay closer attention to the facts of a case. I am not saying this for shock value. I am saying this because it's true and it affects what happens in a courtroom. I wouldn't be doing my job if I didn't evaluate and deal with how others may perceive the likability, credibility, and testimonial effectiveness of the victim, every witness I will call, and every witness the defense will put on the stand.

Please note that I said I must evaluate *and deal with* the biases and preconceived notions that jurors may bring into the courtroom about my victim or the witnesses. That one of my witnesses is a homeless man doesn't mean he is a "bad witness" or he makes for a bad case; it means I have to expect, understand, and counter the biases the jury may bring into the jury box, to the utmost extent that I can. Perhaps this particular street person is not only mentally stable but has a calm, thoughtful demeanor; my questioning will show the jury that stable, steady demeanor. If he has held positions of responsibility in the past, the jury will hear about them. If he was drinking or taking drugs, I face that head-on and find out whether any of that actually affected his ability to see or remember what he saw. Thus, I'm not going to just throw up my hands and quit on a case because my victim or witnesses have some negative baggage. Don't we all? But I have to assess what effect that negative baggage may have on the jury and assess how effectively I may be able to counter it, in determining the likelihood I'll get a conviction using this witness for my corroborating evidence.

Another big risk factor with juries is their tendency to be sensitive to how their decisions will affect the harshness of the sentence that will be imposed on the defendant. Even though juries are admonished that they are not to consider punishment in their deliberations, I have found that they almost always do. Jurors can feel a great deal of responsibility for the result of their decisions—namely, the sentence—even though the only one truly responsible for it is the defendant.

To ease their sense of responsibility, jurors may do something in deliberations known as *splitting the baby*. For example, if there are four charges alleged against the defendant, they will only convict on two of them. And because the jurors don't know the different sentences associated with the different crimes charged, where they will split the baby and therefore how the individual jury decides the counts can leave a big gap in the potential charges. Therefore, what a jury ultimately decides makes the sentencing, the end result of my case, a crap shoot.

In short, a lot of factors have to be considered by both the prosecution and the defense in predicting what the jury is likely to do. Some of those factors are obvious, like the strong evidence of a confession or a DNA match; some are little more than intuition based on years of experience with juries, like whether the jury will like and believe a key witness. Both sides must carefully weigh the strength of their case and decide whether it makes sense to go to trial. But it isn't just the jury risks they must consider; they also have to predict what the judge will do.

WHAT SENTENCE WILL THE JUDGE IMPOSE?

After evaluating the strengths and weaknesses of a case and predicting what the jury will do with it, there also needs to be a separate analysis of the strengths and the weaknesses relative to sentencing. Of which crime will the jury likely convict, and what is the range of sentence for that crime? Are there aggravating or mitigating factors for the judge to consider? And, since judges are human like the rest of us, what are her idiosyncrasies? How will she likely react to this particular crime and this defendant? Does she have a reputation for handing down tough sentences, for sticking closely to the statutory guidelines, for being lenient with younger defendants?

Part of the prosecutor's job in fashioning a plea bargain is to "guess" what sentence a judge might impose. While some states have mandatory sentencing guidelines, other states have a range of possible sentences from which a judge can pick. For example, in California judges often have the ability to pick from the low-, mid-, or high-term state prison sentences.

Or, depending on the charge, the judge can also decide to avoid state prison and give probation, which may include some county jail time and other conditions.

Another factor that can affect what sentence the judge imposes is what's called victim impact statements. During sentencing, the victim and his or her family may attend the courtroom proceedings and present an impact statement to communicate the tangible and intangible impact the defendant's criminal actions have had on them. If the victim is uncomfortable or unwilling to make a statement, she can still write a letter that can be read aloud in court and become part of the court record. Without a full understanding the impact of the defendant's crime on the victim, his or her family, and society, judges may hand out sentences that do not accurately reflect the seriousness of the damage the crime caused. These victim impact statements can be very powerful and can make the difference in whether the defendant receives the maximum number of years the law allows or a lesser sentence.

Different crimes carry different sentences. Because prosecutors choose which charges will be filed, they have a great deal of control over the possible sentence a defendant can expect if convicted. For example, each state has laws regarding which crimes are eligible for probation and which are not. Thus, in some sexual assault cases a court cannot legally sentence someone to probation unless the prosecutor brought a charge that allows for probation, or amends the charge from one that doesn't to one that does as part of a plea bargain.

When I teach detectives how DAs decide what charges to file, I use an insightful bit of advice I once got from Deputy District Attorney Cathie Stephenson: "What you charge is a function of what you want the outcome to be." So, what does this mean?

It means I have to see the end of the case from the beginning and know my bottom-line objective as well as my optimum goal. For example, if I have a strong case, I might bring a charge that doesn't allow probation. The defendant knows that if he chooses to go to trial and loses, he'll be doing time rather than having a chance at probation. On the other hand, if I have a weak case, I may deliberately include a charge that allows for probation.

Why in the world would a DA *want* to include a charge that gave a sex offender the possibility of probation? Because I know my bottom-line objective for the particular case. As I discussed, corroboration is necessary for a case to be filed, but what if the corroboration is weak? For example, imagine two girls who are best friends claim the defendant locked them in one of their bedrooms and raped both of them. He claims they're lying and are angry because he recently dumped one of them. I believe the girls, but I also know my corroboration is weak: the defense will have a field day with the argument that the victims had an axe to grind and cooked up the whole story. The last thing I want is for a person I believe to be a criminal sex offender to go scot-free, plus there is always the chance that an offender who "got off" will feel emboldened to offend again.

So what is the end result I want to achieve, given the facts of this particular case? While I'd love to put him away for years, I'd have to take a big risk of letting him walk to go for all the marbles. Bottom line, what I really want is for the abuse to stop and to create a record so that should the defendant do it again, there would be corroboration in the form of a prior conviction. That's why I am willing, in the appropriate case, to charge and/or plea bargain to a probationary sentence, especially when the charge or settlement includes the requirement to register as a sex offender.

I know what you are thinking: this Sax lady is crazy! Isn't probation basically the same thing as letting him walk? Not hardly. Every probationary sentence has terms and conditions and a probation officer to make sure the defendant complies. If he doesn't, his probation can be revoked. That doesn't mean he now gets a trial. It means he now he goes to jail. He pled guilty as part of the probation sentence so there's no need for a trial and there's no going back from that plea. He stands to go to jail for the maximum time set by the judge as part of his probationary sentence.

Plus the terms and the conditions of probation give the prosecutor, the defense, and the court a great deal of flexibility to tailor the probation to what may actually help the defendant not reoffend. There are certain standard terms of probation, such as being gainfully employed or seeking education, paying fines and fees, not violating any other laws or ordinances, and giving your real name if requested by law enforcement. Other probationary terms may be required that address the defedant's specific past criminal conduct. These case-specific types of terms may be to submit to drug testing, to stay away from a specific person and/or location, to attend anger management or other relevant counseling, to submit to searches of your person or residence and seizure of any evidence of criminal activity, and so on.

Some states have specific requirements for probation in sex offender cases. For example, some require as a term of probation that the defendant register as a sex offender and attend sexual offender counseling. These mandatory probation terms, incidentally, often cannot be plea bargained away.

In fashioning the terms and the conditions of probation, prosecutors and judges consider the gravity of the defendant's conduct, the defendant's prior record, if any, and the need to protect the community. Some of the potential terms and conditions available include:

- Jail time,
- House arrest,
- Community service,
- Alcohol or drug treatment,
- Psychotherapy,
- Sex offender, domestic violence, parenting, or anger management classes, and
- Stay away and protective orders.

By creating terms of probation that address the defendant's actual conduct, the goals of sentencing (retribution, rehabilitation, and deterrence, etc.) may be more accurately addressed than they would be if the defendant were merely put into custody. Plus these benefits may be combined with jail time by specifying the probationary terms that are to apply for a set period of time once the defendant is released from prison.

And remember, perhaps the biggest advantage to putting someone on probation is that if he violates probation (that means breaks *any* law, or violates *any* term or condition of probation), then he can be sentenced to the maximum time set by the judge as part of the probationary sentence, without any trial or worry about having to prove his guilt beyond a reasonable doubt.

When determining whether I'm willing to settle a case and, if so, what bargain I am willing to offer, I consider various factors, which include but are not limited to:

- The likelihood of conviction,
- The victim's feelings about testifying,
- How the victim will be characterized by a jury,
- The safety of the community if the defendant is released,
- The physical, psychological, and emotional harm the defendant has caused the victim,
- Whether the defendant is willing and able to pay restitution for the victim's medical costs and other damages, and
- Whether punishment will act as a deterrent for those who have considered or may now be committing sexually abusive acts against a minor.

There are downsides to plea bargaining beyond just the big one I've mentioned: the victim's pain that the defendant gets a less harsh sentence than the maximum. In addition, there is a risk that innocent people may be coerced into taking deals for crimes they did not commit due to fear of the heavy sentences applicable if they are convicted at trial. Opponents of plea bargaining go further, saying that plea bargaining compromises the defendant's constitutional rights to a trial by his peers and to confront his accusers.

However, there are also benefits to plea bargaining beyond what I have discussed. Plea bargaining reduces the demands on a court system that is already congested and overloaded. It saves witnesses and victims time away from work and school, not to mention the trauma of reliving the event in the stressful arena of testifying in court and being cross-examined. Finally, the taxpayers benefit from the cost savings of fewer trials and fewer courtrooms, plus fewer tax-funded public defenders, judges, clerks, bailiffs, and so on.

MANDATORY MINIMUM SENTENCES—WHAT ARE THEY *REALLY*?

Because prosecutors, not judges, have the first say in how they want to shape a case via their filing decisions, they can effectively "tie the judge's hands" by filing charges that have mandatory sentences attached to the charge. When a legislature attaches a mandatory minimum sentence to a particular crime statute, that means the judge must impose the specific sentence set by the statute on any defendant convicted of that crime. It doesn't matter what the judge or the jurors personally think about how much prison time is appropriate for this particular crime or whether there are extenuating circumstances that otherwise might warrant lowering the sentence. If a defendant is convicted of a crime that carries a mandatory minimum prison sentence, he must get that sentence, period.

In Los Angeles, we call mandatory minimums *One Strike laws*, as a play on the commonly known Three Strikes law. Under a typical One Strike law, a conviction for having committed the crime coupled with certain aggravating factors means the judge must sentence the defendant to fifteen years to life (meaning he'll first be eligible for parole after fifteen years) or twenty-five years to life.

As you can imagine, one strike or mandatory minimums laws can have a big impact on plea bargaining. If the only crime charged by the prosecutor carries a mandatory minimum sentence, then everyone's hands are tied. The prosecutor and the defense cannot negotiate a different recommended sentence, and the judge could not impose it even if he or she tried. The only way for a defendant to be sentenced to a time less than the mandatory minimum is for the prosecutor to change the charge(s) filed against him, which she can only do *before* the jury returns its verdict. After that verdict, the sentence is written in stone. I have often seen defendants who are facing the prospect of a sentence of fifteen or twenty-five years to life if they are convicted jump at the opportunity to take a determinate sentence of twenty-five, twenty-six, twenty-seven, or even thirty-two years just to remove that "to life" element from the sentence. A thirty-two-year sentence on a plea bargain is a pretty good deal in my book.

Although sentencing standards vary state to state, most generally impose longer sentences on defendants convicted of sex crimes than those who commit other felonies, which I think is appropriate. And when the victim of the sex crime is a child, the sentencing generally is—and should be—even longer.

However, the fact there is general agreement that sex crimes against children should be punished harshly does not necessarily follow that all discretion in sentencing should be removed through mandatory sentencing minimums. Despite the nice, get-tough ring to mandatory minimums, there is an ongoing battle between legislators who want mandatory sentencing for offenders who commit sexual acts against minors and others who agree that their punishment should be harsh but nonetheless believe some flexibility should be retained so it may be reduced if the offender is able to rehabilitate successfully. For instance, some states are proposing twenty-five-year mandatory sentences for offenders—regardless of whether or not it is a first-time offense—who commit a sexual assault against a minor under thirteen.

Sex crime sentencing varies not only by the type of act committed and whether the victim was a minor but also by how young the minor was at the time of the crime. Criminals who sexually assault minors twelve to fourteen years of age or younger, depending on the state, receive longer sentences than sexual assaults against minors fourteen years or older. In California, the sentencing guideline for a lewd act on a child, defined as someone under fourteen, is three, six, or eight years in prison.

Another factor that can affect the sentence is whether the criminal used a weapon or otherwise threatened the child with serious physical harm (beyond the sex act itself). If he did, many state courts will add on more years to the defendant's sentence.

Yet another factor that can greatly affect the length of a sentence is whether a child victim has been touched or sexually assaulted by the abuser more than once. In these cases, each act is charged as a separate crime. This can be a difficult call for a prosecutor to make. If the prosecutor believes there is not enough evidence for each individual act, she will likely charge the defendant with a single crime committed over a certain period of time. The defendant may have committed multiple types of crimes during this period, such as touching and forcible rape, which may increase the number of crimes he is charged with and thus increase the maximum sentence.

Mandatory minimum sentences can also affect a prosecutor's decision over whether to file multiple charges. If some charges carry mandatory minimums and others don't and the jury ultimately convicts on only the charges that don't, there is no mandatory minimum sentence. Juries are not informed about which charges carry mandatory minimum sentences, so their tendency to split the baby by picking to convict on only some of the multiple crimes charged, which I discussed earlier, can be especially problematic when some but not all charges carry mandatory minimums.

REALITY CHECK

I hope this chapter has shed some light on the behind-the-scenes issues that affect the sentence a criminal sex offender receives, either through plea bargaining or following a trial and conviction. What I have found is that the reason victims and others involved in a criminal case get upset about plea bargaining is not so much the terms of the settlement in their particular case but rather not knowing the factors and thoughts that went into the settlement in their (or their child's) specific case. When they are informed, they usually agree with the way the risks of going to trial have been balanced with the benefits of the sure conviction with a plea bargain.

While most states have created laws to give victims the rights to be informed about the progress of their cases, present at most of the proceedings and heard through things like victim impact statements, I fear that many busy prosecutors do not spend the necessary time to explain these rights and to keep the victim and the victim's family fully informed and involved in the process. Even when a prosecutor succeeds in getting a lengthy sentence in a criminal child sex abuse case, this does not necessarily assist the victim's or the family's healing and recovery if they are not allowed to be part of the process.

With a little time, understanding, and explanation, victims and society as whole will better understand the system, and the real-life practical factors involved in plea bargaining and sentencing. Without that understanding, it is natural for people to instinctively think that tough, mandatory minimum sentences are good and that plea bargains are bad. But those knee-jerk reactions can be replaced by informed, reasoned opinions about the pros and cons of plea bargaining if someone takes a few moments to explain factors like the strengths and the weaknesses of the evidence in the victim's particular case, the uncertainties inherent in jury trials, the standard of proof, and the range of sentences a judge may or may not impose.

CHAPTER 12
REGISTRATION AND PREVENTION

Ann is a great mom. Though she feels guilty about being a working mom, she manages to stay involved in her kids' lives and schools. With her busy schedule, she must prioritize every-thing, which means separating the "real" worries that parents with kids have from those that are just carpool line hype. To help separate the hype from the truth, Ann comes to me to talk about child safety and ways to prevent her children from becoming vic-tims of sexual abuse. She asks me a question I hear a lot: "How do you let your own kids outside, knowing how many sex offenders are out there?" Ann tells me how she is so overwhelmed by just the idea of a sexual assault against one of her kids that she can't even bear to go online to see whether there is a sex offender near where she lives, let alone how many or who they are or what crimes they've committed. I tell her to take a deep breath, sit down, and let's look together at the information available out there, just waiting for parents like her to use it. That's what I want to do with you in this chapter.

S ay what you will about the Internet, but one thing about it is great—it makes a tremendous amount of valuable information available that can help us better protect our children. One of the best of these Internet resources is the online sex offender registry.

Sex offender registration was established as a means to monitor and track those who have been convicted of a crime that involves some element of sexual conduct or a sexual act. The idea is that by tracking the whereabouts of these offenders, we'll have a better chance of keeping people safe from them.

Sex offender registries did not just arise by happenstance. They are available online due to Congress's passage in 2006 of the Adam Walsh Act (sometimes called simply the AWA, or SORNA for its official title, Sex Offender Registration and Notification Act). The statute is named after a victim of a sexual attack, something we'll see a few more times in this chapter. The legislation sets certain minimum standards for sex offender registration and notification and requires states to have implemented these standards by July 27, 2009.

The SORNA standards make no distinction between sex crimes involving child victims versus those committed against adults. Its registration requirements apply not only to adult offenders but also to juveniles who are prosecuted as adults, and juveniles over fourteen who commit certain aggravated sexual assault crimes.

> As of this writing, there is a huge movement to repeal the SORNA because it is seen as overly restrictive and an infringement on the constitutional rights of offenders. Guess where I stand? Anyway, I'm not going to dip into that fray in this book, but I thought you should know that it's going on right now so you can get involved.

Under the SORNA minimum standards, a qualifying offender must register as a sex offender upon release from prison. Subsequently, the offender must reregister every year on his birthday, as well as within three business days after he moves, changes jobs, or has a status change (becomes a student, homeless, employed, etc.). In some cases, when the crime committed is considered violent in nature, sex offenders must update their registration every ninety days.

As I mentioned, the SORNA and other registration laws have stirred up controversy. In addition to concerns about the standards being too restrictive and possibly unconstitutional, opponents criticize the statute's failure to better distinguish among the various kinds of sex crimes. They point to facts like not all sex crimes are violent, not all require the specific intent to commit a crime, and not all involve equal likelihood of being repeated. For example, an eighteen-year-old male must register as a sexual offender if he is prosecuted and convicted for having "consensual" sexual intercourse with a fourteen-year old female.

On the other hand, proponents of mandatory registration legislation like the SORNA respond by saying that registration is simply another consequence for the offender's criminal actions. They claim that some nonviolent offenses, such as possession of child pornography or solicitation of a minor for sex, should require registration because it was only the arrest for that offense that prevented the offender from executing a more serious crime.

Perhaps a middle ground would be to more clearly define which types of acts should be considered registerable and which should not and to make those criteria uniform throughout the country. For example, here in California, statutory rape charges are not registerable, but lewd and lascivious acts are. If each state uniformly classified registerable sex crimes, I think people would feel more comfortable that registration requirements are appropriate, meaningful, and effective.

Seven-year-old Megan was a lot like other kids her age—sweet, curious, and an animal lover. So it wasn't out of the ordinary for

229

her to accept a neighbor's invitation to come over and see his puppy. Unfortunately, what neither Megan nor her parents knew was that the neighbor was Jesse Timmendequas, a twice-convicted sex offender and by all standards a certified pedophile. What happened when she went to see the neighbor's puppy is any parent's worst fear. He raped and murdered her, then dumped her young body in a nearby park. Looking back, Megan's parents said that they never would have allowed her to travel the neighborhood freely if they had known a convicted sex offender was living across the street.

Does this story sound familiar? It should. The horror of the crime and the lobbying of Megan's parents led to what has come to be known as Megan's Law, the informal name applied to state and federal laws that require law enforcement agencies to notify members of the community about any registered sexual offenders who may pose a threat to the public. As a result of Megan's parents efforts and others inspired by her story, there is a Megan's Law in force now in every state in the country.

Many people think that sex registration began when Megan's home state of New Jersey passed the first Megan's Law in 1994, but actually another tragic case was what sparked the move toward registering sex offenders.

On October 22, 1989, eleven-year-old Jacob Wetterling was bicycling with his brother Trevor, ten, and friend Aaron, eleven, back to their Minnesota home after renting a video at a local convenience store. Suddenly, a masked man stepped out of a driveway with a gun. He ordered the children to throw their bikes into a ditch and lie face down on the ground. After asking the boys their ages, he told Jacob's brother and friend to run into the woods and not look back or he would shoot them. Jacob was abducted. To date, he has never been found, and no arrest has ever been made. Investigators later learned that, unbeknownst to local law enforcement or Jacob's parents, sex offenders just released from prison were being sent to live in halfway houses nearby.

In February 1989, four months after Jacob's disappearance, Jacob's parents, Patty and Jerry Wetterling, set up the Jacob Wetterling Foundation. Patty also served on the Minnesota governor's task force charged with making recommendations on sex offender registration.

After successfully establishing sex offender registration in Minnesota, Patty and Jerry went on to lobby for federal legislation. Their efforts, along with the efforts of many other advocates, resulted in the passage of the Jacob Wetterling Sexually Violent Offender Registration Act in 1994. This statute required all fifty states to establish effective registration programs for convicted child molesters and other sex offenders.

The Wetterling Act also required states to establish more stringent registration standards for a subclass of offenders considered the most dangerous, designated under the law as "sexually violent predators."

How, you may wonder, can the *federal* government pass a law that makes *state* governments pass new laws? Well, as an example, the Wetterling Act provides that states that fail to enact the minimum standards risk a 10 percent reduction of grant funding under the Edward Byrne Memorial State and Local Law Enforcement Assistance Program. This is federal funding allocated to states for improving the functioning of their criminal justice systems, with an emphasis on violent crime and serious offenders. So if the state wants the money, it passes the laws. Of course, many would have eventually passed such laws on their own, but the federal act speeds things up and assures consistent minimum standards.

The Wetterling Act also says that states "may release" information about registered offenders if necessary to protect the public. The carefully crafted "may release" language gave states the *discretion* to publicly release information about registered offenders, but did not *require* it, even if authorities consider a particular sex offender a high risk to public safety.

The Wetterlings were not alone in their efforts to lobby for a uniform federal law to mandate sex offender registration and some form of mandatory public notification. A hearing was called on March 1, 1994, by the Subcommittee on Crime and Criminal Justice of the US House of Representatives Committee on the Judiciary. The hearing was to take testimony about the revolving door of justice in the United States and possible new approaches to combat recidivism, that is, relapse back into criminal behavior. Five panels were called together, and one included victims and their families.

Testimony was given by Marc Klaas; Peggy, Gene, and Jennifer Schmidt; Susan Sweetser, a Vermont state senator and rape survivor; and Dick and Diane Adams, whose son, a store clerk, was killed during an armed robbery. Testimony at that hearing urged the passage of federal legislation to register and notify communities of the presence of sex offenders.

Marc Klaas is the father of twelve-year-old Polly, who was kidnapped at knifepoint from her bedroom slumber party by a career criminal and was later found dead. Marc founded the Klaas Kids Foundation, a nonprofit children's advocacy organization that has been instrumental in working for nationwide and international laws to stop crimes against children. Marc Klaas also founded Beyond Missing to provide law enforcement agencies a secure, Internet-based system to create and distribute missing child flyers to other law enforcement offices, the media, and public and private recipients.

Peggy, Gene, and Jennifer Schmidt are from Kansas and are the parents and sister of nineteen-year-old Stephanie Schmidt. One day, Stephanie had a sore throat and so accepted a coworker's offer of a ride home. But rather than an act of kindness, the coworker's offer was an invitation to tragedy: he brutally raped and murdered her. Stephanie had no idea her coworker was a known sex offender who had served ten years in prison for a prior rape. The Schmidt family founded Speak Out for Stephanie (SOS), the Stephanie Schmidt Foundation. SOS is a nonprofit organization dedicated to changing laws and promoting public safety and awareness about sex offenders. The Schmidt family is perhaps best known for their successful efforts to press for laws in all states that lock up sexual predators indefinitely. These laws are referred to as sexual predator commitment laws or sexual predator civil confinement laws. Nine months after Stephanie's death, the Stephanie Schmidt Sexual Predator Act—empowering a state civil commitment procedure—became a retroactive law for all Kansas sex offenders. The state civil commitment procedure means that under certain stringent circumstances, states can *civilly* confine abusers to mental hospitals, not necessarily criminally. A challenge to the constitutionality of the Kansas statute was rejected by the US Supreme Court in 1997.

These civil confinement or commitment laws are amazing. In California, for example, we call ours a sexually violent predator law (SVP for short). It establishes a process where a person convicted of multiple sexually violent crimes may not be released from prison until a parole board or prison system evaluates his risk of danger to society. After a hearing, if it is found the person would be a danger to society if released, the state prison system has the authority to keep him in custody. This means he may remain in prison for much longer than the original plea bargain or sentence. This is another benefit to plea bargaining. Sometimes we will ask for less prison time but demand the defendant plead guilty to multiple counts, which sets him up to be SVP'd (as we call it).

In 2001 Parents for Megan's Law conducted the first of many national surveys to evaluate the implementation of sex offender registration and notification laws in all the states, the District of Columbia, and US territories. These surveys revealed that all these jurisdictions had enacted registration and notification laws, but the laws lacked uniformity. Where a family lived could determine how well the parents could protect their children from known, convicted sex offenders. Further, a 2003 registration survey by Parents for Megan's Law found that nearly 25 percent of the nation's sex offenders required to register were not complying with state registration requirements. This meant that the authorities had lost contact with over one hundred thousand sex offenders across the country.

Laura Ahearn, executive director of Parents for Megan's Law, presented the results of their surveys, plus descriptions of implementation problems and loopholes at the community level to the Justice Department. That information was used to help craft the newest registration and notification amendments to the federal version of Megan's Law. This became the Adam Walsh Child Protection and Safety Act of 2006, which is the SORNA statute I explained earlier in this chapter. And now we've come full circle.

Adam Walsh's parents, John and Revé, were instrumental in getting this law passed, as well as others. Their work following the murder of their son in 1981 led to passage of the Missing Children Act of 1982 and the Missing Children's Assistance Act of 1984. The latter bill founded the National Center for Missing and Exploited Children.

John and Revé Walsh, along with Ms. Ahearn of Parents for Megan's Law, were invited to the White House to witness the signing of the Adam Walsh Child Protection and Safety Act of 2006 (SORNA) into law, on the twenty-fifth anniversary of Adam's murder.

> *Six-year-old Adam Walsh was abducted on July 27, 1981, outside a Sears and Roebuck store in a mall in Hollywood, Florida. His remains were found in a canal off the Florida interstate, one hundred miles north of Hollywood. Ottis Toole confessed to abducting and brutally murdering Adam Walsh, but three months later recanted, saying he did not kill him. According to* America's Most Wanted, *the television program hosted by Adam's father, John Walsh:*

What may be the most bizarre twist in the Adam Walsh case occurred a few weeks later. The FDLE (Florida Department of Law Enforcement) transferred the carpet samples and Toole's 1971 Cadillac to the Jacksonville Sheriff's Office. Since Toole had recanted his confession, someone deemed the evidence no longer viable and the carpet samples were thrown out. The vehicle was sold to a used car lot and eventually junked for scrap. With the loss of evidence, the opportunity to do DNA testing of the carpets to determine once and for all if Adam was ever in Toole's white Cadillac is now gone. Ottis Toole died at Raiford Prison in September 1996, taking the truth of whether he was Adam's killer or just a false confessor to his grave.[1]

Despite the loss of evidence, the Florida police department announced on December 16, 2008, that Ottis Toole was responsible for the abduction and murder and that the investigation into Adam Walsh's murder was closed.

As I said, the previous Jacob Wetterling Act only authorized states to *release* sex offender registration information. It did not guarantee an active *notification* to the community. So, unless parents regularly checked for released information, which often meant a trip to the police station, they might never know if a sexual predator moved in next door. This will change after all states implement the requirements of the federal SORNA law. As mentioned earlier, states had until July 2009 to comply but may have filed for up to two one-year extensions.

The Adam Walsh Child Protection and Safety Act (SORNA) significantly strengthens registration and notification laws across the nation by increasing the duration of registration for sex offenders; increasing in-person verifications; requiring active sex offender notification programs;

adding requirements that certain juvenile sex offenders register; requiring registration for adults convicted of nonsex offenses if they have prior sex crime convictions that predate the SORNA registration requirements; requiring registration for sex offenders entering the country; making failure to register a federal felony punishable by up to ten years; and providing funding to US Marshals to track down offenders who don't register and update their registrations. SORNA also increased mandatory minimum sentences for sex offenders, increased penalties for crimes perpetrated against children via the Internet, and strengthened child pornography prevention laws. The act also created the Office of Sex Offender Sentencing, Monitoring, Apprehending, Registering, and Tracking (SMART Office) at the Justice Department to administer state implementation of the act's requirements, handle the grant programs authorized in the act to help local governments fund implementation, and coordinate related training and technical assistance.

As a result, in some states, such as California, parents no longer have to go to the police station to look up information about sex offenders who have moved into their communities. Instead, they can access that information on the Internet from the comfort of their own homes. These Web sites have all sorts of useful information, such as a map and address of where the sex offender is currently living, information about the sex offender's previous sexual violations, and descriptive information like his height, weight, and a picture. A particularly important feature for parents is that many of these Web sites say if the offender's victim was a child.

Even with all of these laws and so much progress over just the last ten years in the field of registration and notification, I still feel a tad guilty by thinking that we should do more. But as we go into the future and technology continues to advance, we must address the need for laws as they become necessary and for improved crime-fighting tools. The emphasis is on prevention. So, what would I do? One thing would be to make better use of new technology to provide enhanced supervision of registered sex offenders. Some ideas: requiring registered sex offenders to register their computer and their Internet accounts, IP addresses, and telephone numbers, not just their physical addresses. It may require a waiver of Fourth Amendment rights, but I'd like for authorities to be able to monitor the Internet activity of offenders who have used the Internet to find victims or commit other crimes such as distribution of child pornography. Offenders should also be required to inform authorities of international travel, and there should be an integrated international registration system (like that for known terrorists) to monitor the comings and goings of registered sex offenders from any country. Registered sex offenders should also be subject to lifetime counseling, not merely during the term of their parole or probation. And perhaps most important, those who have been convicted of crimes against children (and are therefore required to register) should not be permitted to live within a set distance of schools, playgrounds, or parks. I realize these laws sound extremely limiting, but why should children be subjected to perpetrators who have a high risk of recidivism?

As you are well aware of by now, sex crimes and protection of children is my thing. It is something that I work on every day and think about constantly. And even as aware of sex crimes as I am, I realized only as I am writing this that it has been at least five or six months since I last checked my state's Megan's Law Web sites. How embarrassing! I have checked my e-mail, my Facebook, my evite.com list, and have even taken a peak on bluefly.com to see if there were any handbags for sale. I do all this regularly, but it's not in my normal Web site surf to check out the Megan's Law Web sites. I know I could tell you to go check it right now and if you are feeling über-diligent you will, but what about next week, next month, next year? Why not bookmark the Megan's Law sites and move them to the top of your favorites?

Trust me, I am not suggesting you live in constant fear, and I certainly am not saying that just checking a Megan's Law Web site will keep your children safe. But it is something that should be in all of our arsenals as a regular part of our parenting routines. With a few strokes of a keyboard we can at least be aware of any sex offenders near our home, our kid's friend's houses, or around her school. I don't want to go overboard here, but I do want to rattle parents out of complacency. The fact is that sex offenders do indeed live just about everywhere, and the database has only those who've been caught for it. Which brings me to one of my gripes about registries, alarm products, cans of Mace, and other "safety tools."

All of these can be wonderful things. There are some great peace-of-mind products out there. But parents need to be mindful that they should not be overly reliant on them. There is no substitute for good parenting. There is nothing that can take the place of good old-fashioned conversations and communication with your children. Parents need to teach their children how to make safe choices on the Internet, on the street, at school, and so on. Let me give you a couple of examples.

Parents are often dumbfounded to learn their kids would even think of engaging in a conversation with some unknown person on the Internet. But predators are successful with their use of the Internet because they provide something it is very hard for parents these days to give their kids enough of—undivided attention. I mean real attention, not just "yes, dear." Predators are patient when they communicate with their online targets. They are good listeners. They shower children with compliments, show intense interest in the their lives, and are unconditional in their sympathy and support.

Predators offer exactly what every young child, and every teenager going through the most confusing time of her life, needs most—someone who listens compassionately and attentively without passing judgment. Internet predators educate themselves about every aspect of children's likes and dislikes (remember the neighbor who knew Megan loved animals?), including the latest trends and lingo. If skateboarding is hip, they know about skateboarding. If it's all about the Jonas Brothers, then they know about them too. They spend time learning the nuances of their target age group, and they know not to talk to a thirteen-year-old like a ten-year-old. They don't multitask; they show their caring by staying completely focused on the child.

After earning the victim's initial trust, the predator will start grooming the victim for in-person contact. He may disclose that "Surprise! I'm not really as young as I said I was." Despite the lie, a child or a teenager is still likely to feel flattered that an older, more sophisticated person is eager to pay so much attention to her and will often keep the contact going.

Just as abstinence is the only 100 percent effective birth control method, children should be taught that the only safe response to getting an e-mail, text, or instant message from someone they don't know is to not respond. If they come show you the message, all the better. And if they do, please, please do not take away their Internet privileges. Give them a hug and tell them you're proud of them. If a child consistently refuses to respond to unknown correspondents under any circumstances, there will be nothing to fear from online predators.

Internet predators are really no different than other predators in how they learn about their victims, build their trust, and groom them for the assault. What is different about Internet predators stems from the nature of the Internet and its use.

The target child sits in front of a computer screen, usually in a private place like a bedroom or study and not outside in the open. The overwhelming use, accessibility, and customization of e-mails, IMs, blogs, and social networking sites has created the impression in young minds that the Internet is a haven to share feelings, discuss taboo subjects, talk with people in distant places, and make friends with people they never expect to meet. (Did you ever have a pen pal you never met? Remember the kinds of things you'd share with him?)

Internet predators are aware of the desires and insecurities of children and prey on them to satisfy their own warped fantasies. So with that in mind I go back to my generic safety tip, which is more important than any registry, product, or service. It is good old-fashioned communication. I like to encourage parents to look for and find "teachable moments," which are opportunities for particularly effective communication.

Teachable moments come up every day. They occur as we take our children to school, when a solicitor knocks at the door, or when a sex crime story breaks in the news. So let's take news stories. I know what you are thinking—"Oh no, not the news! I never want my child to know what's going on." News articles and programs offer parents an excellent opportunity to explain bad behavior and its consequences, and often how no one thought the perpetrator was the kind of person who would do such a thing. (Not a bad basic values lesson—nothing quite like showing kids, rather than just telling them, that there are consequences for one's actions.)

We need to ask our children what they know about a particular news story and then use the facts from the story to show which types of conduct are inappropriate. After the conversation, children should be asked what they learned so you can determine how well they understood the issues discussed. And if you're lucky enough (or good enough) that the child starts asking you questions, give yourself a mental pat on the back and continue talking, one-on-one, until you've answered every question.

Besides talking to our children about sexual abuse cases in the news, we need to teach children how to develop their "creepiness instinct." If some nice-looking stranger in the park smiles at you too much, that's creepy. If someone you don't know wants to give you a present, maybe there is a bad reason. That's creepy. We don't want to make our kids paranoid, but the generic "don't talk to strangers" line isn't going to cut it, not with the sophisticated grooming techniques of today's child abusers and the natural trust of adults most children have.

There are a few lessons that I, as a parent, am not going to wait until a spontaneous moment to bring up. The three most important things children of all ages need to know to help them keep safe from predators are:

1. A child's body is his or her own, and nobody can touch it without asking, especially after the child says no or to stop. We need to emphasize that *no* means *no* and that anybody who argues or is sweetly insistent or refuses to respect the no should be considered dangerous and reported to the police.
2. Anything that feels icky, weird, creepy, or bad should be reported to a trusted adult. (It does not need to be the parent, any trusted adult will suffice.)
3. Adults don't ask kids to keep secrets (with the companion part that they won't get into trouble if they tell their mom or dad a secret that another adult told them not to tell).

These kind of preplanned safety discussions aren't a one-time thing. To really learn any of these, it helps to focus on a particular one and reinforce it over a period of time, say, over a couple of weeks to a month. For example, an appropriate safety lesson for a family with young children (ages five and younger) is to help them memorize key telephone numbers, such as mom's cell phone, the home phone, and grandparents' or caregivers' numbers. Without making it obvious that it's a safety lesson, teaching a child a telephone number can be made into a song or a game and can be easily practiced in the home until the lesson has been learned.

There is no magic age to begin safety discussions. It should be a part of your parenting as soon as your child is able to understand what you're talking about. The only aspect that will change will be the level of discussion you will have with your child.

For example, let's take a discussion about getting a "bad vibe" from someone. Those words might mean something to a teenager, but if you're talking about this with a younger child it would be better to use language like "people who make you feel yucky or maybe a little scared." Discussions about "going to get a grown-up before you answer the door," which would be appropriate for a younger child, can be changed to "how to avoid answering the door when home alone" for an older child, and for a teenager, "always check the peephole."

I know you may be overwhelmed by all of this safety stuff. If you've read this far, you know I'm all about putting the system under a microscope to find places we can make it better. Well, as parents and caregivers we could all be doing better. Like, for example, the old-fashioned "don't talk to strangers" rule I've already mentioned. Who is a stranger? If your kid sees you talking to the checkout clerk at the grocery store, is that clerk still a stranger? Is the paperboy the kid sees delivering the paper every day a stranger? Is a frequent and favorite poster on an Internet bulletin board a stranger?

And what's more, there are people we know whom we would never want our kids to open the door for if we're not around. For example, a new neighbor across the street who comes calling with a cute little puppy in hand. Or I may be okay with our child opening the door for the babysitter, but not for the babysitter's boyfriend.

Same thing is true for some relatives. I recall a case of a fifteen-year-old girl who was home babysitting her sister while their parents went to parent-teacher conferences. The two girls were watching television when an uncle stopped by unexpectedly. The girl felt that it was bizarre that he stopped over but figured that he was a relative and not a stranger. When he sat down on the couch next to the girls and began rubbing the fifteen-year-old's legs, she knew this was not acceptable and knew what to do about it. "Stop it, I'm calling the cops," this mature fifteen-year-old said. And she did it before anything more happened.

Finally and perhaps most important, as parents we need to not only tell our children they can come to us at anytime and about anything, but we also need to make them feel certain they can come to us without any fear or embarrassment. Again, look for the slightest disclosure to turn into a teachable moment, a time when you can demonstrate how pleased you are that she told you and how proud you are of her. If someone does something wrong, like unwanted touching, your child needs to know that it is never his or her fault and never something he or she will be punished for telling you about.

As you must have realized by now, there is no magic formula or secret sauce or surefire tool to keep kids safe from predators. But there are steps to take to reduce the chances your child will be one of the files that cross my desk every day. As Karel R. Amaranth, executive director of the J. E. and Z. B. Butler Child Advocacy Center at the Children's Hospital at Montefiore Medical Center in New York, said:

> Child sexual abuse is something we all have to be concerned about. It really does take a village to raise a child, but much of what will keep our children safe must be learned in the home. And parents need to take that responsibility very seriously.

The more seriously parents take their responsibility to do everything in their power to keep predators away from their children, the more pressure will be brought on Congress, state legislatures, judges, and lawyers to follow suit and help them.

AFTERWORD

I have expressed a lot of opinions and criticisms in this book about how the system handles child sex crimes. Now's the time to quit criticizing and for me to lay out in black and white what I think ought to be done about these problems. I'm a firm believer in the motto that you've got no right to complain if you don't have a fix. This is where I'm going to cover my proposed fixes. I'm going to pretend I'm the legislature, judge, and jury all rolled into one and tell you what I'd do to change our system to better protect children victims and better ensure that the perpetrators are appropriately punished. I don't expect you or anyone else to agree with everything I say, but I hope you'll think about it and maybe come up with some better fixes of your own.

Besides the changes that I have incorporated in the text of this book, here is a summary of some immediate changes I would consider if I had my druthers:

1. There should be mandatory sentencing schemes in all jurisdictions.

2. When a mandatory sentence can be enhanced by certain aggravating circumstances, those aggravating circumstances should not always have to be proven beyond a reasonable doubt. For example, under many current statutes, a case involving two or

more victims would call for a mandatory life sentence. If, however, the jury convicts for the crimes done to one victim and not the other, which can happen if the jury decides to split the baby, then a mandatory life sentence is no longer required. I think that the existence of multiple victims—whether multiple in this case or just one in this case plus convictions in prior cases—should qualify a case for the enhanced penalty.

3. The Supreme Court should overturn the its 2004 *Crawford v. Washington* decision, which held that if a victim dies before trial, even if as a result of the criminal attack by the defendant, the victim's predeath statements to the police or his doctors or nurses are inadmissible on the grounds that letting the jury hear those statements would violate the Sixth Amendment's right to confront and cross-examine one's accusers. I am a proponent of the law prior to *Crawford*, which would allow such predeath statements of the victim to be admitted but only when certain circumstances ensuring their reliability were present. I do not think it is right or fair that a defendant should benefit from having so severely injured his victim that the victim dies.

4. Our jury system sounds wonderful in theory. Under the Constitution, each person charged with a crime is entitled to have his case heard by a jury of his peers. In the United States, this means people selected from the community where the crime occurred.

"A jury of one's peers" is based on the supposed impartiality of a person picked at random from the population at large, and therefore assumes the defendant will be judged by people who are likely to give him a fair shake.

The problem with this theory is twofold. First, those who are not "average"—whether by race, religion, nationality, age, schooling, or whatever—will have a much smaller likelihood of having their peers make up the majority of their jury. Second, the mechanisms of jury selection and the financial and job-related burdens of jury duty increase the problem by creating juries consisting of a disproportionate percentage of poor, unemployed, and often uneducated people showing up in the jury pool.

The solution to this imbalance is a professional jury system. Professional jurors would be laypersons but they would be educated for the task. They would be taught to understand the rules of evidence, the trial process, and instruction, and they would be tested thoroughly on their objectivity.

Most important, a professional jury would have no motivation other than ensuring that due process was followed. The complexities, nuances, and intricacies involved in a child sexual assault warrant a professional jury both because of the difficulty of the case and the great danger of releasing a predator back into society if a jury makes the wrong decision.

5. We need better supervision of registered sex offenders. Some ways to improve supervision include: requiring sex offenders to register their computer Internet accounts, IP addresses, and telephone numbers, not just their physical address. They should be required to inform authorities when they travel out of the country and there should be an integrated international registration system (like that for known terrorists) to monitor the comings and goings of registered sex offenders. Registered sex offenders should also be subject to lifetime counseling and therapy orders, not merely conditions of parole or probation.

6. Money and time should be available to continually update the training of professionals in this field. This includes all the agencies involved: law enforcement, prosecutors, advocates, therapists, judges, probation and parole officers, and so on. Besides helping

them stay current on the latest changes in the law and advances in this area, studies show that continuing training alleviates burn out and serves to inspire and motivate people in this line of work.

7. The norm in assigning prosecutors and law enforcement personnel is to rotate them, so they may be handling sex crimes for a limited time and then rotating to another area of crime. The bureaucratic thinking is that prosecutors and detectives should be cross-trained in all areas of criminal law and that specializing narrows a prosecutor's or detective's skills.

   In contrast, the benefit of being in a vertical unit (handling all aspects of a case from beginning to end) is that a high degree of specialization results from continued experience and training in this difficult area, along with a high degree of accountability. All too often, a prosecutor or detective reaches about a year or so in the unit and then is transferred.

   I believe the sensitivity of these cases and the very special needs of the victims require that lawyers and detectives should be assigned for a minimum rotation of five years. Also, I believe lawyers and law enforcers should be readily allowed to opt from being assigned to these units. This is not the type of work for someone who doesn't have the requisite passion, compassion, and tough stomach to handle it.

8. Specific courts should be designated for child sexual assault (and child abuse) cases so they are 100 percent devoted to the needs and realities of kids who testify. For example, courtrooms can be painted in kid-friendly colors like pastels so they look more like a classroom instead of a large, windowless, intimidating enclosure. The chairs on the witness stand should be appropriately kid-sized and adjustable so that a four-year-old or a fourteen-year-old could comfortably sit and testify.

Further, the judges in these cases need specialized training just as much as the lawyers and other professionals handling these cases. They need to know the laws pertaining to child testimony and how they can use their discretion to protect and assist the child in testifying without trauma but also without suggestion. This system can be modeled after the drug courts that are in place in many jurisdictions, where specific courts are devoted to prosecuting drug addicts. This system has allowed court personnel to develop great expertise in what treatments are available and what works for certain kinds of users, as well as to help gain knowledge of when those alternatives should be used as opposed to punishment.

9. There should be limits to an attorney's ability to cross-examine child witnesses, especially the victim. Aggressive questioning that may be considered good lawyering with an adult witness can be entirely inappropriate when used on kids. Yes, we must protect and preserve the criminal defendant's constitutional right to confront and cross-examine the witnesses against him, whether he is defending himself or has council. But the system already recognizes many limits on how this is done, from not asking questions without foundation to not prying into a rape victim's sexual history. We need to do the same to provide greater protection to the child victim involved in a sexual abuse prosecution.

10. In recent years, legislators have begun to address an important concern: some defendants so intimidate and terrify their victims that the victims are afraid to testify in the defendant's presence, and as a result, the offender may escape prosecution entirely. Some states have enacted special rules that authorize judges in certain situations to allow children to testify via closed-circuit television. The defendant can see the child on a television mon-

itor, but the child cannot see the defendant. The defense attorney can be personally present where the child is testifying and can cross-examine the child. Closed-circuit TV should be allowed whenever it is in the best interests of the child victim.

11. Courts trying child sex crime cases need to let experts educate juries about child psychology and how children react to abuse. The very things defense attorneys claim discredit a child's testimony may be normal, but the prosecution cannot show that unless child psychology experts are allowed to testify. Favorite defense arguments like delayed disclosure, recantation, minimization, self-blame, lying first in order to protect the abuser or fearing being in trouble—these become normal child reactions when put in perspective by an expert in child behavior. Expert testimony should be more readily admitted, with a broad enough scope allowed to truly assist jurors in fully understanding the unique issues when dealing with the behavior of a child who has been sexually assaulted by an adult.

12. Defense attorneys, prosecutors, and judges must be sensitive to difficulties child witnesses have in understanding adult questions. Whether their difficulty is due simply to their age or age coupled with developmentally delayed issues, kids can become very easily confused when badgered by smart, experienced trial lawyers.

13. Cases involving children should go to trial as soon as possible and definitely no later than six months from the filing. Currently, most come to trial roughly a year after charges are filed, which can be weeks or even months after the investigation into the first reports of abuse began. Long or multiple continuances in child sexual assault cases should be discouraged. This is not only better for the case but is critical to the victim's healing process.

14. We shouldn't treat every sex offender alike, any more than we treat every drug offender the same. Like drug rehabilitation, there should be facilities where we can take low-level sex offenders off the street to ensure the safety of the public yet also provide them with treatment that may turn them around. I think we need live-in/lockdown facilities, as an alternative to jail or prison, that are meant to work with, treat, and study sex offenders.

15. There should be amendments to the rule against double jeopardy, which says a defendant can't be tried twice for the same crime, to enable the reopening of a case after an acquittal when compelling new evidence is discovered. This would apply only in cases of very serious offenses, where the public danger from leaving the offender on the streets is especially high.

16. There should be a total ban, or at least limitations, on what a child sexual assault defendant is allowed to do in the criminal process and what private information of the victim he is given access to. For example, he should not be able to personally conduct the cross-examination of the allegedly abused. He should not be given personal access to things like the victims' school records, rape exam photos, and other confidential records. His attorney will have full access to these materials and, as an officer of the court, is bound to follow proper rules for their use and disclosure. But giving a *pro per* defendant access to things like a child victim's rape kit medical report is like giving him porn, in my opinion.

17. If a case is appealed after a conviction, it may take two or three years before a court determines if the defendant is entitled to a new trial. If the defendant is granted a new trial, the prosecution would need to bring the victim in to testify again. Not only is this traumatic, but any inconsistency between the victim's new

testimony and her testimony at the first trial may be argued to cast doubt on the victim's credibility. If the reason for the new trial has nothing to do with a legal problem with the victim's testimony, the victim should not be made to go through the whole process again. The victim's prior testimony should be stipulated and accepted for use in the second trial.

18. Families of victims of child sexual assault (not just the victim himself or herself) should be sent to therapy under the jurisdiction of the court.

YOU HAVE RECEIVED YOUR SUBPOENA. NOW WHAT?

GENERAL CONCEPTS

- Tell the truth
- Answer the question, no more
- Use plain English
- Do not memorize
- Do not guess
- Make a good impression
- Just ask!

As you read these suggestions, keep in mind that these are not meant to be offensive. What you have to say is important, but the way you say it and the way you present yourself have a lot to do with whether or not you will be believed by the jury.

1. Appearance. Dress like you are going to church or interviewing for a job.
   - More specifically, women/girls should wear dresses and men/boys should wear slacks and button-down shirts.

- Do not wear tank tops, flip flops, miniskirts, or clubbing-type clothes.
- Women should avoid wearing too much makeup. You don't want to look flashy or tough. You want to look soft and natural.
- Also, don't chew gum, candy, or tobacco in the courtroom and definitely not on the stand.

2. Always, always, always tell the truth.

3. Listen carefully to each question. Don't try to guess where the lawyer is going with the question and don't assume that you know.

4. Take your time in answering questions.
   - Don't let anyone rush you into an answer.
   - You may be asked the same question several times. Don't assume that you answered a question wrong if you are asked several times in different ways.

5. Answer only the questions you were asked. If the question calls for a yes or no answer, answer with a yes or no. If you want to explain an answer, you can ask if you can explain. If the answer is no, then wait for redirect or "recross." Don't answer yes or no unless you completely agree or disagree with *everything* in the statement.

6. Ask for questions to be repeated or rephrased if you don't hear or understand them.

7. Do not guess.
   - If you don't know the answer, it's okay to say "I don't know" or "I don't remember." But only say that if you really don't know or don't remember.

- Be clear in saying that you are just estimating or guessing about something.
- If you are asked about time or distances and are not exactly sure, tell the attorney that you are not sure, that you are just making an approximation. For example, in this situation you might say, "I don't know exactly what the time was, but it was between 8:30 and 9:00 at night" or "I don't know the exact distance, but it was approximately twenty to twenty-five feet."

8. Ask for a bathroom break, a glass of water, tissue, or whatever when you need it. Do not become angry or frustrated. That's often what the attorney is trying to accomplish. Cross-examination is part of every trial. Don't go for the bait. Stay cool and be polite. The idea is to be on your best behavior, better than the lawyer questioning you. The jury will notice if you stay courteous and the lawyer does not.

9. If you make a mistake in your testimony, don't get flustered or make more mistakes because you're thinking about it. Just say you need to correct one of your answers and say it is as soon as possible. If you feel an overwhelming need to explain or clarify your answer, ask the judge, "May I please explain my answer, your honor?"

10. Don't automatically buy into the words of the lawyer. The only reason a lawyer says, "So your testimony is . . ." or "Do I under-stand you correctly that . . ." or the like is because he doesn't like the way you said it and wants it rephrased. If the words—all the words—are not exactly the ones you think are right or they make you uncomfortable, use your own words. The other lawyer may try to rattle you by being rude, hostile, brusque, or abrasive. But remember, you are the one under oath, not the lawyer.

11. If a question is too long to follow easily, ask the attorney to shorten it.

12. Don't try to memorize your testimony.

13. Don't talk about the case while you are in the courthouse, except when you are on the witness stand.

14. You will probably be asked if you talked to anybody about the case. Don't hesitate to admit that you did. If the other lawyer asks you if you talked to me, tell him yes. If he asks you whether we talked about your testimony, tell him that we did. If the other lawyer asks you what I told you, tell him honestly that I told you to tell the truth, which is exactly what you should do—tell the truth.

15. Try to stay calm. Be courteous to the lawyers from each side and respect the judge. Don't argue with the lawyers or the judge. Don't interrupt the lawyers or the judge. Don't be arrogant. Don't make wisecracks or try to be funny.

16. If the judge interrupts you or if one of the lawyers makes an objection, stop answering immediately. Wait until the judge says that it is okay for you to answer. If the judge doesn't say anything or you don't know if you are supposed to answer, ask the judge, "Your honor, am I supposed to answer the question?" If you don't remember the question after the objection or don't understand it, ask the lawyer to repeat it.

17. Don't say *yeah* or *uh-huh*. Say *yes* or *yes, sir* or *yes, ma'am*, or *no* or *no, sir* or *no, ma'am*.

18. Don't object to answering a question, even if you think it is

improper or stupid. If it's not a proper question, one of the lawyers will object to it.

19. Don't try to fill in moments of silence. If things go silent during questioning, don't volunteer information simply to fill the quiet.

20. Do not stare at the defendant. It will only distract you. Look at the defendant only when asked to identify him.

21. If you have questions, just ask! Remember, there are no mind readers in the courtroom.

APPENDIX:
WHERE CAN I GO FOR MORE INFORMATION?

T here are many resources for sexual assault victims, parents, other family members of sexual assault victims, and those who simply want more information.

JUSTICE INTERRUPTED

Justice Interrupted, LLC, is a media consulting team and radio program that consists of three experts at the top of their fields. Prosecutor Robin Sax, violence expert Susan Murphy-Milano, and police officer Stacy Dittrich provide guidance as three individuals with professional knowledge in criminal cases. Their mission statement is to bring attention to criminal cases that aren't receiving adequate media or law enforcement attention and to help victims find the justice they are seeking through media outlets. Their efforts have contributed to denied paroles for convicted murderers, front-page stories in newspapers such as the *Chicago Tribune* and the *Miami Herald*, and victim's stories brought to the television screen in shows like *48 Hours*.

Together, they bring a powerful force to the airwaves and media. Their weekly radio show on Blogtalk radio, *Justice Interrupted Radio Network*, is one of the highest-rated shows on Blogtalk and is featured weekly. The show is currently being developed into a weekly television show. Their guests to date have included some of law enforcement and the legal field's top professionals who speak to victims looking to have their voices heard. Mark Geragos, Marc Klaas, Diane Dimond, Joel Brodsky for Drew Peterson, David Dimond, Polly Franks, Shawn Chapman Holley, true crime author Diane Fanning, former NYPD detective Gil Alba, Dana Pretzer, criminal profiler Pat Brown, Tina Dirrman, and Joe Hosey are just a few of the television personalities, advocates, authors, and radio hosts who have appeared on the show.

Justice Interrupted provides justice for those whose lives have been interrupted by rape, murder, sexual predators of children, strange and unexplained disappearances, domestic violence, and cold cases yet to be solved.

www.justiceinterrupted.blogspot.com
www.justiceinterrupted.com

GOVERNMENTAL AGENCIES AND PROSECUTORS' OFFICES

Each state and many counties have their own online resources as well as hotline numbers to call for information. The Department of Justice's Web site (www.usdoj.gov) contains excellent information on the law, resources, and links to states' Web sites.

Most prosecutors' offices have a victim/witness program or a victim advocacy office that can provide detailed information on the specific legal procedures for your county or state. To find the prosecutor's office in your county, search your state or county Web site. A national list of district attorney offices is available online at the National District Attorney Association (www.ndaa.org).

CRIME STATISTICS AND LEGISLATION

Bureau of Justice Assistance: www.ojp.usdoj.gov/bja
United States House of Representatives: www.house.gov
Constitution of the United States of America:
    www.law.cornell.edu/constitution
Federal Bureau of Investigation: www.fbi.gov

INTERNET CRIMES AGAINST CHILDREN (ICAC)

The ICAC Task Force Program was created to help state and local law enforcement agencies enhance their investigative response to offenders who use the Internet, online communication systems, or other computer technology to sexually exploit children. The program is currently composed of fifty-nine regional task force agencies and is funded by the United States Department of Justice, Office of Juvenile Justice and Delinquency Prevention. Go to www.icactraining.org for more information.

SEX OFFENDER REGISTRATION

For national information, including links to each state's public sex offender registration, go to http://www.nsopw.gov.

Alabama: http://community.dps.alabama.gov/
Alaska: http://www.dps.state.ak.us/sorweb/
Arkansas: http://www.acic.org/Registration/index.htm
Arizona: https://az.gov/webapp/offender/main.do
California: http://www.meganslaw.ca.gov
Colorado: http://sor.state.co.us/

Connecticut:
   http://www.ct.gov/dps/cwp/view.asp?a=2157&Q=294474&dpsNav=|
Delaware: http://sexoffender.dsp.delaware.gov/
District of Columbia: http://mpdc.dc.gov/mpdc/cwp/view,a,1241,Q
   ,540704,mpdcNav_GID,1523,mpdcNav,|,.asp
Florida: http://offender.fdle.state.fl.us/offender/Search.jsp
Georgia: http://services.georgia.gov/gbi/gbisor/SORSearch.jsp
Guam: http://www.guamcourts.org/sor/index.asp
Hawaii: http://sexoffenders.ehawaii.gov/sexoffender/welcome.html
   ;jsessionid=BECB11F4195AB47FD7770F1C6F7C13E3.lono
Idaho: http://www.isp.state.id.us/sor_id/
Illinois: http://www.isp.state.il.us/sor/
Indiana: http://www.insor.org/insasoweb/
Iowa: http://www.iowasexoffender.com/
Kansas: http://www.accesskansas.org/kbi/ro.shtml
Kentucky: http://kspsor.state.ky.us/
Louisiana: http://www.lsp.org/socpr/default.html
Maine: http://sor.informe.org/sor/
Maryland: http://www.socem.info/
Massachusetts: http://sorb.chs.state.ma.us/search.htm
Michigan: http://www.mipsor.state.mi.us/
Minnesota: http://www.doc.state.mn.us/level3/search.asp
Mississippi: http://www.sor.mdps.state.ms.us/sorpublic/
   hpsor_search.aspx
Missouri: http://www.mshp.dps.mo.gov/CJ38/search.jsp
Montana: http://www.doj.mt.gov/svor/
Nebraska: http://www.nsp.state.ne.us/sor/
Nevada: http://www.nvsexoffenders.gov/
New Hampshire: http://www4.egov.nh.gov/nsor/search.aspx
New Jersey: http://www.njsp.org/info/reg_sexoffend.html
New Mexico: http://www.nmsexoffender.dps.state.nm.us/
New York: http://criminaljustice.state.ny.us/nsor/search_index.htm
North Carolina: http://sexoffender.ncdoj.gov/

North Dakota: http://www.sexoffender.ncdoj.gov/
Ohio: http://www.sexoffender.nd.gov/
Oklahoma: http://docapp8.doc.state.ok.us/servlet/page?
    _pageid=190&_dad=portal30&_schema=PORTAL30
Oregon: http://sexoffenders.oregon.gov/
Pennsylvania: http://www.pameganslaw.state.pa.us/
Rhode Island: http://www.paroleboard.ri.gov/sexoffender/agree.php
South Carolina: http://services.sled.sc.gov/sor/
Tennessee: http://www.ticic.state.tn.us/sorinternet/sosearch.aspx
Texas: https://records.txdps.state.tx.us/DPS_WEB/Portal/index.aspx
Utah: http://corrections.utah.gov/contenthome/homepage.asp
Vermont: http://www.dps.state.vt.us/cjs/s_registry.htm
Virginia: http://sex-offender.vsp.virginia.gov/sor/
Washington: http://www.icrimewatch.net/washington.php
West Virginia: http://www.wvstatepolice.com/sexoff/websearchform.cfm
Wisconsin: http://offender.doc.state.wi.us/public/
Wyoming: http://wysors.dci.wyo.gov/

INTERNET SAFETY AND RESOURCES

Wired Kids, Inc.: www.wiredkids.org
National Center for Missing and Exploited Children: www.cybertipline.com
GetNetWise: www.getnetwise.com
SafeKids.com: www.safekids.com
Under Your Thumb: www.underyourthumb.com

SEXUAL ASSAULT NURSE EXAMINERS (SANE) OR SEXUAL ASSAULT RAPE TEAMS (SART)

SANE and SART (www.sane-sart.com) are the common acronyms given for the multidisciplinary teams in each city, county, or state. Local teams can be based in a hospital, a clinic, a forensic interviewing center, or even a law enforcement office or a prosecutor's office. Any member of a multidisciplinary team can direct you to the right person to give you more information.

NONPROFIT ORGANIZATIONS

Some organizations throughout the country are wonderful at not only providing educational information in sexual abuse prevention but also have a contact list showing to whom or where one can go to learn more or get help. Some of my favorite organizations are the following.

THE AWARENESS CENTER

The Awareness Center (http://www.theawarenesscenter.org) creates an international organization to address the issue and ramifications of sexual victimization to both adults and children in Jewish communities.

BEYOND MISSING

Beyond Missing was founded by Marc Klaas on June 8, 2001. Klaas began to pursue an aggressive child safety agenda for the nation's children following the kidnap and murder of his twelve-year-old daughter, Polly. Mr. Klaas provides the vision and the day-to-day leadership for the organization. Beyond Missing has wonderful resources, including online tools to create "missing person" flyers for free.

Twenty-four-hour support and business phone 415-339-0923
info@beyondmissing.com
www.beyondmissing.com

CAROLE SUND/CARRINGTON MEMORIAL REWARD FOUNDATION

The Carole Sund/Carrington Memorial Reward Foundation is committed to raising public awareness for the issue of those who have gone missing under suspicious circumstances and of innocent people who have fallen victim to the most violent of crimes. This foundation offers support and resources to aggrieved families in an effort to bring them hope and resolution. Under qualifying circumstances, the foundation posts rewards for families of victims who lack the financial means to do so themselves. These rewards provide a tool to help law enforcement find missing persons and bring perpetrators to justice.

209-567-1059
www.carolesundfoundation.com

CHILDHELP USA

Childhelp USA is a nonprofit organization "dedicated to meeting the physical, emotional, educational, and spiritual needs of abused and neglected children."

Its programs and services include this hotline, which children can call with complete anonymity and confidentiality.

1-800-4-A-CHILD
(1-800-422-4453)
TDD: 1-800-2-A-CHILD

CHILDLINE (UK)

According to its Web site, "ChildLine is the free helpline for children and young people in the UK. Children and young people can call us on 0800 1111 to talk about any problem—our counsellors are always here to help you sort it out."

THE INNOCENT JUSTICE FOUNDATION

The Innocent Justice Foundation (http://innocentjustice.org) is dedicated to helping rescue children from sexual abuse. The foundation strives to significantly impact and reduce child sexual abuse in the United States through education on Internet crimes against children, victim legislative advocacy, and essential material support to law enforcement and governmental agencies that prevent, investigate, prosecute, and criminally adjudicate sex crimes against children.

The Innocent Justice Foundation
132 N. El Camino Real #483
Encinitas, CA 92024
760-585-8873
888-698-8873
info@innocentjustice.org

i-SAFE

Founded in 1998, i-SAFE Inc. is the leader in Internet safety education. Available in all fifty states, i-SAFE is a nonprofit foundation whose mission is to educate and empower youth to make their Internet experiences safe and responsible. The goal is to educate students on how to avoid dangerous, inappropriate, or unlawful online behavior.

www.i-safe.org

THE INTERNATIONAL SOCIETY FOR PREVENTION OF CHILD ABUSE AND NEGLECT (ISPCAN)

Founded in 1977, ISPCAN is the only multidisciplinary international organization that brings together a worldwide cross section of committed professionals to work toward the prevention and treatment of child abuse, neglect, and exploitation globally.

ISPCAN's mission is to prevent cruelty to children in every nation, in every form: physical abuse, sexual abuse, neglect, street children, child fatalities, child prostitution, children of war, emotional abuse, and child labor. ISPCAN is committed to increasing public awareness of all forms of violence against children, developing activities to prevent such violence and promoting the rights of children in all regions of the world. ISPCAN invites you to join forces with its members around the world to protect children in need—their bodies, minds, hearts, and rights.

The International Society for Prevention of Child Abuse and Neglect
245 W. Roosevelt Road Building 6, Suite 39
West Chicago, IL 60185
1-630-876-6913
www.ispcan.org

NATIONAL CHILDREN'S ALLIANCE

Call the Children's Advocacy Center nearest you for a referral to a nearby support group or therapist specializing in child sexual abuse.

National Children's Alliance
1612 K Street, NW, Suite 500
Washington, DC 20006
800-239-9950
202-452-6001
info@nca-online.org

NATIONAL DOMESTIC VIOLENCE/ABUSE HOTLINE

This is a twenty-four-hour-a-day hotline staffed by trained volunteers who are ready to connect people with emergency help in their own communities, including emergency services and shelters. The staff can also provide information and referrals for a variety of nonemergency services, including counseling for adults and children and assistance in reporting abuse. It has an extensive database of domestic violence treatment providers in all fifty states and US territories. Many staff members speak languages besides English, and they have twenty-four-hour access to translators for approximately 150 languages. For the hearing impaired, there is a TDD number. This is a good resource for people who are experiencing or have experienced domestic violence or abuse or who suspect that someone they know is being abused. All calls to the hotline are confidential, and callers may remain anonymous if they wish.

1-800-799-SAFE
1-800-799-7233
1-800-787-3224 TDD

NATIONAL CENTER FOR MISSING AND EXPLOITED CHILDREN (NCMEC)

The National Center for Missing and Exploited Children's mission is to help prevent child abduction and sexual exploitation, help find missing children, and assist victims of child abduction and sexual exploitation, their families, and the professionals who serve them.

National Center for Missing and Exploited Children
Charles B. Wang International Children's Building
699 Prince Street
Alexandria, Virginia 22314-3175
703-274-3900
1-800-THE-LOST (1-800-843-5678)
www.missingkids.com

PARENTS FOR MEGAN'S LAW

Parents for Megan's Law, Inc. (PFML) is a nonprofit 501(c)3 community and victim's rights organization dedicated to the prevention and treatment of sexual abuse through the provision of education, advocacy, counseling, victim services, policy and legislative support services.

www.parentsformeganslaw.org

PAVE: PROMOTING AWARENESS, VICTIM EMPOWERMENT

PAVE is a national grassroots nonprofit organization. It uses education and action to shatter the silence of sexual and domestic violence. www.pavingtheway.net

PEACE OVER VIOLENCE

Peace Over Violence is a nonprofit, feminist, multicultural, volunteer organization dedicated to building healthy relationships, families, and communities free from sexual, domestic, and interpersonal violence. To achieve this mission, the agency manages five departments delivering the services of emergency, intervention, prevention, education and advocacy.

Twenty-four-hour hotlines
310-392-8381
213-626-3393
626-793-3385
877-633-0044 (stalking hotline)
www.peaceoverviolence.org

Rape, Abuse, Incest National Network (RAINN)

RAINN has an automated service that links callers to the nearest rape crisis center. Rape crisis centers are staffed with trained volunteers and paid staff members who also understand sexual abuse issues and services (though sometimes they are not adequately prepared to refer male callers). All calls are confidential, and callers may remain anonymous if they wish.

1-800-656-4673
www.rainn.org

Texas EqquSearch

The Texas EquuSearch Mounted Search and Recovery Team was started in August 2000 with the purpose to provide volunteer horse-mounted search and recovery for lost and missing persons. Texas EquuSearch is a professional organization that takes notification of a missing person very seriously.

www.texasequuusearch.org

Blogs and Current Legal Articles and Information

Robin Sax	www.robinsax.com
Justice Interrupted	www.justiceinterrupted.com
Women in Crime Ink	www.womenincrimeink.blogspot.com

STATE CHILD ABUSE HOTLINES

Alaska (AK)
  (800) 478-4444

Arizona (AZ)
  (888) SOS-CHILD
  (888-767-2445)

Arkansas (AR)
  (800) 482-5964

Connecticut (CT)
  (800) 842-2288
  (800) 624-5518
  (TDD/Hearing Impaired)

Delaware (DE)
  (800) 292-9582

Florida (FL)
  (800) 96-ABUSE
  (800-962-2873)

Illinois (IL)
  (800) 252-2873

Indiana (IN)
  (800) 800-5556

Iowa (IA)
  (800) 362-2178

Kansas (KS)
  (800) 922-5330

Kentucky (KY)
  (800) 752-6200

Maine (ME)
  (800) 452-1999

Maryland (MD)
  (800) 332-6347

Massachusetts (MA)
  (800) 792-5200

Michigan (MI)
  (800) 942-4357

Mississippi (MS)
  (800) 222-8000

Missouri (MO)
  (800) 392-3738

Montana (MT)
  (800) 332-6100

Nebraska (NE)
  (800) 652-1999

Nevada (NV)
  (800) 992-5757

New Hampshire (NH)
  (800) 894-5533

New Jersey (NJ)
  (800) 792-8610
  (800) 835-5510
  (TDD/Hearing Impaired)

New Mexico (NM)
  (800) 797-3260

New York (NY)
  (800) 342-3720

North Dakota (ND)
  (800) 245-3736

Oklahoma (OK)
  (800) 522-3511

Oregon (OR)
  (800) 854-3508

Pennsylvania (PA)
    (800) 932-0313
Rhode Island (RI)
    (800) RI-CHILD
    (800-742-4453)
Texas (TX)
    (800) 252-5400
Utah (UT)
    (800) 678-9399

Virginia (VA)
    (800) 552-7096
Washington (WA)
    (800) 562-5624
West Virginia (WV)
    (800) 352-6513
Wyoming (WY)
    (800) 457-3659

NOTES

CHAPTER ONE

1. Thomas D. Lyon and Martha Matthews, "Model Points and Authorities Regarding Questioning of Child Witnesses," http://works.bepress.com/cgi/viewcontent.cgi?article=1037&context=thomaslyon (accessed August 4, 2009).

CHAPTER THREE

1. Kathleen Coulborn Faller and Ellen DeVoe, "Allegations of Sexual Abuse in Divorce," *Journal of Child Sexual Abuse* 4 (1995): 1–25.

2. Ibid.

3. Kathleen Colburn Faller, "Possible Explanations for Child Sexual Abuse in Divorce," *American Journal of Orthopsychiatry* 4 (1991): 86–87.

4. Elizabeth A. Sirles and Colleen E. Lofberg, "Factors Associated with Divorce in Intrafamily Child Sexual Abuse Cases," *Child Abuse & Neglect* 14 (1990): 165–68.

5. Charles Schulbert, Kathi Makaroff, William Holmes, and Sharon Cooper, In *Sexual Assault: Quick Reference for HealthCare, Social Service, and Law Enforcement Professionals* (St. Louis: G. W. Medical Publishing, 2003).

CHAPTER FOUR

1. William C. Holmes and Gail B. Slap, "Sexual Abuse of Boys," *Journal of the American Medical Association* 280 (1998): 1855–62; US Department of Justice, Bureau of Justice Statistics, "Recidivism of Prisoners Released in 1994 Study," 2002; US Department of Justice, Bureau of Justice Statistics, "Alcohol and Crime Study," 1998; US Department of Justice, Bureau of Justice Statistics, "Sex Offenses and Offenders Study," 1997; US Department of Justice, Bureau of Justice Statistics, "National Crime Victimization Study," 2003.

2. Badgley Royal Commission Report, 1994.

CHAPTER FIVE

1. Amy Hammel-Zabin, *Conversations with a Pedophile: In the Interest of Our Children*, 28th ed. (New York: Barricade Books, 2003), p. 28.

2. Erna Olafson in *Sexualized Violence against Women and Children*, ed. B. J. Cling (New York: Guilford Press, 2004).

CHAPTER NINE

1. Kathryn Brohl, *When Your Child Has Been Molested* (San Francisco: Jossey-Bass, 2004), p. 33.

2. The Warren Washington CARE Center's mission is "to recognize that the children in our communities are by nature, vulnerable and need our love and protection." Content from www.wwcarecenter.org.

3. Ibid.

CHAPTER TEN

1. Donald E. Shelton, Young S. Kim, and Gregg Barak, "A Study of Juror Expectations and Demands concerning Scientific Evidence: Does the 'CSI Effect' Exist?" *Vanderbilt Journal of Entertainment and Technology Law* 9, no. 2 (2007): 360.

2. Court TV, "O. J. Simpson: Week-by-Week," http://www.courttv.com/trials/ojsimpson/weekly/16.html.

3. Robert R. Hazelwood and Ann Wolbert Burgess, eds., *Practical Aspects of Rape Investigation: A Multidisciplinary Approach*, 4th ed. (Boca Raton: CRC Press, 2009), p. 298.

CHAPTER TWELVE

1. "The Story of Adam Walsh," www.amw.com (accessed August 4, 2009).

ACKNOWLEDGMENTS

I t takes a village. It really does. This book could never have been written without the support, care, guidance, and love of a wonderful family members, friends, and professionals who have stuck by me through the roller-coaster ride of being a prosecutor, an author, a legal commentator, and a mom. In each area of my life I am indebted to the kindness and hard work of those who have allowed this book go from an idea to a reality. I am going to try really, really hard not to forget anyone. But anyone whom I do inadvertently forget, I thank you for your friendship and most important, your understanding.

First, I must recognize my family, the small but mighty bunch who have always stood by my side with love, patience, and ironclad loyalty. I thank each of you for not rolling your eyes when I said I was writing this book, for always supporting me by pushing my books on your clients, and by designing my artwork.

To my husband, my CEO, my rock, Andy Katzenstein. I am so lucky on so many levels to have someone who can put up with me and all of my crazy ideas, plans, and endeavors. I thank you for not only believing in me but also for encouraging me to do everything I dream up. Not many people can have a husband who not only puts down the toilet seat but knows more about the criminal justice system than any world-class estate planner should. Andy Katzenstein, you are husband of the week and your picture does hang on every wall, playing hide and seek. Let's always be each other's Kelton.

To Jeremy, Mr. Connoisseur of the English language and grammarian. Whilst I wrote this book, I felt so lucky to know that you would occasionally look over my shoulder to make sure I didn't confuse my who's from my whom's. Jason, thank you for challenging my ideas, questioning my material, and always offering the other side of life's most important issues. While we may not agree on everything, like where Hannah will go to high school, I do know that I can count on you for unconditional love, interesting opinions, and good humor. To both of you boys, I also apologize for ruining two perfectly good spring breaks to Cabo with my book deadlines.

To Hannah, as I write this I know the names we have for each other will be exchanged for new ones by the time the book is in print. But for now Ms. Clavel loves her Banana, Plátano, the boss, bundles, Nanner, to the moon and back. And no matter what you say, I love you more . . . because I am bigger and I say so.

To Mom, Rikki Sax, director of Graphic Design for Operation Robin Sax. I am so lucky to have a mom whom I cannot only call anytime to vent, cry, and laugh with, but a mom to whom I can send html questions, banner ideas, flyer concerns, and pictures that need updating. I am thrilled that your hard work can be seen in the photos of this book. I thank you for all of your professional contributions but more than anything, for your mothering.

To Dad, I so appreciate you spreading the buzz of my projects and books among your clientele. See, there was an upside to the stock market plunge: the extra years at the office have allowed you to be the world's greatest promoter. I so appreciate everything you have done for me on the career level, but more important, for the unwavering love you wrap around me, my mom, my children, my sister, and our husbands. You are as loyal as they come and I thank you for being you.

To Heather, let's hope this book makes enough so I can buy you a house right next door. Sure, that would drive Andy and Scott crazy, but that's how much I love you. I thank you for being the best sis in the whole wide world but more important, I thank you for going into the medical profession so someone can answer all of my medical/pharmaceutical questions.

To Scott, I never had a brother and I am so honored that I can call you my bro. Not only can we chat about the legal system but I can always share a good laugh with you about the trials and tribulations of life as part of the Sax family!

To my aunts Vic and Mary and uncles David and Royce, I love that you guys have been part of my crazy ride through life with good humor, smiles, and lots of yummy new restaurants to try. I appreciate your unwavering support in every project.

Bill, Dolly, and Danny, I am so lucky that my family has grown to include wonderful people who not only have taken me in as a daughter/sister, but also as a friend. I love you guys.

To Erica, what would I have done without you? This and all of my projects could not have been completed without you keeping me on track, being there in a pinch, and caring for our family like we were yours. Thank you. Thank you. Thank you.

Claire Gerus, so what book are we on? Never in a million years would I have dreamed that I could write and sell this book, and the others too. It would not have happened without your hard work and tenacity. I love having you as my agent, and thank you for our friendship.

Rex Browning, in another million years I would never have dreamed the amount of support and work you have given me. Your gift with words and the English language have helped make this book go from okay to awesome. Thank you for your edits, comments, and queries. You rock.

To Steven L. Mitchell and everyone at Prometheus Books, I hope you know how thankful and appreciative I am for you believing in me and my projects. Our thought-provoking conversations have made this book better than I could have hoped. Thank you for everything, particularly those deadline extensions.

ACKNOWLEDGMENTS

To Jaime Williams, research assistant extraordinaire. You always have gone above and beyond the call of duty. For your hard work and ability to speedily turn things around, I thank you and appreciate you more than you will ever know.

To Stacy and Susan, my partners in crime at Justice Interrupted, I am honored to know you, work with you, and have your guidance and advice in every project I pursue. You guys are vastly under-recognized for the amazing work you do each and every day. But I know it and see it! You are the best 'yatches ever!

Mark Geragos. Oh Mark, you have been there for me in so many ways I can't even begin to thank you enough. Whether in handling my own legal affairs, being a mentor and advisor, or just being a solid friend, you have shown that you are a true mensch. I not only appreciate but am also honored that you took time away from your unbelievably hectic schedule to write the foreword to this book. Thank you from the bottom of my heart.

No woman can write a book without the support of girlfriends, the ones who have kept me going with words of encouragement, great suggestions, and the occasional stiff drink just in the nick of time. The girls who do all of the above and way more include (of course, and as always, in alphabetical order): Kathryn Cavanaugh, Beth Christopher, Stephanie Cornick, Joanna Cowitt, Mandi Dyner, Stacy Dittrich, Victoria Gold, Dana Guerin, Mary Hanlon Stone, Heather Karpf, Tamara Miller, Susan Murphy Milano, Rikki Sax, Jillian Straus, and Eva Stodel.

And then there are the SaxFacts ladies, the ones who have pulled through with articles, material, and information to keep me and society in the know. Thank you for your hard work and dedication, especially as I was rushing to get this book in on time. Each of you is amazing: Jenn Berman, Wendy Bice, Kathryn Cavanaugh, Linda Cobarrubius, Erica Jaimeson, Kawai Matthews, Anna Rajo-Miller, and Jill Roberts.

And then a big thank you to all the women I have met who are out there making a difference in our world and doing amazing things! You guys are fantastic and I look forward to our continued friendships. Especially to Robyn Ritter Simon and Rebecca Simon, thank you.

To Cassie Nelson, I would never have made it through the summer of 2009 without you. You have been my daughter, my law clerk, my travel companion, my fashionista, my critic, and my friend. I have valued each and every minute with you and I can't wait to spend many more years together.

To Steve Cooley, John Spillane, Curt Hazell, Richard Doyle, John Lynch, Jane Blissert, Michelle Daniels, and every single employee from the Los Angeles County District Attorney's Office for truly being there for me in all aspects of my career. Every day you guys are not only making sure justice is done, but you have also made it your mission to see that the deputy DAs thrive, with our caseload and in our personal lives. I am honored to be part of such an esteemed group of individuals.

Last and never least, thank you to all the people—the advocates, the victims, the lawyers, the judges, the legislators, the news commentators, the shrinks, the social workers, the doctors, the cops, the investigators, and all the other people who toil so diligently to make sure justice prevails. There are too many people to name but you know who you are: you are my e-mail buddies, my Facebook friends, my blogging friends, my colleagues, and my heroes. Thank you.